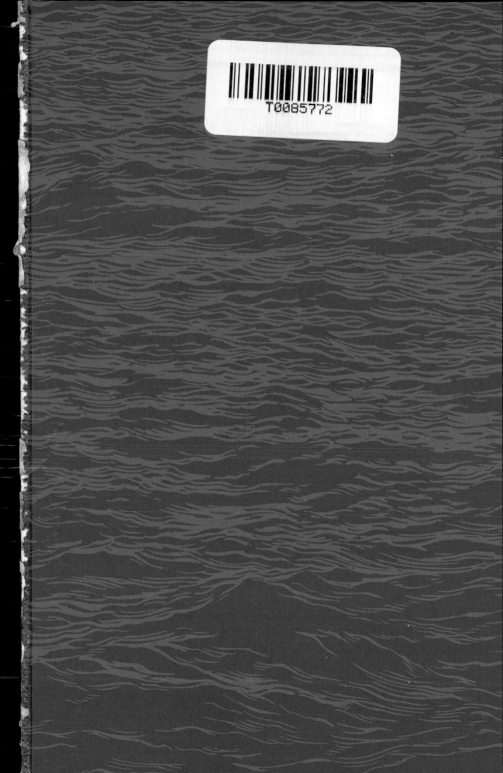
T0085772

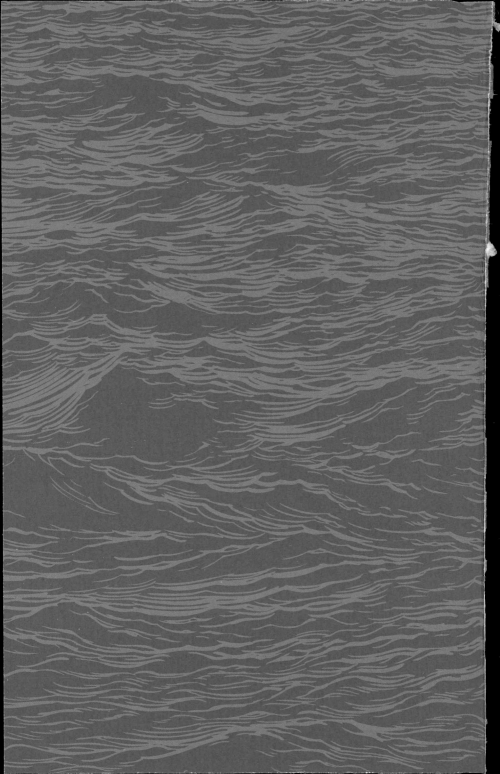

CROSSING THE RIVER

SEVEN STORIES THAT SAVED MY LIFE

A MEMOIR

CAROL SMITH

ABRAMS PRESS, NEW YORK

The stories in this book are based in part on ones that first appeared in the *Seattle Post-Intelligencer*. They are used here by permission of Hearst Corp. Some passages included here were also previously included in the essays "Middens," which appeared in *Literal Latte*, and "Spider Silk," which appeared in the anthology *Pooled Ink* published by Northern Colorado Writers. Thank you to the publications that gave this work an early home.

Jacket © 2021 Abrams

Library of Congress Control Number: 2020944850

ISBN: 978-1-4197-5013-7
eISBN: 978-1-64700-096-7

Printed and bound in the United States
10 9 8 7 6 5 4 3 2 1

Abrams books are available at special discounts when purchased in quantity for premiums and promotions as well as fundraising or educational use. Special editions can also be created to specification. For details, contact specialsales@abramsbooks.com or the address below.

Abrams Press® is a registered trademark of Harry N. Abrams, Inc.

ABRAMS The Art of Books
195 Broadway, New York, NY 10007
abramsbooks.com

FOR CHRISTOPHER
AND THOSE WHO LOVED HIM

"Real isn't how you are made," said the Skin Horse. "It's a thing that happens to you when a child loves you for a long, long time, not just to play with, but Really loves you, then you become Real."

"Does it hurt?" asked the rabbit.

"Sometimes," said the Skin Horse, for he was always truthful. "When you are Real, you don't mind being hurt."

—The Velveteen Rabbit, *Margery Williams*

This is a book about trauma and grief. But it's also a book about love, about living, about persistence and joy. It's about reinventing, finding purpose, and discovering strength you didn't know you had until you were called upon to use it.

Every one of us fears there is something we could not survive. For me, it was the death of my only child when he was seven years old. He died suddenly, during what was shaping up to be the best year of his life. A kidney transplant had given him a second start on a healthy childhood. That dream ended when, without warning, he collapsed in cardiac arrest at his grandparents' house. I was not with him when he died, a fact that haunts me to this day. After his death, I woke in shock to an utterly changed world. I couldn't read the map to find my way out of the vast, harsh landscape of my grief.

In a similar way, the coronavirus pandemic has forced so many of us into unfamiliar territory. And its signature wound is that people die alone without their loved ones near, the thought of which still brings me to my knees.

The feelings in those early days of the pandemic, the way time blurs, the obsessive search for any bit of news that might change the outcome, the sinking realization that control had slipped from our grasp, the sense of dislocation, the daily struggle to breathe—all these perfectly mirror feelings of grief.

So, too, does the panicky sense that we don't know yet what we've lost, only that it's something we didn't know how much we'd miss. Or the sense of foreboding that even if something awful hasn't happened yet, it will soon—what I heard one person call "the grief before the grief." And there is this, too: the grief after the grief, the way one trauma calls back another in the echo chamber of the heart.

People can't give you hope, can't dispense it on an as-needed basis like a prescription. But I believe hope can be learned, and it's learned through the experience of others. It happens through our shared stories. After my son died, I needed hope. I found it through reporting the stories of others who had faced down hard circumstances of their own. These were stories of survival and transformation, of people confronting devastating situations that changed them in unexpected ways.

I learned how to live after loss from their stories. Many more of us are facing unimaginable losses in the long tail of the COVID-19 crisis. I hope these stories will provide as much courage and insight for others as they did for me.

—Carol Smith, May 2020

PROLOGUE

I did not go to my son Christopher's school the day the nurse came to speak. Instead, I lay fetal-like on his bed, my face pressed to his sheets. The trace scents of crayons and Band-Aids, mud and baseball leather, kept me breathing. I squeezed my eyes shut. Images clicked by like a reel in his View-Master:

Christopher, riding a therapy horse, showing off his "tricks," his arms sticking straight out, his head thrown back, laughing.

Christopher, hiding rocks and shells under his bed, the found treasures of a seven-year-old.

Christopher, nestled next to me on the bed as we read books together in sign language.

"Again, story," he would sign, tapping the fingertips of one hand into the palm of the other, then drawing his hands apart like he was pulling taffy. I'd laugh, knowing this was a tactic to avoid the dreaded bedtime, and turn back to the beginning.

We'd spied this bed together early one Sunday morning as we wandered the Rose Bowl flea market in Pasadena, California, near where we lived. Both of us had fallen for its vintage pine headboard, festooned with fading decals of saddles and spurs. Sometimes he drifted to sleep in blue pajamas with comets on them, still wearing his red cowboy hat. The bed was his steed and his rocket ship. Now I clung to it for fear of drowning.

It was the first day after winter break, and overcast, the sun locked behind a scrim of gray. Fifteen miles away at George Washington Elementary School in Burbank, my friend Kathy, the mother of one of Christopher's best friends, stood in front of their first-grade class. A pediatric nurse, she'd dealt with young children on cancer wards. Her wide smile and warm voice would have been steady and reassuring.

I could picture her signing as she spoke, by habit as the mother of a deaf child herself, and because many of the children were deaf like

Christopher. I'd left my newspaper job in Seattle to move to Pasadena when Christopher was four years old, partly so he could go to this school with its side-by-side teaching in oral and sign traditions. Hearing children in the classroom learned to sign. Deaf children learned to read lips and use their voices. Together, they made a seamless language of childhood. I asked Kathy later to tell me what happened next.

The children fidgeted in their blue-and-red school uniforms as a clutch of adults hovered around the edges of the classroom. They must have thought it strange to see so many grown-up faces in this space for play and learning. Along with Kathy, their principal was there and a psychologist from the hospital where she worked, as well as the director of the preschool many of the students had attended the previous year, and both their teachers. The teachers' eyes were red from crying. In the middle, Christopher's small wooden desk sat empty.

The therapist—a man the children didn't know—held up a Raggedy Andy doll. Kathy asked the class what they observed about it. The children pointed out his red yarn hair and triangle nose, his sailor hat and embroidered heart. The man put the doll out of sight.

"Even though Raggedy Andy isn't here anymore, can you still remember things about him?" Kathy asked.

The game excited the kids. They shouted out the various adventures of Raggedy Andy and Raggedy Ann from memory. Then one of the adults—Kathy no longer remembers which—stepped forward to break the news. Something very sad had happened. The children quieted. Christopher had gotten sick and wouldn't be coming back to school. Doctors couldn't help him anymore.

"Christopher died."

Christopher died. The bed beneath me seemed to pitch and rock. I clutched my knees to my chest to keep from throwing up. I could not grasp the words. Each time I tried, they shattered into piles of indecipherable letters like a child's alphabet puzzle spilled to the floor.

I'd feared these words for seven years. Christopher was born with a tiny developmental defect in utero that had blocked his urinary tract, damaging his kidneys. That seemingly insignificant error set in motion a kind of butterfly effect, a cascade of medical sequelae we later could not escape.

Yet he had survived. Against odds, medical crisis after medical crisis. Until now. Until this. An abdominal obstruction that unexpectedly claimed his life during the Christmas holidays while he was visiting his grandparents with his father. I could not forgive myself for failing at the only thing that mattered. I had survived. Christopher had not.

And I wasn't there to say goodbye.

In my fugue of grief, I could barely leave the house. Kathy had volunteered to help tell his class, sparing me the impossible task. She told the kids they could still talk about Christopher, about how he wore a *Lion King* costume for Halloween that year, how his eyes were the golden brown of maple syrup, how he loved trains. She asked the class to write down their Christopher stories.

Weeks later, I received their brief memories, printed with crooked block letters on lined paper, illustrated with hearts and stars and stick-figure children with oversize hands.

"He was my best friend," read one. "He played tetherball with me."

"When I hurt my knee, he got me a Band-Aid," read another.

Some were written with the curious syntax of a deaf child: "Chris heaven go." In some of them, Christopher hovered in the right-hand corner of a bright blue sky.

I envied them the comfort of these small tales. I had no language for stories, no words at all. Even the simplest statements didn't make sense anymore. Christopher *is* my son. Christopher *was* my son. I couldn't make either be true. The void of his loss was as indescribable as the darkness between stars.

The dictionary offers little help when it comes to grieving. There is no word for bottomless well or unanswered prayer, no word in English, like "orphan" or "widow," for a parent who has lost a child. In Sanskrit, *vilomah* means "against the natural order." Portuguese has *saudade*, an untranslatable word that describes a deep longing for a person who will never return. In Spanish, *madrugada* is the word for the ineffable dark between midnight and dawn. But what noun did any of those make me?

IN THE WEEKS AND months after Christopher died, people stepped in to help. One of my old colleagues from the paper wrote Christopher's obituary when I couldn't. Other friends advised me to move home to Seattle to be near family. But that would mean packing up his room, and I could not bring myself to give his things away. When Christopher was little, I would sometimes discover my watch missing, usually when I'd been getting ready to leave for an errand or for work. I'd find the watch later, tucked into one of his many secret compartments for hiding schoolyard finds. Psychologists would have called this a "linking object," something to soothe the separation.

Now it was my turn to need a linking object. But what single, magic talisman could conjure Christopher back for me? I clung to them all—his windup dinosaurs and Slinky, his Batman Band-Aids and his red fanny pack with the blue asthma inhaler, his beloved View-Master.

Instead of packing, I cleaned his room the way I would when he left for school breaks with his father, my ex-husband. I threw out the dried-up Magic Markers, boxed the outgrown clothes and toys for recycling, tidied up the art supplies, and gathered the ephemera of a seven-year-old's life for his scrapbook. I folded his clothes, put them in his closet, turned the calendar, and stacked his homework. I sorted puzzle pieces into their proper boxes and spent time playing with the things he'd been outgrowing—my ritual for remembering the stages he was passing through.

Afterward, the room felt ready, ordered, welcoming. That made it worse. I craved the happy swirl of his energy when he'd come rushing home and the ensuing disarray. I missed the "campsite" he set up each night, preferring the adventure of sleeping on the floor to the comfort of his bed. I missed the lumpy piles of clothes and endless rearranging of toy train tracks that threaded through the room. His unchanging room taunted me with the truth of his absence.

This is the paradox of grief. At first, I could not bear the thought of moving. Later, I could not bear to stay.

I.

THE GIFT OF CHILDHOOD

(SETH)

CHAPTER 1

The drive from my house to the *Seattle Post-Intelligencer* each morning took me across the old Evergreen Point Floating Bridge, then the longest span built on pontoons in the world. Its bridge deck hovered so close to the surface of Lake Washington that any major windstorm forced its closure. People at the paper used to say the bridge was held together with gum and shoelaces. They were only half kidding.

Traffic often stalled on the bridge midspan. On clear days, it was a spectacular place to be stranded, Mount Rainier emerging to the south, the sun lighting the tops of the Olympics to the west. The water was my space between. Cocooned in my car, I could shake off the remnants of the dreams that unsettled my nights and haunted my mornings. Frantic, sweaty dreams that Christopher wasn't really dead, that I'd forgotten to pick him up from school, that he was lost in a snowstorm without a jacket, that his father had taken him away and I didn't know where.

I carried little of my old life with me—a few of Christopher's favorite Batman Band-Aids tucked in my wallet, along with his dog-eared library card. I wore a small gold star around my neck for all the times we'd counted the stars in the sky together. By the time I made it across the bridge, I'd assembled my professional mask, put up the guard I needed to get through the day.

When I'd left the paper six years earlier, I'd worried I might be derailing my journalism career for good. I'd left a solid newspaper job, covering aerospace and tech, for the vagaries of working for myself, taking whatever freelance gigs I could get. Coming back to a salaried job at the *P-I*, I wasn't sure I wanted that career anymore.

I'd originally started at the *P-I* in my midtwenties, thrilled to get my first big newspaper job after toiling at a small daily in the suburbs for a few years right out of grad school. Back then, the *P-I* was still in its old home at Sixth and Wall in downtown Seattle, a building designed to hold a thirteen-ton spinning blue globe on its roof. Giant neon-red letters rotated its equator, boasting, IT'S IN THE P-I. An eagle outlined in neon yellow perched on top. The building itself was squat and solid, built with the hopeful modernism of the 1940s. It took up a whole city block and used to shake when the presses ran. When I arrived to work each day, I looked up at the globe like I was Lois Lane, like I had a world of possibilities ahead of me, like I could conquer anything.

A few years before I'd moved to LA, the paper had moved to a sleek office building on Seattle's waterfront. The new newsroom looked less like something out of an old movie set and more like a messy insurance office. Hearst, the paper's owner, had split the globe in half like a plastic Easter egg one night and trucked it down from the old building to the new one on extra-wide flatbed trucks. Plopped on top of its new home, the globe looked anachronistic and out of place.

I felt the same when I returned to the newsroom two years after Christopher's death. I bumped into my old self in every corner: the stairwell where I'd first whispered to a colleague I was pregnant and she'd squealed, clapping me in a big hug; the restroom where I'd hidden after finding out, two weeks before his due date, that Christopher might not survive his birth; the desk where a gravelly-voiced consumer columnist coordinated meal deliveries for me during Christopher's long months in the intensive care unit as an infant.

The newsroom was a maze of memories. Every morning on the way to check the staff bulletin board by the coffee machine, I passed the glass office of the managing editor who'd wished me well when I'd resigned to move to Los Angeles. "Taking care of your family is more important than any job," he'd said back then. Now I had my job back, but it gave me no pleasure. I had failed at the most important thing.

Each night after work, I closed myself in my study, wrung out from getting through the day. I slumped on the floor next to the heat register, my back against the wall, and poured my feelings into journals. I wrote in gasps, as though a formless beast had seized my throat. Metaphors fill the pages, my attempts to name this thing, this inexpressible grief, this raw, wild feeling of being lost. What had happened to that young woman who gazed up at the globe and could imagine anything but this?

I wanted to go back and be her again, wanted to rewind to the part where I was young and in love with the prospect of caring for a new baby, fixing up an old house, and planning for a future filled with family. I wanted to be that person who'd cooked Thanksgiving dinner for my whole family each year, who had friends over for summer evening barbecues and made flourless chocolate tortes for their birthdays, who spent nights weaving baby blankets on an eight-harness loom. I wanted to rewrite the script so that Christopher didn't die, so that I could poke my head into the next room and tell him to finish his homework, or hop on his bed to read him a book. My life would cycle in flashbacks until I'd fall asleep on the floor, all cried out. There were days I wanted the long *madrugada* to end. I didn't care if the bridge sank on my way to work.

WHEN I FIRST RETURNED, my desk was in the business section, the same back corner of the office where I'd worked before. It had the advantage of being out of the main circulation of the newsroom. Long stretches went by when I could hide in my cubicle and avoid tripping on my memories.

Some reporters had sweeping views over Puget Sound, where winter sunsets would distract them from their deadlines. My desk looked the other way, south over the railroad tracks that ran along Seattle's working waterfront. Freight trains rattled the building several times a day. Without thinking, I'd find myself counting the cars as they rumbled by, something Christopher and I had loved doing whenever we saw a train.

Mostly, though, I tried not to think about Christopher so I could work. There were no pictures of him at my desk. I made no mention of him when other parents talked about their kids. Still, he shadowed my conversations. Unconsciously, my hand would form his name sign—the shape of a C circling over my heart. Signs I'd used over and over with Christopher—hot or stop or happy, please and thank you and sorry—would slip out, too. Sometimes my hand would form the C of his name and go to my throat, then fall to my sternum. The sign for hunger. The sign for wish. *Saudade.* Out of context, most people didn't notice the signs. They probably thought I just gestured a lot when I spoke.

Within a year of my rejoining the paper, Tom Paulson, the medical reporter, went on a fellowship leave, and Kathy Best, the city editor, asked me to move out to the main city room to cover medicine. I was glad, by then, to give up my business beats. The machinations of corporate America held little interest for me. As a younger reporter, I had broken a national story about a business con artist that had landed me in *Forbes.* There was a picture of me, very pregnant, to go along with the article. I'd added it to the brand-new "baby memories" box I was assembling, joking back then that it was my baby's first co-byline. Later, I'd covered the early development of recombinant DNA technology and the dawn of injectable biologic drugs, including erythropoietin, a hormone that boosts red blood cell counts, and human growth hormone—two drugs I would eventually give to Christopher to counter the effects of kidney failure. Now, though, business stories no longer excited me the way they once had. Medicine had consumed so much of my life already, I thought covering it might be a better fit. Except for one thing: It would mean leaving my safe hiding space in the back of the building.

The main city room of the *Seattle P-I* was a large open space lined with glass offices for senior editors. The ACEs—assistant city editors—sat at desks on a dais in the middle of the room, where they could see everyone. That way, when news broke, they could yell assignments and get people out the door quickly. The reporters were clumped in small pods throughout the space. My desk was in a pod right next to the giant conference table that served as the "bullpen"—the place editors gathered each morning to decide what stories to assign that day and which ones had front-page potential. The newsroom had a kind of kinetic music.

Ringing phones and the rat-a-tat of teletype machines, which spit out the wires, punctuated the low and urgent hum of talking. That hum was our electricity. The newsroom ran on it.

Each morning at work, I made rounds of calls and sifted through piles of papers for story ideas. I looked for small mentions of accidents in the briefs inside the newspaper, wondering about the rest of the story, or searched through the obituaries, wondering about survivors, or heard about people going through life-changing circumstances from colleagues and sources. I was obsessed with finding those moments on which a life turns. The ones that divide time into before and after. I couldn't help myself. These were the stories that interested me—the moments we can't control and didn't see coming.

ONE APRIL AFTERNOON, I was about to leave for lunch when I ran across an announcement from the National Institutes of Health. I sat back down. Scientists had found a genetic mutation responsible for progeria, a rare disease that causes children to physically age many times faster than normal and leads to premature death, often before age thirteen. My heart faltered. It had been more than eight years since Christopher's death by then, and normally, I could separate my past from my daily work. This time, though, the news slashed open that familiar wound.

I shoved the paper to the bottom of a pile and pretended I hadn't seen it. But it was too late. Already, a flash flood of memories threatened to drown all my other thoughts. My lungs clenched down like fists. I got up from my desk and went to the windows that banked the bullpen to stare out over the waters of Elliott Bay and try to remember how to breathe.

Showers blew down in breezy splashes, the sun peeking out between. A stately container ship, stacked high with bright blue boxes, glided toward the port at the far end of the bay where a flock of tall, orange cargo cranes stood like giant metal shorebirds awaiting a meal washed in by the tide. Slowly, my breath returned, and I went back to my desk to scour the wires for another piece of breaking news, anything to distract me from my ghosts.

Hours passed, or maybe it was only minutes, but no matter how much I worked to forget it, the progeria story tugged at me. I fished the press release back out of my pile.

On my second read, I tried to approach the story the way I would any other, with professional detachment. The announcement implied that scientists were coming closer to understanding this childhood disease, which had, until then, eluded their grasp. It meant doctors might be able to develop effective treatment, or maybe even a cure.

The scientific implications should have intrigued me. I should have begun pitching the story to my editor right then. As I read, though, I kept imagining all those families who knew their children were going to die before becoming adults. Families who likely wouldn't see their children graduate from high school, or realize their childhood dreams, or start families of their own. They were families who would miss their children's nerve-racking first driver's tests and awkward first loves. I couldn't imagine how they could bear it. I didn't know how I was still bearing it. So I did the only thing I could do: I lost myself in research.

The disease, which was random and not inherited, had baffled researchers since 1886, when it was first identified. There'd been only one hundred documented cases since, making it exceedingly difficult to study. What scientists had just discovered was this: A certain gene mutation caused a flaw in a key protein found in the scaffolding of the nuclei of cells, which made the cells break down more quickly. Discovery of this gene offered researchers a place to target a potential treatment and possibly even cure what they thought to be an incurable illness. I scrolled through the wires to find that the national press was already buzzing about what the research might also tell us about the process of aging in general.

The story had front-page potential, if I could locate a family to profile. Major genetic findings with implications for the general population were always of keen interest, especially in Seattle, a city full of medical researchers. Front-page stories were currency in the newsroom.

I would be a fool not to pursue this one. But I couldn't stop thinking what it would mean for me if I did. I would have to face a mother who knew she was losing her child.

My life already teetered on the edge of that unnameable, bottomless well. It took all my energy not to fall over, not to spiral back to those early days when I thought I would die from the pain of Christopher's loss, when I pleaded for that relief. During the day, a busy job and deadlines kept me away from the lip of the well. Nights, though, my mind betrayed me.

In my nightmares, I lost Christopher over and over. In these night terrors, he was always pedaling away from me on a little blue tricycle in his favorite red-and-turquoise camp shirt, a Bell helmet like a turtle on his head, a cliff in front of him. I couldn't see his face. No matter how fast I ran, no matter how much I yelled for him to stop, he could not hear me. I could never catch him before he fell into the darkness.

In the months that followed, I tried to put the story out of my mind, but it wouldn't release me. It pulled at me like a bowline in a gathering storm. In an attempt to once and for all cut the idea loose, I finally called the NIH and the Progeria Research Foundation, looking for leads on families. There were fewer than forty children with progeria in the world, and only seven of them lived in the United States at the time. The odds of finding a child with progeria near enough to me to make a story feasible were minuscule. Still, my pulse raced as I ran my finger down the list that popped up on my computer screen. My finger stopped on one line, and I felt the little elevator-drop sensation of my heart missing a beat, a sensation my doctors had more than once assured me had nothing to do with a murmur. One of the seven children in the United States with progeria lived in Darrington, Washington.

Darrington is a mountain town in the North Cascades an hour and a half north of Seattle. Bordered by rivers, the town had once served as the portage between them. Now it served the people who fished and logged in the surrounding woods. Darrington, as I learned that day, was also the home of a ten-year-old boy named Seth Cook.

There was no information about his health or condition, just the stark fact he belonged to the unlucky club of children born with a random mutation that dictated their future.

My hand shook as I took down the details on the yellow legal pad that lived by my phone. I told myself it didn't mean anything. I didn't have to call. I ripped the number off the pad and turned it facedown where it wouldn't stare back at me.

That night, though, I couldn't sleep. Memories crowded in on me: Christopher crowing the first time he hit a T-ball. Christopher snuggling into my arms to read a book. Christopher in the hospital, unconscious and tethered to monitors. *I wasn't there to say goodbye.* I tried to bury the thought. It was no use.

I got up and paced around my darkened living room, stepping on the long shadows that had turned all the colors black and gray. I wondered what Seth's life was like, what it would be like to see the world through the eyes of a child who knew, at a deep bone level, he was going to die. To understand what Christopher might have thought.

THE NEXT MORNING, I talked to my editor, Laura Coffey, about doing a documentary-style story about a boy with progeria. I made the case we could all learn something about confronting mortality from a boy who was aging faster than the rest of us. I proposed that I follow Seth for a year—enough time to really get to know him.

Laura had red hair and a hearty laugh. Enthusiastic and tender-hearted, she loved human interest and animal stories. Her emails to me were always peppered with multiple exclamation marks. She was on board with a story about Seth immediately, as long as pursuing it didn't prevent me from covering the more mundane aspects of my beat—the blood drives and flu counts, hospital mergers and research findings.

Not all my editors knew about Christopher, but Rita Hibbard, the metro editor, did. She knew me from when I'd first worked at the paper. I'd brought Christopher to Rita's baby shower years earlier and we'd bonded as mothers of sons. When I'd come back to the paper after Christopher died, she was the one who'd suggested recruiting me off the business desk to cover medicine. When Rita heard about the story I'd pitched, she pulled me aside, a grave look on her face. We sat in her glassed-in office while she asked me about my plans. Rita wasn't one to flinch from difficult stories. As a young reporter, she'd covered the sadistic attacks of the South Hill Rapist, who'd terrorized the city of Spokane, Washington. She'd been a medical reporter before me and had done her share of stories about human suffering. She'd risen through the editor ranks at the *P-I* with a reputation for making tough calls on hard stories. Yet she didn't seem to think this was one I should pursue. It took me a few minutes to realize it wasn't the story she was worried about, it was me.

"Think about what you're doing," she said, her blue eyes bright with the suggestion of tears. She didn't say the thing we probably both were thinking—the thing about Christopher, the thing about me having reasons for pursuing this story other than journalistic curiosity.

For me, though, there was only one choice I could make. The idea for the story kept running through my mind. I kept trying to picture Seth—what he looked like, what he sounded like. I wondered whether he was joyful, like Christopher, or somber with the weight of knowing he had a fatal disease. I didn't know whether Christopher had been afraid of his own death. Maybe this story would give me a second chance to find out.

CHAPTER 2

The morning I was to drive up to Darrington to meet Seth for the first time, I checked and rechecked to make sure I had the directions Seth's mom, Patti, had given me. A quarter mile from the paper, I discovered I'd left my notebook and questions back in the newsroom. I turned around, picked them up, and rushed off, wondering if it was a sign that maybe Rita was right. Maybe this was a bad idea.

Patti and Kyle, Seth's parents, had tentatively agreed to my doing the story, with one caveat: It would be up to Seth, which meant I had to travel to Darrington to seek a ten-year-old's approval.

I'd spent very little time around children since Christopher's death. I was clumsy even around my own young niece and nephew, awkwardly trying to be cheerful when I could see so much of his face in theirs. Now I was going to be talking to a boy not much older than Christopher had been when he died, and I was going to have to pretend it would not gut me.

Darrington was tiny—fewer than three hundred families. There was one main street with one grocery, a café, and a bank. The one school campus served kindergarten through twelfth grade. Still, I got lost trying to find Seth's house and had to stop for directions in the town itself. The waitress at the café knew Seth's family. As soon as I asked, she pointed me up a road leading out of town into the woods.

Seth's house sat at the end of a long gravel driveway, hidden in a nest of trees in the hills above town. Kyle had built the house in a clearing with Whitehorse Mountain in the view beyond. A deer leapt off at the sound of my tires. I parked and grabbed my notebook, my hands shaking. Then, before I could second-guess myself, I knocked on the door.

I thought I'd known what to expect, but as the wooden door swung open and I looked down to meet Seth, I still had to stop myself from gasping. At age ten, he looked like an eighty-year-old man in a toddler-size body. He was bald and wrinkled. His veins showed through his skin, and his blue eyes were cloudy. He barely came up to my waist. It took a few heartbeats to recover my composure.

"You must be Seth," I said. My throat was so tight that my voice came out strangled and thin. Despite their vastly different appearances, there was something in Seth's face that reminded me of Christopher's, just for a flash—a kind of eager curiosity to meet the world.

Seth nodded politely and held out a bony hand. I shook it gingerly. He smiled and led me to the couch in the family's small living room. He perched on the edge of the cushions and sized me up behind my notebook. The skin of a bear his dad had hunted for meat one winter hung on the wall. It looked vaguely menacing.

"Sometimes the bears come right into the front yard," Seth said, following my gaze. His voice was high and tinny, like he'd sucked the helium out of a balloon.

I started to say something about how scary that must be, then stopped. It seemed the wrong thing to say, considering what a frightening situation he already faced. I swallowed hard and said something noncommittal about that being cool. I hoped I sounded convincing.

Seth scooted off the couch. "Want to see my room?"

An image of Christopher dragging my parents to his room first thing whenever they came to visit flitted through my mind. I glanced at Patti, who nodded her permission. My stomach lurched as I stood.

Seth led me down a hallway lined with department-store portraits of him growing up. They reminded me of the ones I'd had done of Christopher, posed with toys or balls, and parsed out to relatives' wallets. Except looking at this gallery of Seth was like watching a time lapse. In his earliest picture, his hair was silky blond and his blue eyes were bright above chubby cheeks. In each subsequent portrait, made a year apart, he looked a decade older.

Seth caught me staring and shrugged. "I age faster than other people," he said, "like dog years."

Just then, a large black spider hopped along the hall toward my leg. I nearly jumped.

Seth beamed. "Don't worry." He showed me the button he'd hidden in his hand that made it work.

Despite my nerves, I laughed. The sound of it startled me. Since moving back to Seattle, I'd arranged my life carefully to avoid encountering children. No going to Woodland Park Zoo or Shilshole beach, where families swarmed on weekends. No trips to Seattle Center, where kids flocked to the spray of the International Fountain. It was as though there were a cheerful, alternate city—a "children's Seattle"—I'd shut myself out of. It seemed like years since I'd laughed spontaneously around a kid. Maybe it had been.

I don't remember what we spoke about, or whether I said anything cringe-worthy from a ten-year-old's viewpoint, but when my interview was done, Seth saw me to the door. He grinned. "See you next time."

It took a moment for it to sink in, and then I smiled back. Somehow, amid all my awkward fumbling, I'd passed his test. And mine.

I drove away elated, eager to get to know him better and confident I could assure my editors the story would be worth the investment of the paper's time. I drove through the forest that surrounded Seth's tiny community, winding down along the old highway that paralleled the North Fork of the Stillaguamish River. Occasionally the woods gave way to wide, sweeping views of the rising Cascade foothills, the landscape lush and rugged at the same time. I could feel the hold it had on its small and self-sufficient population of loggers and fishers, artists and recluses. It was a world away from the traffic and commotion of Seattle.

But as I turned back onto I-5 heading south and the forests gave way to outlet malls and tribal casinos, my excitement began to fade. I thought about what lay ahead for Seth and his family. My metronome of regrets started up again: the conversations Christopher and I had never had; the game of Candy Land I'd told him we'd play later and never gotten around to; the Dodgers games we hadn't seen, kites we hadn't flown, and camping trips we hadn't taken. All the things we hadn't had time for.

When I finally got back to the office, I wanted to collapse, as though a heavy stone had landed on my chest. I didn't think I could do the story after all.

"How'd it go?" Laura asked.

I was too tired to tell her the truth. Instead, I headed home and crawled into bed, exhausted. I pleaded for a night with no nightmares.

MY COURAGE, IN THOSE first months after meeting Seth, was a fickle thing, dipping away and swinging back to me, like a pendulum whose rhythm I couldn't predict. Each time I'd decide to visit him again, I'd find something else to do that seemed more pressing. That was the good thing about the news business. There was always something else that needed covering.

I'd plunged into reporting on a horrible case about a young woman who had gone into a coma after an anesthesiologist allegedly removed her breathing tube too soon during a routine procedure. The anesthesiologist, who'd been fired in another state, later admitted he'd been stealing and using narcotics intended to treat his patients. I tracked how state medical boards kept such information secret, allowing addicted doctors to move from one state to another without the information following them. The story consumed most of my attention, but every so often, I'd find myself wondering about Seth.

A few months after that first meeting, when I'd at last regained my resolve, I made a plan to visit him again. Seth was going to be reading to a class of kindergartners, and Patti had suggested I go along with them. It was something they did every year for the newest batch of students.

I set off in a hard November rain, giving myself extra time in case my nerves failed me again. I got as far as Arlington, the point-of-no-return exit toward Darrington, before I had to pull over. I sat in the car on the corner of a gas station lot and went over my questions, bracing myself for the interview to come. I'd be asking Patti questions this time—about how they'd discovered Seth's diagnosis and what it had done to their lives. I worried about how difficult it might be for her to relive those moments. Or for me to listen.

By the time I arrived, I'd worked myself into a state of high anxiety. Patti greeted me warmly, as though I'd been there just a few days earlier. I gulped down the glass of water she offered me, willing my throat to open so I could talk without gasping. I looked around to buy time. A row of ceramic angels rested on a windowsill in her kitchen. On the wall, Patti had hung the framed verse "Love is patient. Love is kind. . . ." Seth's most recent spelling test was posted to the fridge: "crises, knives, pianos, waves, wishes, armies, heroes, tomatoes, canoes." He'd gotten 100 percent and a five-dollar reward.

Patti had light brown, honey-streaked hair that fell to her shoulders. Her face was unlined, and she laughed easily. While Seth got ready for school, she stood there making peanut butter sandwiches like nothing was wrong. Each time she smiled, a sharp pain corkscrewed beneath my sternum. Seth's future was already written. He was going to die while still a child. How could she be smiling? How could her bones hold her up? I looked down at my notes so my face would not betray me, and quickly, before my thoughts could spiral any further, I asked her to tell me how she and Kyle discovered Seth's diagnosis. She nodded and began.

Seth was just three months old when she'd first sensed something was different about her only child. When she picked him up, she could feel his baby fat already melting away. *Maybe it was just new-parent jitters*, she thought, but it didn't seem right. She and Kyle took Seth to the pediatrician, but doctors couldn't find an explanation. They tried not to worry. By six months, Seth's skin seemed thinner and his veins were showing. The first seed of panic took root.

"He was falling off the growth chart," Patti said. Measured against other growing babies, Seth was losing ground. By one year old, he was completely bald. "We kept getting more tests," she said. But no test explained what was wrong.

All the questions doctors had never been able to answer for me raced through my mind. They couldn't say what caused the original birth defect that had critically damaged Christopher's kidneys, or why he had seizures, or why he was deaf. They couldn't say how we were supposed to survive without him. Even though Patti couldn't have known it, I understood the helplessness she must have felt.

When Seth was eighteen months old, Patti and Kyle sent his records, along with photos of him, to a doctor in New York who specialized in children's developmental diseases. A few weeks later, Patti received a letter from the doctor.

She was alone in her living room when she opened it. The word "progeria," printed in crisp black ink, leapt up at her. She knew what it meant. The diagnosis came with one simple, irrefutable reality: Children with progeria died of old age, usually in their early teens. Few had crossed the threshold of twenty-one. At the time, Patti was only twenty-one herself.

Shock is the body's best defense against a coming blow.

Patti drove, letter in hand, to the lumber mill where Kyle worked. They each read and reread the letter, searching for words that weren't there, words that would make this monstrous prophecy untrue. But no relief came. Patti was not prone to crying. It was a point of pride. Her dad was in the military, and she called her mom a "tough Mexican lady." Patti had bounced around a lot as a kid and considered herself pretty tough as well. The night she got the letter, she cried, the first of what would be many times that year.

Patti lowered her voice so Seth wouldn't hear her in the other room. "I thought, *What do I do? How do I deal with this?*"

As she spoke, my stomach twisted with the same sickening sensation I'd had when I found out Christopher might not live past birth. I looked down at my notebook and clenched my jaw to keep from crying.

With no cure and no treatment for progeria, the only thing doctors could do was put the Cook family in touch with other families through a group called Sunshine Foundation. The foundation, which had been started by a former Philadelphia cop to grant wishes to critically ill children, sponsored annual reunions for children with progeria. Although Kyle didn't like to travel, he knew this was something his family needed. In Darrington, he and Patti were surrounded by "typical" children— kids who were growing like weeds, plowing through clothing sizes, and attempting more and more daring skills on the playground, while their own child grew more fragile by the day. That summer, they went to their first reunion in Florida, and for once, Seth wasn't the kid who was different.

I pictured Seth at a reunion full of children who looked like him, small and wizened, doing the regular things kids did but without pity or stares. I'd been so happy the first time I'd seen Christopher signing in a room full of other deaf children. It had been such a relief to know he wasn't alone.

In the next moment, though, the image slipped away. One of the first kids Patti and Kyle met at the Sunshine Foundation event died when he was six. Seth was only three at the time. He didn't comprehend what this meant, but Patti did. She understood then, in a visceral way, what she hadn't before: that her time with her son would run out. With Kyle's support, Patti quit her job at the Station, a combination gas station and store in Darrington, to spend more time with Seth. Kyle worked "dark to dark" at the mill, pulling double shifts so one of them could be with Seth as much as possible.

Kyle, a soft-spoken man most comfortable in the woods, took his son with him wherever he could, spending long weekend days on the river, teaching him a woodsman's skills. Both parents knew it could never be enough time. Patti tried to ignore her fears, but they crept in anyway. "I was a wreck, crying all the time. Kyle heard it all. He did his best to comfort me," she said. "He was a lot of what got me through."

Sitting at Patti's kitchen table, I wanted to blurt out that after Christopher was born, I, too, was terrified my son would die. That at night I still dreamed I had time to stop it. I started to speak, but Seth emerged from his bedroom just then, a gray hoodie pulled over his head against the chill. He asked his mom where his school pack was before turning to smile at me.

Something in my chest pulled tight. In the few months since we'd first met, his face seemed pinched even smaller. His big-kid-size teeth seemed too large for his tiny receding jaw. When Seth finished loading his pack, he went to brush his teeth. I trailed behind him. For the first

attitude, slouching low in their chairs, baseball c
trading insults. I took a seat in the back of the classro
imagine what Christopher might have been like at that a
few rows ahead of me, hunched over his desk. His feet dan
the floor. The brim of his baseball cap was bigger than his face,
barely bigger than a man's wrist.

Seth's teacher, Mr. Gerring, tried valiantly to focus the class on
morning's math lesson. He had curly, gray-streaked hair and a mildl
exasperated air that verged into amusement behind his glasses. Occasionally he'd turn and fix a kid with a look to get them to stop talking.
He threatened a pop quiz, and a round of groans filled the room. The
fidgety energy in the class built like rocket fuel until, finally, he ordered
everyone out of their seats for jumping jacks.

Seth hopped to attention along with his classmates. The other kids
began to jump, their bodies jackknifing the air. If any one of them
bumped into Seth, it would have sent him sprawling. I sat forward in
my chair, anxious for Seth, wondering what he would do next. Across
from him, I noticed a poster on the wall with a lesson in problem
olving: "Choose a plan. Examine your choices. Pick a strategy." Seth
ng on to the back of his chair and bobbled up and down until the
count. Then he plopped back into his seat and resumed his math
on as if it were no big deal.

Weighing twenty-seven pounds and coming up belt-high to his
mates did dictate certain realities for Seth at school, though.
the course of that day, Seth had to scoot a chair under a water
n to get a drink. He asked his cousin Emily, who ate lunch with
ry day, to pop open the top of his apple juice for him. "My can
Seth called her, and they both giggled. While the other kids
ut in PE, he power-pressed a broomstick. "I have the body of
year-old and look what I can do!"

recess, Seth headed to the computer lab. "Wanna see some-
" he asked, settling in at his computer for a virtual frog
peeked over his shoulder as he labeled frog body parts.
hed programs and showed me how to deconstruct "owl

---

time, I noticed a little limp. His arthritic fingers had trouble opening
the toothpaste tube. I wanted to jump in and help him, but I stayed
back. He wasn't my son, and he hadn't asked for help. I had to remind
myself my job was to observe. Finally, he wrangled the cap off, then
threw his whole weight into turning on the water faucet. His veins
showed purple in the bathroom light.

"Let's go!" he said. "I don't want to be late." He headed out the door,
his coat drooping off his shoulders, dragging a book bag nearly as big
as he was. I had no choice but to follow.

OUTSIDE THE CLASSROOM, I hesitated, my nerves buzzing like high-
tension power lines. This would be the first time I'd been around
kindergartners since Christopher had died. I'd already nearly cried
in Patti's kitchen. I'd already nearly told her too much about my life. I
wasn't sure how I'd handle this. But it was too late now to turn around.

Seth limped in ahead of me with a picture book tucked under one
arm. A baseball cap covered his bald head. Patti and I stood at the edge
of the classroom while he took his place at the center of the kindergarten
circle. He hopped onto a pint-size chair, skinny shins dangling from
arthritic knees swollen to the size of tennis balls. The kindergartners in
the room loomed around him like linebackers. Seth, however, seemed
nonplussed. He opened the book with gnarled fingers.

"I'm a wide-mouthed frog and I eat flies," he began. His jaw worked
visibly beneath his translucent skin. As the story unfolded, the squirm-
ing five-year-olds pointed to the animals and squealed. Seth played to
his audience, waggling the pop-up illustrations for dramatic effect, all
the way to the last page.

Seth closed the book and waited. "Any questions?"

I held my breath, my stomach as jumpy as the frog in the book.
Children could be unexpectedly cruel. Kidney failure had stunted
Christopher's growth, and the steroids he took after his kidney transplant caused his body to bloat. Whenever I dropped Christopher off in
a new classroom, I'd worried that kids would make fun of his moon-pie
face behind my back or mock him because he couldn't talk like them.

Ten hands shot up. My body tensed in preparation.

"I like the crocodile," one child said.

"I like Seth's reading," said another. A chorus of "I likes" ran around the circle. The unasked questions hovered like trapped balloons. Patti looked on quietly from her spot outside the circle. Finally, she raised her hand.

"I like how all the animals are different from each other," she said. The children turned to look at her. "Does Seth look the same as you?"

I stiffened. My pen dug a hole in the paper of my notebook.

"I can see his blood pipes," a little boy said.

The hole widened.

Patti's voice was calm. "Yes, that's because Seth has a disease."

"How did he get it?" another child asked.

"He was born with it," she said, as though it were the most natural thing in the world. "It's a very special disease that makes him stay smaller."

I looked up to see the children nodding as though this all made perfect sense.

"How are each of you different?" Patti asked.

"I was born in China," a tiny girl chirped.

"I have glasses," a boy said.

"Me, too!" another said.

"He's been on the Earth more than us," a girl chimed in, pointing to Seth. "When he was in preschool, I wasn't even born." A dozen tiny mouths fell open in momentary silence. Age was relative. At five years old, ten seemed ancient.

I clapped my own hand over my mouth to keep from laughing out loud. My heart stopped tripping over itself and my jaw unclenched. I closed my notebook, and my body relaxed for the first time all morning.

CHAPTER 3

The next time I visited Seth, I arrived during breakfast to find him presiding over two of his younger cousins from the head of the kitchen table. His cousins, five-year-old Tristan and one-year-old Jaedan, had the rosy cheeks and sturdy bodies of children raised in the country. Seth barely scraped three feet tall. He held court from the booster seat he needed to reach the table.

"Can you open this?" Seth handed me a bottle of gummy vitamin

I was there that day to go with Seth to his regular fifth-gr classroom, not do manual labor, but as I was quickly learning, impossible to be a passive observer around Seth.

"Which should I take first?" he said to Tristan, pointing to aspirin and his vitamin C. Not waiting for an answer, he po both into his mouth at once. Then he slid down from t headed to his room to get his stuff for school.

I followed him into his bedroom, jotting down the to get his books into his bag and the way he stuck behind him when he bent down. I was concentratin notes that I didn't notice when Tristan came into

"Jaedan's not being nice to kitty," Tristan sa

Seth hopped up and went in search of his kin. "Hey buddy, buddy. Enough of that," Set his layers of baby fat, looked like he could again for the cat's tail, but Seth distracted I chuckled. Clearly, despite his size, Se

BEING TEN—POST-KID, PRE-TEEN—
fifth-grade classroom, the girls w
puberty baby fat spilling out of h

pellets" on the screen. "This is what's in their poop," he said, using his computer's mouse to extract bones from the pellet and reassemble them into a virtual rat.

The rest of his class interrupted us fifteen minutes later, pouring in to join him for typing practice. Much as I enjoyed our one-on-one time, I could see that being in the middle of a bunch of other kids was what Seth liked best. He seemed to grow an inch, pulling himself up to his full height and puffing out his narrow chest.

"Gimme some skin," said one of the girls, high-fiving Seth as she passed by. She had long, center-parted hair and the beginnings of a Britney Spears pout. The lab filled with loud banter and the chatter of computer keys.

Seth had to stand to type because the chairs were too low for him to reach the desk. His hands weren't wide enough to stretch all the way across the keys, but he pecked away. "Ink, kink, brink, drink," he typed. "Bunk, hunk, junk."

Seth's mannerisms—his little strut and the way he laughed—reminded me so much of Christopher. I was sure he and Seth would have made great friends, could imagine them getting up to no good together, playing practical jokes and inventing games. For the first time in a long time, the thought of Christopher didn't contract a piece of me. Instead, it made me smile.

When the teacher wasn't looking, Seth played with images on his computer, manipulating and enlarging them. "I like making things grow," he whispered.

My smile faded. Seth seemed so cheerful and unselfconscious, but unselfconscious wasn't the same as unaware.

AFTER SCHOOL, SETH WANTED to show me the woods that bordered the scrubby meadow surrounding his house. He found a rock for us to kick as we went along. I was glad to have some quiet time with him at last. I wanted to know what he thought about having progeria and whether he understood what it meant for his future, a conversation I couldn't have with his classmates blundering around us. But it made me nervous.

We kept going, passing the rock between us. Asking Seth if he ever thought about dying seemed wrong. What if he didn't know he would likely die before any of his friends, had never really computed that fact? I didn't want to precipitate a conversation his parents had yet to have with him. Every time I tried to frame a hard question to Seth, an unseen hand seemed to grab my throat and choke the words back down. All my reporter instincts failed me at once. I shaded my eyes against the weak December sun and looked up at Whitehorse Mountain, snow settled on its shoulders, a distant sentinel in the sky. The mountain had looked down for centuries while the lives of the people in the valley below flitted by like butterflies, briefly beautiful in their passing. The thought steadied me.

"Look!" Seth pointed as something scuttled away from our feet. He shrugged. "Lizards are too fast," he said. "They won't let me catch them."

When Christopher was about five years old, I'd opened the door one day to find a lost cat on the front porch of our bungalow. I picked it up and let him pet its silky coat. "Kitty, my," he signed, slapping his chest to emphasize the "my." He stroked the cat, his expression rapturous. But as soon as we put the cat down, it darted back out the door, as fast as Seth's lizard. Christopher's face had crumpled in shock before dissolving into piercing, throbbing sobs. I tried picking him up to comfort him, but he shoved his arms straight against my chest, pushing me away. His grief was pure and inconsolable, as though he were crying out the sum of all his losses. It stabbed hard at my heart, even now, all the things I could not give him.

I needed a way to shunt my pain. "How does having progeria affect you?" I blurted the question before I could reconsider. My heart began to race. I held my breath and looked down at the ground beneath us, at the star-shaped calyx on a thimbleberry, the late-season wild rose hips and feathery horsetails that brushed my knees.

Seth kicked the stone a few times before he answered. "I can't tie my shoes because I have arthritis," he said. "And I have to take an aspirin for my heart. That's about it."

I searched Seth's face for more answers, but he'd already moved on.

"I'm going to get a dog." Seth said it in a stage whisper, like it was a secret.

I laughed and the breath trapped in my chest escaped at last. "Do your parents know?"

Seth nodded and giggled, then resumed his little stiff-legged swagger as he told me about the other things of importance going on in his life. He was trying to earn money for new electronic gadgets. He'd already bought his own Xbox with proceeds from garage sales, shelling out 220 single dollar bills that he'd counted every night until he had enough. There was also homework to avoid, especially math, his least favorite subject.

I nearly picked Seth up and hugged him. My memory of Christopher's sorrow burned off like winter mist. Christopher had probably cried so hard because he'd just wanted to pet the cat. Because he'd wanted a cat of his own. Not because of all the other things he could not have in his life, his health, his hearing, a certain future, the things I wished for him. I wanted to fall down with relief.

IT HAD BEEN SO long since I'd been on the roller coaster of life with a sick child that I'd almost forgotten that for every climb up, there was always a plummet down.

At work, much of my job was doing the grunt work of covering a beat—writing up small items for the briefs column in the local section, making rounds of calls to find news to fill the paper that day. "Feeding the beast," we called it. I rotated through weekend duty, making cop calls to see what calamities had befallen the city the night before. Readers sometimes called to complain about stories, or that the paper had missed their front porch, or we'd canceled their favorite comic strip. Being polite sometimes took effort. But as Seth crept into my thoughts more and more often, I found myself being nicer, more patient than usual. I'd catch myself smiling.

Tom, the other medical reporter, who had returned from his fellowship leave by then, sat across from me in our pod. One day, he offered me a square of chocolate from the stash he kept in his drawer for deadlines. "You're in a good mood," he said. "That's not allowed." Tom wore a Hawaiian shirt and baseball cap to work every day but prided himself on being a "grumpy Norwegian." His self-proclaimed curmudgeonly ways were a running joke in the newsroom. I knew he wanted an explanation for my lifted spirits, but I couldn't tell him the truth. I couldn't even explain it to myself. I took the chocolate but deflected his unasked question.

A few weeks later, I answered the phone to hear Patti on the other end of the line. "Carol?" Her voice was even, but something in it sounded different. Seth was in the hospital overnight for observation. She thought I'd like to know. Instinctively, I shielded my face with my hand to create a sense of privacy in the all-ears newsroom. Patti and Kyle weren't sure what was going on. Her voice was even, betraying no other information.

I hung up the phone and stood up from my desk, knocking over one of my stacks of files. My mind clicked to the morning nine years earlier when Christopher had gone with his dad to visit his grandparents. The worst of Christopher's medical ordeal seemed behind us at last, and I'd been savoring all the possibilities that lay ahead. Then the phone ringing. Then his grandmother's frantic voice and his father's stunned one, saying the words I could not understand, words that still seemed impossible to me all these years later.

In the abstract, I'd understood that Seth could die, but not now. I had the panicky sense I'd forgotten something critical, like giving Christopher his medicine. I'd let my guard down. I'd been fooled by Seth's nonchalance. I'd forgotten he was a little boy who was dying.

My breath jetted out in tight bursts. I told myself Patti hadn't said anything overly alarming, certainly nothing about Seth dying. My body didn't care. It was already surging with adrenaline and cortisol, the way it had whenever Christopher had gone to the hospital and I couldn't be sure he'd be coming home.

I rushed out into the cold without a coat, letting the rain pelt against me. I bent forward, bracing my hands against my knees, and heaved for air. Above me, the blue globe on top of the building spun slowly. I looked up. *Anything but this.* The cold water on my face slapped me back to the present enough to make a plan. I went back into the newsroom, grabbed my keys and coat, and headed for the hospital.

Seattle Children's sat at the top of a long drive in the northwest corner of Laurelhurst, one of the city's oldest neighborhoods. Christopher had been in and out of its ICUs when he was a baby. The hospital was designed with children in mind, its various wings named for animals and its waiting rooms stocked with bead toys. The gentle thwack of beads moving through the wire labyrinths was a soothing distraction for impatient children and anxious parents alike. But its emergency entrance was like the entry to every other emergency room I'd taken Christopher into, a threshold beyond which you surrendered your care, your fate, and especially your future. Where no answers were certain, where whatever you had planned for your life, that day, that month, that year, was now placed like a bet on a table.

As soon as I walked through the doors, the astringent smell of Hibiclens and alcohol wipes knocked me right back to the day in the neonatal intensive care unit when, all washed and gowned up, I was finally allowed to cradle Christopher in my arms for the first time. I tried to stay in that moment with his warm body against my breast, but the lobby floor began to tip beneath me, as though I'd stepped onto one of Christopher's little cardboard games of tilt-the-ball, as though at any minute I would drop through the little hole in the maze of all that came after.

By the time I got to Seth's room, I was shaking. Seth was hooked up to monitors, an IV line snaking to bags of fluids above him. The veins on his head protruded, the blue of them a stark contrast with the white hospital sheets. A limp GET WELL balloon drifted from the corner of his bed. Seth opened his eyes briefly as I came in, and gave me a weak smile. I wanted to hear him tell some silly ten-year-old joke, like the ones he'd told me before: *What do you call a dinosaur with a big vocabulary? A thesaurus!* But there were no jokes today. He'd already slipped back into a semi-sleep, his body nearly lost on the gurney.

Countless times I'd seen Christopher similarly dwarfed by the hospital apparatus that kept him going. I wanted to reach out and touch Seth's hand, stroke his forehead, soothe him the way I'd once soothed Christopher, but I clasped my hands together instead, like a prayer.

Patti was calm in the way I'd once been calm in hospitals to protect Christopher from my panic. Her voice was cheerful, the way mine had once been cheerful—as long as I didn't sound scared, there would be nothing to be scared of. An enormous weight pressed against my chest, the weight that had landed there the day Christopher died, the weight that made it hard to breathe.

It had been only minutes since I'd arrived, but I backed away from Seth's bed. "You all must be worn out," I said to Patti. "I'll leave you some privacy." Without waiting for her response, I fled to my car.

In the parking garage, I pressed my forehead against the steering wheel. Patti had called me, yet instead of being a comfort or distraction, I'd run out on them. I'd run out on Seth. My other failing clawed at me, a hibernating pain that reared up and threatened to crush me every time I thought of it. I'd let Christopher down in the most unforgivable way, was absent when he needed me most. And here I was, in an endless loop of history, repeating my failure.

ONLY SETH DIDN'T DIE. This time, I had a chance to redeem myself.

At Seth's follow-up appointment a few weeks later, I steeled myself and got out of the car, notebook in hand, to join Patti and Seth, who were waiting for me. I didn't want a repeat of the last time. I needed to restore Seth's and Patti's trust. I needed to restore my trust in myself.

"Come on," Seth said when he spied me. He pointed the way to the elevator. I followed as he and Patti led me to a part of the hospital I hadn't been in before. I was relieved. It meant fewer memories for me to stumble over.

As we got off the elevator, I looked instinctively for the little door off the waiting room through which doctors took parents to deliver bad news in private. Most hospital units Christopher had been in had such rooms. When doctors nodded me toward them, my stomach would drop and I'd march, stiff-backed in terror, past the averted gazes of anxious strangers awaiting their own news.

To my surprise, there didn't seem to be a room like that here, or at least if there was, it was hidden. The doctors who strode through this lobby weren't wearing scrubs and worried looks. Instead, they appeared like busy office workers in street clothes and lab coats. I sank into a chair and prepared to wait. I wondered what Seth and Patti were thinking, whether they were worried about what doctors might tell them. I'd always hated the waiting, wanted to know right away, for better or worse, what I would be facing. It was an illusion, maybe, but I figured the quicker I knew, the better I could prepare for what was to come.

Seth busied himself folding paper airplanes. He and Patti tossed the planes at each other from a short distance apart.

"One, two, three." Seth counted down so they could release their planes at the same time. Most missed their targets. Seth scurried across the floor to retrieve his. His swollen joints made him do a kind of awkward curtsy each time he picked one up. "On your mark," Seth said, trying one more time. "Get set. Go!" He let his plane fly. In the stop-time of a heartbeat, the planes' paths crossed, and each of them— Seth and Patti—caught the other's midflight.

"Yes!" Seth threw his arms up in a victory V.

"Yes," I whispered to myself. Late afternoon sun streamed through a stained-glass mural of stars and planets that formed the window wall of the lobby. Sunlight pooled on the floor and made the colors of the window glow. I watched Seth and Patti play, the light of the universe at their backs, and something heavy inside me lifted.

I don't remember what the doctors told them that day, only the sense of calm that scene left me with. The happiness lingered as I transcribed my notes into the computer file where I was drafting scenes for the story as I went along. I thought about how Christopher was always laughing as he reached out for life and grasped at language. "Fast boat," he'd signed one day, eyeing his grandfather's ski boat when we were home for a visit. My dad lifted him in and took off slowly from the dock. Christopher, barely visible beneath his orange life jacket, poked his hands out from the bulky vest. "More fast," he signed.

Being with Seth that day reminded me that children measure happiness differently than adults. Their preoccupations are not ours.

AS MUCH AS I wanted to stay with Seth in that world with its childlike preoccupations, the truth was Seth was running out of time.

By the end of winter, Seth had begun showing signs of heart disease and eye problems. His arthritis was worsening, and he was in danger of having a serious stroke. His pediatrician in Darrington had referred him to a specialist, so one icy winter morning, Patti drove him down from the mountains to his first gerontology appointment. I met them at the hospital.

In the exam room, Seth had to be lifted onto the table. His bony arms poked out of his red shirt, the wrinkled skin folding delicately along their length. He sipped from a water bottle nearly as long as his torso and looked around, his eyes huge on his pale face. There wasn't much to look at. A few green oxygen cylinders leaned against the wall. A sign reminded elderly patients: CALL. DON'T FALL.

The ultrasound technologist poured slick gel on the detector. "Are you ready for the slime?" she asked. I guessed she must have had young children who watched a lot of Nickelodeon. Seth didn't answer.

The tech ran the detector over Seth's head and neck to check the blood flow to his brain, a measure of his risk for stroke. A landscape of gray furrows and valleys leapt and twitched on the screen. Seth perked up. "Cool!" He scanned the screen, which looked a lot like an Xbox game world.

The sound of Seth's pulse amped up like an electronic drumbeat, filling the room. "Here's your peduncle, in the middle of the brain," the tech said. "You didn't know you were so noisy in your head, did you?"

Seth didn't miss a beat. "That's the sound it makes when math starts." We all laughed, the air in the room suddenly less static.

The ultrasound finished, we headed to his next appointment, which was in the stroke clinic in a different wing. Seth rode in a portable stroller Patti had brought for longer distances. When we got to the clinic, he hopped out and parked it. "My ride," he said, like he was talking about a Harley. We sat down next to a table stacked with copies of *Prime Times*, a weekly paper for seniors. If Seth noticed them, he chose to ignore their implications.

In the exam room, the nurse tried to take his blood pressure, but the cuff was too big. Flustered, she kept trying until, finally, she called the front desk for an infant cuff to better fit around his bony arm. She seemed awkward around Seth, not sure what to make of him. "How old are you? Six?" she asked, extra brightly, as we waited.

I sucked in my breath and wished she'd stop talking. I didn't want Seth to see himself the way she seemed to.

Seth drew himself up, squaring his skinny shoulders so his wing bones nearly touched behind him. "Ten," he said, a hint of defiance in his voice.

"No way. You look too young."

Seth sat up very straight and looked her in the eye. "I'm ten."

I felt a shift. My nerves fizzled into stillness. I'd been looking at age from the standpoint of loss of years, not gain. Christopher would never be ten. Never have an Xbox. Never be sixteen. Never get a driver's license. Never get married. Never have kids of his own. Sometimes the "nevers" nearly strangled me.

But he had not known that. He'd been proud of his age, the way Seth was proud of his. Whenever Christopher met someone new, he would cup his hand into a C and circle it over his heart, the sign for his name, then he'd add a number for his age. "Chris, six," he introduced himself to our seatmate on a plane ride back to Seattle one day. He turned and pointed toward me. "Mama," he signed, spreading his fingers and tapping his thumb against his chin. Then he added *my* age.

No secrets were safe.

Maybe this had been his stand against mortality, claiming each year as an accomplishment. I closed my eyes and imagined Christopher's life through his, which couldn't conceive of being my age, let alone miss it.

The past, with those eyes, looked quite different.

CHAPTER 4

In May, I made a trip up to hang out at home with Seth. Being with him made me feel close to Christopher again. I looked forward to my visits, making excuses to tell my editors I needed to go do "some reporting."

"It won't take long," I'd tell Laura, hoping she'd forgotten by then that a visit meant disappearing for most of the day.

Whenever I drove to Darrington, I imagined Christopher in the seat beside me. I'd glance over, half expecting to see him in his favorite red school sweatshirt, his brown eyes merry, signing the sights as we went along.

For so long, I'd had to turn down the dimmer switch on my memory just to get through my days. But in the car, Christopher felt alive to me again. I could almost reach over and brush the sandy hair from his forehead, almost hear him whoop at the cows and horses once we'd left the city limits. I practiced finger-spelling words on road signs I passed as I drove, a habit left over from the years I'd spent crawling along LA freeways with him. I spelled his name, the shape of the letters as familiar as a signature. Or I would think how to sign things the way he might have, using our limited vocabulary. Ferry became a "car boat." Dandelion, a "wind flower." A fountain, "water dancing."

My mind would roam over our life together until I turned up the narrow winding road that led to Seth's house. The sound of my car crunching into the gravel driveway brought Seth to the front door, eager to lead me to his room.

A boy's bedroom is a universe of his own construction. Seth's room, with its black light and pop psychedelic poster on the door, doubled as central headquarters for his fan club of young cousins. They came to plop down on his racing-car bed and admire his various valuables—a scorpion encased in resin, a bleached alligator skull from Florida, his dad's "Mini Logger" football trophy.

On that day in May, Seth came flying out the door to tell me he had a big surprise. He escorted me to his room. "Look," he said as he cracked open the door, and a tiny puppy, no bigger than a teacup, scrambled over his tennis shoes. Seth scooped him up and spilled the wiggly blob into my hands. "He's a mixed rat terrier," he said proudly.

"What's his name?" I asked, juggling my pen between puppy kisses. I sat down on the edge of Seth's bed and pulled out my notebook.

"I thought about naming him Hulk," he said. "Or Goliath. But I chose Bullet." The pup clambered over Seth, who wrestled him until he fell asleep snuggled in a baseball cap on Seth's lap. I put down my pen. Watching the two of them filled me with a kind of contentment I hadn't known in a long time.

The phone rang just then. Seth took the call, wrapping his hand around the mouthpiece to keep his mom, who was in the kitchen, from hearing.

"All seven of them?" he whispered into the phone. "Get them all and I'll pay you back."

"What was that about?" I asked when he hung up.

He leaned close to confide his secret: "The complete set of The Chronicles of Narnia." He planned to give them to his mom for Mother's Day. She'd first read the books to him when he was six years old. Fantastic voyages were a special interest of his. His favorite book of the Chronicles was the final one, *The Last Battle*.

I racked my brain, trying to remember the plot. I knew he was interested in epic battles and outsize adventures he could lose himself in. But what was it about that one?

That evening at home, I retrieved a copy of the book from the ba of my own shelf of childhood favorites. I turned to the last page began t read. Then I remembered—how C. S. Lewis led his cha of one journey so they could begin a new one in a t he called the beginning of "the Great Story."

I had put my hand against the bookshelf to steady myself. The implication was inescapable. Seth's parents were preparing him to die and Seth must have known it, too.

I stumbled to my bedroom and curled into a fetal position on my bed, wrapping myself around the memory of Christopher's warm body sleeping next to mine. I gasped for air, sobbing until my ribs hurt, until my body, spent, couldn't do it anymore. *I wasn't there to say goodbye.* The refrain circled endlessly on its well-worn track in my brain.

It was dark by the time I finally went back to my study to return the book to its shelf. Another book caught my eye. I pulled *The Little Prince* from its spot nearby. In the years since Christopher's death, I'd turned to it often for solace. Nights when I couldn't sleep, I'd go outside and stare at the stars and think about the words the Little Prince had left behind:

> *In one of the stars I shall be living. In one of them I shall be laughing. And so it will be as if all the stars were laughing, when you look at the sky at night. . . .*

I walked into the chilly spring night and looked up, reflexively searching for the Big Dipper, the way Christopher and I had always done together. I touched the star I wore around my neck and remembered the drawings his classmates had sent me after he died, the ones with hearts and stars and stick-figure children, the ones with Christopher drawn in the upper right corner.

I searched for the right-hand corner of the sky.

RRINGTON IS A PLACE of rivers, cradled between the Sauk and the ɡuamish. One spring afternoon, Seth and his parents launched ʳift boat at a favorite spot along the Sauk. Fishing expeditions ʒ part of the family's life together, and Seth wanted to show could catch a fish.

ʲe boat skid down the ramp into the river. He fished tʰ

waters in all seasons—for chum and pinks and kings. He wanted more than anything for his son to catch a steelhead, to play the line and feel that heavy silver body lift into the light. "Steelhead fight a lot better," Kyle said as we pushed off, his faint drawl giving away his North Carolina roots.

Kyle had fished his whole life, since he was smaller than Seth. Family lore had it he clung so hard to his first catch, he took it to bed with him and the fish had dents in its sides from his clutches. I laughed when I heard the story, but it also told me something about Kyle, how when he loved something, he loved it hard.

I sat up front with Seth and his mom as Kyle rowed against the current, his oars marking the tempo like a metronome. Silver-trunked alders arced over the river, its banks piled high with remnants of floods from past seasons. Lines of merganser ducks arrowed into the distance. Patti looked content on this river, her family tucked close around her, Seth snug on her lap. I still hadn't told her about Christopher. There never seemed to be a good time, a time when it wouldn't rip back the curtain on what she and I would have in common someday.

Kyle searched for the slots where fish might hide, with no luck. "Fishing's no good in an east wind," he said. It didn't appear to matter to Seth. As we slid farther down the river with no hits, we played movie trivia to pass the time, then the conversation floated to stories about "Dog Skull Island," so named by Seth for a skull he'd found and planted at a favorite camping spot one year, and to planning what they would do when they finally caught a fish. You have to let it go, Kyle told Seth. "Catch and release."

I studied his face, trying to read what else he might have meant.

I WAS SWIFTLY COMING to the end of my time with Seth, and in an effort to be with him as much as possible, I persuaded my bosses to fly me and Dan DeLong, the photographer who was documenting Seth's life alongside me, to Florida for the annual reunion of kids with progeria.

Dragging and dehydrated, we arrived at the Renaissance Airport Hotel in Orlando after a nearly six-hour flight. I wasn't sure how I'd handle being around so many kids. I didn't know what to expect. Seth was just Seth. I'd grown comfortable with him, but the thought of a room full of kids who likely wouldn't make it past their midteens shook me up. That and facing all their parents.

Patti and Kyle's strength had carried me through much of my reporting. They didn't fall apart, so I couldn't, either. However, there were no guarantees with other parents, especially those coming to terms with the prognosis for the first time. Just inside the lobby doors, I tensed imagining those new parents seeing children in the later stages of progeria. Even worse, the parents who would notice which kids hadn't come back this year. Then, suddenly, Seth appeared before me. He'd been up waiting since three A.M. and was practically vibrating with excitement. He ushered me into the hotel, and before I knew what was happening, he gave me a shy hug.

The hug surprised me. Usually, Seth gave me a polite handshake. I was more than content to just shake his hand back. That was what reporter protocol called for, anyway, keeping distance between myself and my subject. This time, though, he'd hugged me, and I hugged him, too. Then, before I could even register the feeling, Seth turned around and announced to the small group of parents and kids who had gathered: "My reporter's here!"

I flushed with pride. *My reporter.* I couldn't stop smiling as Seth introduced me around.

Back when Christopher was in school, I'd taken for granted the affection of other children, of his friends and classmates. Being part of a child's world opened the door to so many other kids and their love. Seth had cracked that door open again.

Seth worked the revolving entry like a carnival ride, greeting each new family as they rolled up. Children arrived from all over the world, from Australia and Belgium, Argentina and the United Kingdom. Kids with bald heads, bony limbs, and wrinkles caromed around the lobby behind him. It looked like an old-folks home where all the miniature residents were having fits of giggles. Jesper, a six-year-old Danish boy at his third reunion, approached Seth and pointed to his name tag. He didn't speak English, and Seth didn't speak Danish.

"Seth!" he said, sounding out the name tag. Then he pointed to himself. "Jesper."

Seth nodded and made a game of mismatching other people's names and identities. "Alicia," Seth said, pointing to his dad, Kyle. The real Alicia, a little girl with progeria who was watching nearby, dissolved in giggles. I scribbled furiously, trying to get it all down.

For the next few days, the kids ricocheted from one activity to the next on a schedule that sandbagged the adults but didn't seem to slow the children down. There were visits to various theme parks, all-you-can-eat ice-cream-sundae buffets, long stretches of play in the pool. Watching the kids constantly, trying to anticipate how they might hurt themselves, plunged me back to an old familiar state of vigilance. Soon exhaustion crept up on me. I caught myself wishing for breaks.

At the end of one muggy afternoon, I headed up to my room to take a nap before that evening's scheduled dinner dance. I collapsed onto the bed, relishing the cool air-conditioning and the silence. I sighed deeply and waited for sweet sleep to take over, but my brain wouldn't let it. I stared at the ceiling. It turned into a white screen, my mind a projector. Christopher's life played across its surface like the jumpy reel of a home movie. The images, instead of being a comfort, tormented me. I tried turning onto my side, but it didn't help. The thought of all the times my body had begged for sleep when Christopher was young pierced me with guilt. I kicked and twisted in the sheets, trying to get comfortable. Kyle's words floated back to me: *Catch and release.*

Over the years, friends and counselors had talked to me about "letting go." Moving on. But moving on implied leaving Christopher behind, something I couldn't fathom doing then or in the future. I didn't want to let go. I believed letting go was the same as forgetting, and forgetting meant that Christopher's life had never mattered at all.

I got up, fighting back tears, and took a shower to compose myself. Then, my limbs still heavy, I went back downstairs. There would be no rest on this trip.

BY LATE THAT EVENING, the hotel had transformed a generic banquet room into a ballroom. The kids, dressed up for the "formal" occasion, milled awkwardly on the dance floor. Parents stood around the periphery, chatty and relaxed. I searched for Seth until I spied him in the corner beside a tiny girl in a pink dress with a matching scarf wrapped around her bald head. She leaned in and kissed Seth on the cheek. His eyes widened—whether in mortification or delight I didn't know. But later they did an awkward, junior-high kind of slow dance under the twinkly lights. A little tingle of recognition ran through me as they shuffled side to side.

I imagined the bundle of emotions Seth must have felt, the combination of shyness, nerves, and excitement that lights up the neural circuits so that even years later, each of us can locate the exact moment we first felt this way ourselves. As I watched the kids dancing, with each other and with their parents, I thought how a life that sped by so fast on the outside—too fast—could feel slowed way down in the moment. From a child's perspective, the night must have seemed so long. Perhaps this was the way Christopher's life had felt to him.

I slept deep and dreamless that night, waking to bright Florida sunlight cracking through the hotel curtains, a sunshine that at last felt a little like hope.

BEFORE I KNEW IT, my deadline was upon me. The first draft of my story was due in a month. My editors had green-lit a special section, which meant my story could run magazine-length—more than a hundred inches—a luxury for a newspaper reporter. Our bread and butter were the ten- and twenty-inch stories that filled the daily paper. I had most of the story drafted, but I was running out of time to ask Seth the one question I'd set out to in the very beginning.

Patti knew I wanted to talk to Seth about dying and she had already said it was fine. Death was a recurring part of the conversation in their household. They didn't dwell on the future, but they did talk about life and death, and life after death. Religion was a deep part of the family's life. It's what had eventually gotten Patti through the darkness after Seth's diagnosis. It had gotten them through the losses of Seth's beloved grandfather and several of his friends from the reunions. Seth attended a weekly after-school Bible class. He and his parents went to church on Sundays. Every evening, the family prayed. But I'd never found the nerve, or the right time, to talk to Seth about dying. I knew I wouldn't have many more chances to do it.

On my next visit, I asked Seth if he wanted to go for a walk. It was a hot July day and Seth was eager to visit the fishpond at the bottom of the hill. We set off on the road toward town, our pockets full of dimes to buy worm pellets to feed the trout. Along the way, Seth peeked through a barbed-wire fence to check whether the neighbors' horses were out. He stopped to examine a lizard on the pavement. "Dead," he pronounced.

I reached for my notebook in my bag. If I didn't do it now, I never would. Sweat pooled under my arms. "What do you think death is like?" I tried to sound casual.

Seth fell quiet. My blood pounded out the moments I waited for him to answer. I immediately regretted asking. What if he said it would be a nightmare? That he was terrified of dying? If he was afraid, perhaps Christopher had been, too. I couldn't bear to think that. I wanted to stop Seth and say, *You don't have to answer.* But I didn't. I needed to have the conversation with Seth that I'd never had with my own son.

I once tried to talk to Christopher about death. He was in preschool at the time, and his classroom hamster had died. He used to love showing me the hamster in its sawdust nest when I picked him up from school. I didn't know how to tell him it was gone. The school had sent home a one-page, single-spaced list of instructions for discussing death with children:

- *Do pick a quiet time together to talk.*
- *Do say it's OK to be sad.*
- *Don't say the pet went to sleep or went away.*
- *Don't lie.*

The list went on. But it did me no good. Despite my sign language classes, my vocabulary had remained stunted. I'd achieved the fluency of a five-year-old, able to sign the names for dinosaurs and not much else. I didn't have the words for what I wanted to say.

I wanted to tell Christopher that dying was something that happened to all living creatures and that he didn't need to be afraid, that he would always be in us and us in him. That heaven was a place we go to in our hearts. But I couldn't. It was as though all my words had been taken away and I was trying to explain the moon.

At last, Seth broke his silence. "My house in heaven has got lots of rooms for people and some for pets. And it has a zero-gravity room. You go hunting for gummy bears and chocolate rabbits, and when you fish, you're guaranteed three a day." Seth reached the floating dock at the pond, his fists full of pellets. Blue dragonflies skimmed the water like slivers of sky. Seth scattered the pellets across the pond. Fish flipped and splashed near his feet with every throw. When he finished, he tossed a dime in and made a wish.

"What did you wish for?" I asked.

He paused. "I wish my birthday would come sooner."

A FEW DAYS LATER, I got a party invitation from Seth. His birthday celebration was to be on a Saturday afternoon at his grandmother's log house in Darrington, down the road from his own. His cousin Tristan's birthday was the same day, and they were going to share the limelight. My story was almost finished, which meant this would be one of the last times I would likely see Seth. I had to go.

On the drive up, though, I nearly turned back, struck suddenly by the same fears that had gnawed at me when I'd first met him. The prospect of Seth's party reminded me of all the birthdays I hadn't had with Christopher—ten by then, more than I'd had with him when he was alive. Spending time with Seth had let me relive many of the feelings I'd had when Christopher was with me. I was afraid this birthday party would break the spell, that the mended parts inside me would rip open at the seams.

Halfway there, I pulled off the freeway and sat in the car in a gas station parking lot, an empty notebook on the seat next to me. The refrain started up again. *I wasn't there to say goodbye.*

I didn't know if I'd ever see Seth after this. Usually, once a story was finished, I moved along to the next one—it was what we reporters did. If I turned back now, I wouldn't have a chance to say goodbye to him. I put the car back in gear and drove on.

Seth shouted when he saw me. Practically bouncing, he led me to a picnic bench and offered me a paper plate for hors d'oeuvres. "I made these myself," he said, holding up a tray of neatly skewered chunks of cheese. Children milled around us, the din of their voices rising and falling. Seth left me with my cheese and plunged back into the middle of the action, driving a toy car through sprinklers set up on the grass, tossing water balloons, and decorating boxes of favors.

I hunched on the bench, trying to make myself as inconspicuous as possible, and fought back tears as I watched the children play. Soon their whoops and cries cross-faded in my memory with Christopher's as he whooshed down slides at the park and splashed in swimming pools. I saw him in my mind's eye, waving gleefully from the cockpit of a small plane while he "drove" it around the tarmac, sitting on his grandfather's lap. Christopher had known as much joy as these children racing around before me. The memories strengthened me. This was Seth's party, but seeing Christopher as a lucky boy once more was Seth's gift to me.

After a supper of salmon and ambrosia salad, and after patiently letting his younger cousin Tristan open his presents, Seth started in on his own pile. Stray bills fluttered out of cards. He tucked them neatly into his baseball cap, which he immediately slapped back onto his head.

"Can I hold your cap for you, Seth?" asked Dan, the photographer.

"Nice try," Seth said.

Each gift—the CD player he'd been wanting, the giant soaker water gun, the glow-in-the-dark jigsaw puzzle of dragons—got a "Wow!" I *oohed* and *aahed* with the rest of the crowd and felt, almost, like one of the family.

As the mosquitoes came out and the guests headed home, Seth sat on a white plastic chair, surveying his gifts.

"I hit the jackpot," he said. "I'm eleven."

This time, the smile that spread across my face was as big as his.

I FINISHED WRITING THE story a few weeks later. When I turned it in to my editors, I felt a peace I hadn't known since before Christopher died. For the first time, I began having happy dreams with Christopher in them. Sometimes he was older in the dreams, driving or playing basketball with friends. Sometimes he spoke to me, his voice sweet and bell-like. Sometimes I dreamed in sign. The dreams didn't end with him riding his trike away from me toward the edge of a cliff.

For the first time since he died, I woke up each day remembering how to breathe. For the first time, I didn't need to screw up my courage on the bridge to work each day.

After Seth's story ran, hundreds of people called or wrote to tell me how his life had touched them. I printed out the emails to share with his family and read them in my cubicle at work. Some made me smile. Others made me cry. They reminded me of the notes I'd received after Christopher had died.

"He broke my heart and then mended it at the same time," wrote one reader. I understood exactly what she'd meant. I was supposed to be the reporter, the objective observer, and to therefore stay uninvolved. But Seth had worked a little magic on me. What seemed tragic at first—a child cheated of a long life—had turned into a life of wonders. Seth had helped me remember Christopher's that way, too.

When I first lost Christopher, the thought that his childhood had been overshadowed by pain and illness consumed me. I was sick with worry that he'd been afraid of dying and that I hadn't been there in the moment when he may have needed me most. My guilt and shame kept me from seeing his life for what it truly was—one filled with love and lots of joy, despite the hardships he'd faced.

Seeing Seth as a regular ten-year-old kid with a ten-year-old's take on life showed me that children are focused on living, not dying, even when they're sick. And it's this focus, not the length of a life, that makes it feel rich. I learned from watching Seth, too, that a life well lived is not dependent on its length, but rather measured by the love it generates. And by that measure, Christopher's life had been as full as any other. Seth forced me to slow down and see that children live their lives in moments and that a life can feel long in experience—no matter how long it is in days or weeks or years. You can see a life as cut short. Or you can see it as completed. They are two different things.

That didn't take away my anguish. I still needed to learn how to live with that. But it did help me see it for what it really was—my missing him, not my having failed him. Those left behind mourn the loss of time with the ones we loved, the loss of our dreams for them, our wishes for the way things had turned out. The pain is real. The hole in my heart was real. But I began to take comfort in knowing that Christopher knew how well loved he was. I stopped obsessing over the trauma of Christopher's life.

Years later, I would read in the *New York Times* that in the Khmer language, the term for giving birth—*chhlong tonle*—means "to cross the river."

The phrase startled me. I put the paper down, then picked it up and reread it. *Exactly*, I thought. This gave me a way to describe my life back then. Losing Christopher was like having to make the dangerous journey back across the river. Every day felt like drowning. There were times I wanted to yield to it, to go into the stillness below the rush of the current and watch the light fade from beneath the surface.

Reporting stories like Seth's became my lifeline. It kept me above the waves, kept me from giving in. These people I reported on were the ones who showed me the way back across the river.

II.

THE ALCHEMY OF MOTHERHOOD

(JOHN & BILLY)

CHAPTER 5

"Do you have children?" The question startled me from my trance in the salon where I was getting my hair cut. I shifted uncomfortably under my black plastic cape, sending a cascade of damp hair clippings to the floor.

It was the first time I'd been to this hairdresser. Her silver scissors had paused above my head, and her eyes stared expectantly at mine in the mirror. Behind her I could see a line of other chairs filled with women of various ages, their hair festooned with foil or hidden under bubble dryers. The hum of women's chatter and the whine of blow-dryers filled the room. Fragments of conversation floated toward me—snippets about college applications, preschool drop-offs, the problem with video games. My throat felt suddenly dry. I coughed to cover my hesitation.

"No." I kept my face composed.

She immediately went back to snipping.

"You're lucky," she said, and launched into a tale about her teenage son, who had recently taken her husband's car for a spin without permission and crashed into the neighbor's fence. "It was quite a scene." She chuckled as she ran through the details. I tried to smile along, but catching a glimpse of myself, it looked more like a grimace. Two high spots of color had bloomed on my cheeks, and my eyes were burning. I closed them and was glad she couldn't see my hands beneath the drape, my fingernails digging into my palms to keep from crying.

Each time someone asked me about kids, I struggled for what to say. There was always a split second of reckoning as I considered whether the person asking needed to know. Saying yes meant the conversation could go nowhere without explaining that my son had died. By the time it sunk in, there would be an awkward silence all around. I could see people wishing they hadn't asked, see them trying to rewind the moment. "Oh, I'm so sorry," they'd say, and make excuses to end the conversation. They clutched their own children tighter, as though my misfortune were somehow contagious. *Vilomah*. I had violated the taboo.

If I said no, it was like denying Christopher had ever lived, a second kind of death. Daily life was a minefield. The question came all the time, especially if children were around—at parties, in line at the grocery store, at the post office.

The question always led to another, unspoken one. I stared at myself in the mirror. *Who was I if I wasn't a mother anymore?*

THE YEAR BEFORE I got pregnant with Christopher, my then husband Frank and I had done a budget trip to Europe with friends. We were in our twenties, loose in a big world, aimless and adventuring. None of us had children, or responsibilities beyond our jobs.

One night in Provence, we were at a small café, eating bouillabaisse and drinking wine, when I noticed a family across from us. The mother had long straight hair cascading down her back. Her four dark-haired children chattered and beamed at her. She didn't appear much older than me at the time, but her bearing gave her a kind of gravitas. She seemed serene, despite the chaos of small children. She radiated. She was the center of a small universe, her children orbiting around her. I watched her surreptitiously throughout our meal, an unexplainable envy growing inside me. I wanted to stroke the children's hair and their cheeks. I craved belonging to someone the way she belonged to them. I left the restaurant excited, as though I'd crossed a threshold of some kind. For the first time in my life, I wanted children. Really wanted them, not just in the "of course, you're a girl, you're expected to" way, but deeply, viscerally. I wanted my life to be that central axis, to have a purpose.

When I became a mother, it was as though all my molecules rearranged, changed state, the way water locks into place and becomes solid, becomes ice. I was made of the same elements, but everything in my world was different.

Mothers joke about it—how your vanity takes a hit. You go through your days, hair half-combed, dried vomit on your shirt, sour milk off-gassing from your skin. You understand with a fierceness you didn't know you had that you would throw yourself into traffic to save your child. The fierceness frightens you sometimes, on playgrounds or in classrooms when you perceive a threat—another child biting yours, say, or a teacher who doesn't "get" your child's learning style. You learn to tune that fierceness, adjust it to the situation, but it's always there.

It was there when medical technicians poked my son with needles, and I'd ask them how many more times they had to try. It was there when strangers asked what was "wrong" with my son. Christopher was small for his age. Dark, downy hair covered his arms and legs, a side effect of one of the medications he was on. He often had some kind of medical appliance attached to him, a wheelchair, gastrostomy feeding tube, hearing aids, an oxygen tank.

"There's nothing *wrong* with him," I'd say. Now, though, when people asked me whether I had kids, more and more often I said no and changed the subject. To protect them. To protect me from the truth.

At home, I put away all of Christopher's pictures and moved most of his things, the ones I'd brought from his room in Pasadena, into storage miles from my house. Every evening, I drove home from work, parked in my driveway, and sat, sometimes for an hour or more, listening to the radio. I dreaded walking into the house. I didn't know which was worse—an empty house, or an empty house with no reminders.

It's no coincidence that the word for "mother" sounds similar in many languages—ma, *mère, moeder, madre*. Linguists say "ahh" is the first sound a baby makes because it is easiest—an exhalation. The "mmm" sound comes from pressing the lips together, the way babies do when nursing. Mama. Our first word derives from the urge to suckle. To survive. I feared I could not survive this—un-becoming a mother.

I didn't know where to put the fierceness. The only thing I could do with it was work.

"HEY, TOM." I AIR-KNOCKED in the space above our two desks to get his attention. I'd just gotten off the phone with Susan Gregg, my contact at Harborview Medical Center, who'd told me burn surgeons there were experimenting with a newly developed form of artificial skin. They hoped a skin substitute could reduce the need for the excruciating grafts that severe burn patients had to undergo. Just the thought of skin grafts made me squeamish.

"What do you think?" I asked Tom. He'd spent a fair amount of time in burn wards for his own reporting, and I was curious for his opinion about the story's prospects. He squinted at me from under his baseball cap and launched into a description of the "tank" room at Harborview where nurses scrubbed off patients' dead, burned skin in steel bathtubs, a necessary step before healing and grafting could begin. He described patients so swollen and swathed they looked like the Michelin Man. I shuddered, but he was just getting going. I couldn't tell whether he was enjoying watching me squirm. By the time he was done briefing me on the gory details, I was convinced I couldn't handle being around such horribly wounded patients.

I got up from my desk to shake off the images and went to retrieve my yogurt from the mini fridge next to the office coffee machine. I chatted with a couple of other reporters while they waited for the coffee to brew. These little routines, wearing work clothes, getting coffee, commiserating about deadlines, made me feel almost normal, like I really was the person I appeared to be—a single, childless professional. I could forget for a moment that my life outside work wasn't like the lives of the people around me, or so I believed. As I peered into the crowded fridge, trying to find my yogurt, I heard a young woman behind me tell another reporter how she was using sign language to communicate with her baby. The heat rose in my face. I turned to look.

"She goes like this for 'more,'" she said, imitating her baby milking the air with its tiny fists. Other moms, whose rosy-cheeked baby pictures I'd seen propped up on desks and pinned to cubicle walls, soon clustered around the coffeepot to share how their toddlers had already picked up signs from *Sesame Street*.

"They say signing will help them read faster," one of the moms said. The others nodded.

A bolt of anger surged through me. My body started to quiver, strung tight like a wire. I wanted to lash out, to smash the coffee cups from their hands. Instead, I turned and rushed away before they could see my face. I stumbled to the paper's second-floor lactation room, the only private place I could find, and locked the door. I lay down on the couch in the dark with my heart hammering in my ears. *How dare they be able to sign to their hearing babies—babies who don't even need it—when I can't even smile at mine.* My whole body ached to reach for Christopher. To hold him against my breast. To hear his cooing "ahh, uhhh, ooh," *I love you,* one more time.

When I finally made it back to my desk, I wanted to feel something, anything, besides this crushing emptiness. I picked up the notes I'd taken about the burn story. I called Susan at Harborview back and asked to observe a graft surgery. A week later, she said yes.

HARBORVIEW MEDICAL CENTER LOOMED over the city from the top of Seattle's "Pill Hill." Harborview was where the sickest and most damaged patients went. Helicopters circled a landing pad on its roof day and night, bringing the burned and broken from afar. The city's morgue occupied its basement.

I showed up for the surgery early in the morning and changed into scrubs supplied by the hospital, then tucked my hair into a blue paper cap, donned paper booties and a yellow mask. Surgeries usually fascinated me, the glimpse inside the clockwork of our bodies. I'd watched brain surgery and open-heart surgery, even watched a surgeon with huge hands fashion a tiny new thumb for a baby born without one.

Walking into the burn operating room that morning, though, something felt off. The OR, usually chilly for surgery, was cranked up to a womb-like ninety degrees. I shed my long-sleeve scrub jacket for the loose top underneath. A nurse explained to me that they kept it that way because the damaged skin of burn patients could no longer help them regulate their own body temperature. Skin is the largest organ of the body, a complex protective layer that also fends off infection and helps the body retain fluid. Without it, we die, period. Doctors used to calculate a patient's odds of survival by adding her age to the percentage of burn. That number roughly equaled her chances of dying. The reality was, if a burn covered more than 50 percent of a body, there wasn't enough skin left over to harvest for grafts. Doctors hoped a skin substitute could change that calculus.

I knew going in that day that the patient was a child, a toddler named Maria, who'd been reaching for some candy hidden in a cabinet when she accidentally tipped over a pot of boiling beans. The scalding water landed on the back of her head, then flooded over her shoulders, searing most of her back and parts of her chest, neck, and face. The burn covered more than 30 percent of her body. I did the math. One in three—those were her chances of dying. My hands started to shake.

I tried the trick I'd used for other surgeries—not focusing on the patient beneath the drape—but it was impossible not to see there was a little girl on the table. Sweating and clutching my notebook, I girded for the procedure. I made myself as invisible as I could, standing against the wall as a team of three surgeons and four nurses moved in a tight choreography around Maria. They had to work quickly. Dr. Nicole Gibran, the lead burn surgeon, steadied the air-powered blade of a dermatome and began the graft harvest. She lifted each sheet and ran it through a meshing machine that cut slits in it so it could be expanded like a fishnet stocking. Next, surgeons laid down a layer of Integra—a skin substitute made from cow collagen and a carbohydrate derived from shark cartilage—on top of the areas where Maria's dead, burned tissue had already been cut away. The skin substitute mimicked the substructure of dermis, the lower layer of skin that can't regenerate once destroyed. Then the surgeons spread the grafts from Maria's body on top. The combination allowed them to use thinner grafts and far less of her own skin. The air vibrated with the shrieking of the blade, setting my teeth on edge. My stomach roiled and bile burned my throat. I forced myself to keep taking notes.

Four hours later, the grafting finished, Dr. Gibran sank onto a step stool, her back against the operating room wall, her head in her hands, to dictate orders for Maria's aftercare. I ripped off my mask and raced from the room, gulping for air. My legs wobbled and my stomach heaved. I closed myself in the toilet of the OR locker room and dropped my own head into my hands to keep from throwing up.

An image of Christopher flashed through my mind: Just before Christmas, the year he turned seven. We'd spent the afternoon rolling sheets of beeswax into candles and pressing them in glitter. We worked in the coved dining room of our rented bungalow in Pasadena. A few days later, we'd be flying to Seattle to spend Christmas with my family. Rolling beeswax candles was something I'd done as a child with my mother. Passing the tradition on to Christopher was going to be as much my surprise gift to her as the candles were. Christopher, who loved any kind of craft project that involved taking over the whole dining room table, had thrown himself into the task. He'd proudly stacked his batch like Lincoln Logs. Now he wanted to light one.

"Matches," he signed, his index finger striking against his palm. I lit the candle.

"Hooh," he said, the little whoop he made for emphasis when something delighted him.

"Little fire," he signed, waggling his fingers like a flame. We kept working, the room redolent of pollen and honey, the light making a lantern of the honeycomb. Our hands sparkled. Before I could stop him, he reached toward the light to blow the candle out. A few drops of melted wax landed on his hand. He yelped, surprised, and looked at me as though betrayed before bursting into tears. I scraped the little flecks of wax off and kissed his fingers.

I wished I could protect him from the world, even though I knew I couldn't, knew I shouldn't. Dealing with hurt, from the minor insult to the major blow, is what forges children into strong adults. Still, watching him bent to the task of rolling his candles, I wanted to wrap him in my arms and keep him safe forever. I choked down a sob and squeezed my eyes shut against the memory.

Two weeks later, he died.

I leaned against the porcelain sink in the OR bathroom, splashed my face, and rinsed the acid from my mouth. I dressed as though under water, my limbs moving in slow motion.

A few minutes later, Susan led me to the ward where Maria would recover. I averted my gaze from the patients swaddled in dressings in their rooms. As we rounded a corner, though, a patient out walking the halls loomed in front of me. I sidestepped quickly to avoid a collision. "I'm sorry," I mumbled, ducking my head. I couldn't tell their gender beneath the shapeless hospital gown. Their face was sheathed in a tight beige pressure bandage with holes for their eyes and mouth. The mask erased their features, the way a nylon stocking rubs out those of a thief. I shivered despite myself.

A nurse smiled at the patient. "Doing your laps?" The patient nodded and kept going.

Whenever I went to the burn ward to check on Maria after that, I noticed the face patients in their eerie masks. The delicacy of facial skin and the way it scarred made face burns among the most complicated to treat. If a patient came in with a severe facial burn, they often left with a vastly altered face. In a strange way, they mirrored how I felt—like someone whose inner and outer realities were at odds, who had become unrecognizable to herself. *Who was I if I wasn't a mother anymore?*

I wondered about them and what their lives were like afterward.

CHAPTER 6

A few years after I first visited the burn ward, surgeons began seriously discussing the possibility of face transplants. The ethics of doing them, and the implications of reentering the world with someone else's facial features, had touched off huge debates. Faces are so bound to our sense of identity, the idea of switching them felt like messing with something sacrosanct. I pitched Laura on a story to look at the relationship between faces and identity. I wanted to tell a dual story. First, from the point of view of someone with a severe facial injury who was at the beginning of the process, to understand what they went through as they came to terms with knowing they would never look the same way to the outside world. But I also wanted the perspective of someone who had already been through it, someone who had lived their life in the world with their new face, their new identity. Finding two subjects who would let me follow them would complicate doing the story, and it would take more time, but it also seemed like the best way to fully explore the experience and the debates that went along with it. Laura was intrigued. When she gave me the green light, I knew where I would have to go.

Harborview's eighth-floor plastic surgery clinic was one wing over from where I'd met Maria and her family. I sat down to wait, notebook in my lap, for a man named John Swanson. I wasn't sure what to expect. John had suffered a horrific burn eight years earlier. He was due for yet another surgery on his face and had agreed to meet me there. I fiddled with my pen and tried to ignore the parade of haunting faces from books and films that kept stealing into my mind: the Phantom of the Opera, Freddy Krueger, the English Patient. I wondered whose I'd see when John walked in.

John bounded into the clinic waiting room a few minutes later, wearing blue jeans and deck shoes, his brown hair cropped short. I stood up, flustered, dropping my notebook in the process.

"Hey, sorry I'm late," he said with a rueful laugh. "Doctor's appointments are kind of a low priority for me right now." He and his dad owned a charter boat business together, running fishing and wildlife tours up the Inside Passage of Southeast Alaska. They were in the midst of repairs, getting the boat ready for the summer tourist season. He'd come straight from the dock.

"What kind of boat is it?" I stammered, trying to make eye contact but not stare. John's face was tight and masklike. He had no wrinkles or expression lines. No eyelashes. His grafted eyelids were like slits, and his thickened lips didn't close completely.

My question turned out to be the magic one. He was off and running, describing the storied life of *Discovery*, the classic wooden yacht he and his dad had gutted and repaired together. It had originally been built for William Morris Jr. of talent agency fame back in the thirties, and its mahogany staterooms had been filled with the luminaries of the time. But its glamour era ended when the US Navy commandeered it during WWII, painted it gray, and put it on patrol up and down the coast to Alaska. When the war was over, *Discovery* ended up ferrying Washington's most notorious prisoners back and forth to the McNeil Island Federal Penitentiary in Puget Sound. John was just getting to the part where *Discovery* was finally rescued by the Sea Scouts when the nurse stuck her head out and motioned us into the clinic.

As we stood up, I noticed the sideways glances for the first time. People, who had been pretending to read magazines, looked down quickly or stared over our heads like they were checking for a clock on the wall.

John must have sensed me taking in the other people. "Don't worry, I'm used to it," he said. "People are always taking a second look and I think, *What are they looking at?* Then I remember: *Oh yeah—you look different.*" He laughed. "Sometimes they ask questions," he continued as he settled on a chair in the middle of the exam room. "Usually it's when I'm cashing out at a bar, after they've had a few drinks in them."

John had already had dozens of surgeries by then. Mostly, he didn't care anymore what his face looked like, except for his mouth. Scar tissue kept it from opening very wide or closing properly, which made dental work a challenge. That was why he was there that day. His doctors were running out of tricks to try. This time, they'd called in a new plastic surgeon.

John leaned back in the exam chair while the surgeon, Dr. Joseph Gruss, began poking and prodding at his face. He hooked a finger in the corner of John's mouth and tried to pull on his upper lip.

"There's not much give here," Dr. Gruss said. He proposed taking a flap of tissue from John's lower lip and temporarily sewing it to his top lip to close the gap when his mouth shut. He would remain so-called lip-tied, with the two sections attached that way, for a few weeks while the flap of tissue grew new circulation. Once doctors were sure the transplanted piece would survive, they would cut the lips apart.

"It sounds promising," John said noncommittally. I couldn't read his face, but something in his tone told me—he knew the difference between hope and promises.

THE NIGHT OF THE burn, John had been tinkering under the hood of his old Ford Courier truck in the garage of his rented house in Edmonds, a town on the shores of Puget Sound eighteen miles north of Seattle. He was twenty-two years old and good with his hands. Good-looking, too, with the chiseled features and dark hair and eyes of Christopher Reeve in his *Superman* days. It was a chilly February night and John's roommate, T.J., hung out with him, his motorcycle also parked in the garage. The two had plenty to talk about—they'd been dating a pair of identical twins.

Neither noticed when a droplight broke free behind them and plunged into an open container of gasoline. They heard the whoosh as the bucket flashed into flame. John tried to grab it, but the handle melted in his hands. The burning bucket crashed to the floor, spewing a river of flaming gasoline across the garage toward T.J.'s motorcycle, waiting there with a full tank of gas.

T.J. raced for water, but he was too late. The bike blew like a bomb. John ran toward him, engulfed in flames.

"Get down," T.J. yelled as he doused John with water.

The odd thing is John felt nothing at first. A flash burn incinerates so deeply it obliterates the nerves. There was no immediate pain. That would come later.

John remembers the smell of burning flesh. He remembers trying to put the fire out with a garden hose even after he'd been burned. When the fire finally died, he turned to look at T.J., who was staring at him, shaken.

"Is there something wrong with my face?" John asked.

T.J. considered John's ash-white face. It didn't look too bad, he said later. Not compared with John's hands. The latex gloves John had been wearing to work on the motor had fused to his skin. But that's not what he told John.

"Your eyebrows are singed," he said.

DR. GRUSS CONTINUED WITH his exam of John's face. The irony was plain. More than a dozen reconstructive surgeries later, John's eyebrows were the only things on his face that had remained the same.

After a burn, the body weeps. Blood vessels leak. Fluid rushes into the space between cells and blood volume drops, blood pressure with it. The inflammatory reaction is extreme, like what happens when you hit your thumb with a hammer, except over the whole body. Tissues swell. The heart and kidneys begin to fail. The body consumes so much fuel trying to stay alive, it's the equivalent of running marathons twenty-four hours a day without stopping.

I went to find Dr. Gibran, the surgeon I'd met when she'd operated on Maria, to learn how the body heals from an injury like that. She looked younger when not in her scrubs, but no less intense as she walked me through the healing process.

Because of their calorie needs and difficulty eating, burn patients used to die essentially of starvation, she told me. They wasted away until they didn't have enough strength to breathe, or cough, and succumbed to pneumonia. Modern techniques had changed that outlook, but they still had to fight the body's worst tendencies.

I nodded, taking notes.

"One of the ways the body restores itself is by contracture," she said. "The body uses the mechanism it has." It evolved to heal injuries it had to close quickly, like lacerations. When a wild animal has torn your flesh apart, the most important thing was to seal the wound as quickly as possible. My pen paused over my paper as I took in what she'd said.

When a wild animal has torn your flesh apart.

My vision started to tunnel. Darkness crept in from the periphery. I could feel myself dropping through the wormhole of memory to the moment nine years earlier when I learned of Christopher's death. Ripped open. Torn apart. It's how I'd felt. In the surreal days that followed I convinced myself it was something I'd done, or failed to do, that had caused his death. *I'd killed him.* The agony was unbearable. I could not sleep or eat or breathe. If a wild animal had dragged me away, I would have let it.

I could barely hear Dr. Gibran. Her words sounded jumbled and disconnected—"graft," "shrink," "scar"—like they were coming from very far away. I forced myself to look at her face so I could read her lips, concentrating until her words started to make sense again.

The mechanism of contracture, however it evolved, didn't serve burns very well, she was saying now. Pulling the sides together made grafted skin shrink, especially in the T-zone—the eyes, nose, and mouth—where most of our expression happens. It's these shrunken grafts that give burn-injured faces their Halloween mask appearance, as though unseen hands had clapped their cheeks and pulled the skin taut. If the shrinkage is severe, patients end up needing repeated grafts as doctors attempt to restore function to the features. A lower lip that's pulled down can't hold a drink. A shrunken eyelid can't cup a tear. Scarring compounds the problem. The human body scars in a way unique in the animal kingdom. Deep burns, especially, could lead to "hypertrophic" scarring, an excessive wound response that gives burned skin its warped and melted appearance. These were wounds that couldn't heal by themselves. Damage from such injuries accrues long after the initial burn is over, the way a smoldering fire continues to scorch.

Like grief. The thought flashed by. The pain of Christopher's death seemed to worsen with each passing year, though well-meaning people had assured me things would get better with time. I thought again of John, sitting in the doctor's office. The difference between hope and promises.

I tried to keep up with Dr. Gibran's words, but my hands felt stiff and clumsy. I looked down at the scrawl on the page of my notebook and asked her to repeat her answer, borrowing time to compose myself.

I couldn't wait for the interview to be over. When it was done, I thanked her and left quickly. As I drove back to the office, the poem "For What Binds Us," by Jane Hirshfield, kept running through my mind with its reference to how love is like a scar that binds two people together, a "black cord . . . that nothing can tear or mend."

The thick, ropy cord that trailed out of my body as Christopher was born, the cord through which our hearts once beat together, had joined us then. Now we were bound by only this, the black cord of his death *that nothing can tear or mend.*

I seldom cried anymore. When I did, the tears came hard and sudden. As I drove, my eyes flooded with mascara. They stung so badly I could barely see. I pulled my car over under the viaduct that ran along the Seattle waterfront a mile from the office. The pounding of cars running over the expansion joints above me matched the pounding in my temples. I banged my head on the back of the seat again and again until the words stopped, until I had no emotion left to wring out. Then I gathered myself and drove back to the clatter and hum of the newsroom, a place where few people knew I'd ever had a son.

DRAWING THE WOUND CLOSED didn't work for grief, either. Yet that was what I'd tried to do. I'd avoided talking about Christopher's death for so long, it meant I no longer talked about his life, either. I pretended I had no scars.

I sidestepped people whenever I could. When colleagues headed to lunch and asked me along, I'd skip out and go swimming instead. I'd head up to a community center at the top of Queen Anne Hill above the paper, slip into my suit, and sink into the water, where there were no ringing phones, no newsroom chatter. I'd swim laps until my arms burned. Then I'd dive and flip over, my back to the bottom of the pool, and watch the light waver through the water, wishing I could stay below, waiting until the last moment before the need for breath would force me to the surface.

After one swim, I'd gone to change when I heard some women talking in the locker room. I turned to look. "I don't care what it is, as long as it's healthy," a young woman was saying. She'd peeled off her wet suit, and her pregnant belly glistened under the fluorescent lights. The two women changing on either side of her didn't even try to disguise their naked baby hunger. They peppered the pregnant swimmer with questions about her due date and doctors, discussed the merits of doulas and epidurals. In the other corner, I noticed a woman dressing a small child. A red scar zippered the length of his torso. One side of his face drooped. As she spoke to him, he searched her face eagerly. His eyes never left hers.

By habit, my hand went to the little star I wore around my neck. I felt the pressure of its points against my fingers and thought how Christopher had seen my face—always as his mother's first—how no one else would ever see my face that same way. I toweled off quickly, not sure whether it was chlorine stinging my eyes or tears.

Somebody dropped a makeup bag on the cement floor just then, sending bottles and tubes scattering. The women in the corner paused their conversation a beat, then resumed discussing another woman they knew who'd found out her baby had Down syndrome.

"I don't think I could handle it," the woman on the right was saying now. "It was awful. The husband didn't want to keep it, but she did anyway. They split up after that."

"I know I couldn't do it," the pregnant woman said.

Which? I wondered. *Have a baby who wasn't what you were expecting? Or keep her?*

I wanted to rush over and shake them. Tell them they were worried about the wrong things. That any baby, no matter what challenges she has, brings her own well of love with her into the world. That the things that most scared them were also the things that would bring them joy they couldn't imagine. That they would someday give anything, their money, their health, their life, to have that baby back.

In my agitation, I dressed hastily, my tights twisting uncomfortably against my damp skin. I gathered my things and headed to the door, anxious to get out of there. The woman with the little boy caught my eye as I rushed past. She smiled at me. For an instant I thought maybe she recognized me, or maybe just something in me, something in common. I hesitated a moment, drawn inexplicably to make some conversation, thinking she would understand, then thought better of it. I smiled back instead. Stepping into the cool Seattle air, I felt suddenly buoyant.

A handful of the older reporters at the paper did know my history. They remembered me from the days I'd worked there before I'd left for California. Merry Nye, warm and funny, who handled the letters to the editor that poured into the office every day, had swum with me at the pool as my own belly grew when I was pregnant. A mother of three girls, she'd talked me through my pre-baby jitters about becoming a mom. Mary Lynn Lyke, one of the paper's feature writers, wrote me long letters of encouragement after I moved to California. She'd been through her share of pain. Pain, she told me, is what makes us wise. I didn't believe her then. Pain was something I was doing my best to run away from.

Rita, too. And Tom, my fellow science geek, who made it his job to keep me from taking myself too seriously. I drew these people around me at work. They motivated me, straightened me out, made me laugh. Tom never failed to produce some chocolate to share across our desks around deadline time in the late afternoon. He shared tips with me as well. He was the one who'd told me about John.

A FEW WEEKS AFTER meeting John, I went to speak with Dr. Loren Engrav, who'd operated on him multiple times. He ushered me into his Harborview office, wearing his signature bow tie, and watched, bemused, as I took it all in. A small herd of pigs—ceramic, jade, plastic, and paper ones—had taken over nearly every surface. On the side of a piggy bank, someone had written, "Engrav's research fund. Donations welcome." They came from patients, well-wishers, and colleagues, he said when he saw me looking. Among animals, pigs scarred the most like humans and had been instrumental in developing treatments for burns.

"To really fix burns we would need an ointment to stop contracture, ugly scarring, and pigment abnormalities," he said. "If we had those three ointments, we could win a Nobel Prize."

He thought for a moment, then added a wished-for fourth ointment. "Mind scars. I wish we had an ointment for that, too—for PTSD, depression, guilt. But then again, an ointment wouldn't work."

Dr. Engrav took me to a darkened conference room and started up a slide projector. He'd taken a snapshot of John after every surgery to record his progress, starting with his first. Image after image flared onto the screen, a grim procession of raw and distorted features. I flinched with every clunk of the carousel. In each photo, John faced the camera head-on, unsmiling. Dr. Engrav had fixed hundreds of faces, but John's still haunted him.

When John first got to the operating room after the explosion, his face bore the signature red, white, and black mottling of an extensive third-degree burn. The white areas were the deepest. His eyelids and one ear were burned off. Dr. Engrav and his team used temporary grafts of cadaver skin to buy time until his face was healed enough to accept permanent grafts from elsewhere on his own body.

The burn surgeon's goal is to rebuild a face that both functions biologically and is socially acceptable. It's a tricky business. Reconstructive surgeons know how precise the facial recognition response is. People notice if the realignment of someone's shattered jaw or brow bone is even a millimeter off, just as they notice when celebrities or friends have had "a little work done," no matter how subtle the cosmetic surgery.

Like the wound response, there is likely an evolutionary reason for this. We're hardwired to recognize faces for survival, in order to tell friend from foe. Starting between six and nine months, even babies can tell one stranger's face from another.

There were problems with John's grafts from the beginning. The first ones didn't take, and with 47 percent of his body burned, the surgeons used nearly all his remaining skin for patches.

"One of the reasons he's not a perfect result, and few are, is he makes terrible scars," Dr. Engrav said. The slides kept clicking. "Then a thing happened I never quite understood." He paused the projector. "He began showing up with a significant other and a kid."

More often, Dr. Engrav had seen the opposite after a traumatic injury like a burn. Typically, the circles of people's lives closed in on them. They didn't expand.

That had been my own experience. I seldom reached out to my old network of Seattle friends. After Christopher was born, they'd sat with me in waiting rooms, fed me, taught their children sign language. Now I let the Christmas cards slide and their children's birthdays pass. It was easier not to see them, not to remember the life I'd had before. They were busy with their own lives, facing challenges that I would never face. They reminded me how much I wasn't a mother anymore. Nor did I try to make new friends. Talking about Christopher made most people sad and uncomfortable, so I didn't bring him up. I couldn't make new ones without feeling I was constantly guarding a lie.

The same wasn't true for John. His first son, Michael, was born two years after the burn. "Look at this," Dr. Engrav said as the next picture popped onto the conference room wall. As a surgeon, he was never 100 percent satisfied with his results. This one, though, he confessed, made him happy. "It's two and a half years post-burn," he said. "We got a little smile."

A FEW DAYS LATER, I drove up to Lynnwood, a shopping suburb a few miles north of Seattle, to meet the woman who'd started showing up with John at his appointments. Her name was Jamie Cooper. She'd been eighteen and an aspiring model when she and her twin sister had first met John. She thought he was funny and smart. She hoped he'd call.

He thought the shy girl with long wavy brown hair was nice, maybe a little too innocent for him. He didn't call her for six months. When he finally did, she remembered him immediately. "There was something about him," she said. "He had a good sense of humor. He got along with people." Within a year, she was in love.

They were just getting serious about their relationship when she got the call about the fire. She rushed to the hospital, not knowing what she'd find. At first, doctors blocked her from the room. When they finally let her in, she was stunned speechless. John's newly grafted eyes were sewn shut. Doctors pulled her aside and told her his face would never be the same. That they might have to amputate one hand. That he would have to wear a mask for two years, twenty-three hours a day.

She started a journal that night: "The nurse said that you were asking for me. When I saw you I almost started crying. But I know that I have to be strong."

She came to the hospital every day, whenever she could get away from her job working at Albertsons. She sat by his bed and watched him in silence. She struggled with what to say.

Five days after the burn, she wrote:

> I walked into your room about 5 pm. I saw you lying there so still, wrapped up and hooked up to 3–4 different machines. Your dad told me to talk to you. I couldn't. I just started crying. He told you he loved you and it hurts him to see you like this. I told him it hurts me too. He took my hand, placed it on your chest, placed his on my hand, and told me that you would like that. We both cried. Then your mom came in for about 15 minutes. She didn't say anything, just held your foot. Then she left. I stayed, held your arm and just touched you. Then I finally said, John, it's me Jamie. You're doing good.

After that, her days toggled between working the deli counter and visiting the hospital. Other guys asked her out. She turned them down.

She couldn't sleep. Friends tried to distract her with activities. She ran errands to keep her mind off John's injuries. She kept his watch and his belt beside her bed.

By mid-March—a little over a month after the burn—John's father wrote his own unspoken fears in his log: "His face is horrifying right now. . . . I don't know what the future holds. . . ."

Two weeks later, Jamie went to the hospital as usual, but John's room was empty. He hadn't called to tell her he'd been discharged. He'd just vanished. Shocked, she tried repeatedly to call him but got no answer. He didn't call for what seemed like weeks.

Finally, she learned from the hospital that an infection had threatened John's fresh eye grafts, and doctors felt he stood a better chance of recovery at his parents' home. But that didn't explain why he was shutting her out.

John came into the living room in time to hear her say that. "I was giving her space, letting her make her own decision," he said. "I didn't want her to be with me out of guilt."

At first, John feared what he might look like. He'd overheard the whispers on the ward that he'd "burned his face off." Images of monsters filled his head. Weeks after the accident, he still hadn't faced the mirror. He hated pity. Self-pity most of all.

Then, one morning, fifty-seven days after the burn, he slipped into the bathroom by himself. Looking down at his hands, he turned the faucets at the sink. His eyes flicked to the mirror, a habit from years of shaving. The face staring back at him was raw and red, seamed where the new grafts had been laid in place. Its features were different. But that wasn't what he saw.

"I looked in the mirror," he said, "and I saw myself looking back at me."

CHAPTER 7

About the time I met John, I'd also asked the hospital for an introduction to a second burn patient, one with a more recent injury, who could help me tell that part of the story. As it happened, one had just been airlifted from Alaska a few days earlier.

Billy was so young when I met him, just fifteen, the age boys should be skateboarding and hanging out trying to impress girls, which was what he'd spent his time doing before the burn. Instead, the boy in front of me peered through the eyeholes of a pressure bandage that hooded his whole head.

"Hi." I automatically finger-spelled the greeting. Something about a boy in the hospital triggered my instinct to sign, even though I knew he could hear. Billy's hands were covered with pressure gloves, so he couldn't shake mine. He wore fuzzy moose slippers. A catheter bag dangled by his leg.

"Hi," he said back.

Billy was soft-spoken. Polite. I sat through his physical therapy appointments and hung out while he aimed snowballs at targets in a virtual reality game called *SnowWorld*. The game, a pilot project, was designed to keep patients' minds off their wounds during dressing changes. He talked about his interest in marine biology. He was charming in a fifteen-year-old kind of way. "I can't help it if I'm the ultimate ladies' man," he liked to say.

Before the burn, he'd been a cute guy with peach fuzz and a cool haircut, short on the sides and long on top. He was popular with the girls at school and liked to hang out at the radio station in his hometown of Ketchikan, a fishing community in southeastern Alaska that bills itself as the "Salmon Capital of the World." When he tried, he did well in school; he didn't like doing homework.

"After school should be my time, you know?" He looked at me, gauging whether I was a sympathetic listener. I almost said what I was thinking, which was that of course he should do his homework *first*, but I bit my lip to keep from answering. This was the tricky part of reporting—trying not to reveal how I felt about whatever people were telling me, at least not in the moment. Sometimes it was hard, especially with young people. My instinct was to protect them—even if from themselves.

The night of the fire, Billy had had an argument with his parents. It was the day after New Year's, still winter break. Billy was supposed to be catching up on schoolwork during his time off. He'd had a pleasant dinner with his parents, then planned to go down to the radio station to hang with his friends. He still had homework to do. His mom told him no, not until he finished.

"That made me mad," he said.

The argument over his homework wasn't a big one. Nothing out of the ordinary. At about ten P.M. Billy came in from outside. He reeked of gasoline.

"I found what I was looking for," he told his mother. He carried matches.

Shock has a way of lengthening time.

I tried to imagine the horror his mother must have felt in that instant as the realization dawned on her with no time to stop it. How with one strike of a match, every illusion she'd ever had about keeping her child safe from harm would vanish. I ached for her. I ached for myself. I thought about Christopher's Band-Aids in my purse, how flimsy our protections.

The burn lasted a few seconds, maybe. Long enough to be forever. His frantic parents rolled him in an area rug and beat at the flames.

"Do you think I'll be ugly?" he asked his mom right before the ambulance arrived. "Will I be able to grow a mustache?"

By the time I met him a week or so later, the reality had begun sinking in. He wanted me to know he hadn't meant to do it.

"I mean, I wouldn't have done it normally," he said. "I wasn't thinking properly."

I knew as much. Scientists had established by then that the adolescent brain, particularly in boys, lacks the ability to make adult-style judgments and calculations. It's why teenage behavior has vexed adults forever.

That didn't change the facts, though. I wished I could assure him everything would be all right. But I couldn't. I left the hospital feeling useless and unhappy.

IN FEBRUARY, I AGAIN suited up to watch a surgery, this time Billy's. Surgeons planned to harvest most of the skin from his head for grafts because it most closely matched that of his face. They'd take sections from his thighs as well, to graft his hands, which had burned, in some places, down to tendon and bone. Once again, I braced.

Fiddle tunes played through the operating room's sound system. The music seemed to match the complexity of the task ahead. Dr. Engrav orchestrated the actions of two other surgeons and three nurses as they worked simultaneously on multiple operating sites on Billy's body. They operated quickly to minimize blood and heat loss through his open wounds. At the same time, the work couldn't be hurried.

Dr. Engrav peered out of gold-rimmed glasses protruding from beneath his blue surgical hood. "We only get one shot at it," he said to the surgeon harvesting the graft for Billy's face. The familiar screech of the dermatome filled the room.

"Beautiful," Dr. Engrav said as a swath of skin the thickness of a chamois cloth emerged from the dermatome. He draped the skin like a bandage across Billy's raw, excised forehead. "This one's an A-plus." He tapped his feet to the music, his head bent over his stitching. No snippet of skin got wasted. He used small pieces to contour a new nose, smoothing them in place. A piece from behind Billy's ear became a new eyelid. He laid the seams in the folds of the face where they would appear most natural.

No matter how painstaking the surgeons' work, though, it couldn't make the burn injury disappear. Grafts could heal but they couldn't be invisible. They mended, but they also scarred.

A FEW WEEKS LATER, the hospital called to tell me Billy was about to head home to Alaska for the first time since having his face grafted. I rode with him and his mom to the airport to say goodbye.

For the trip, the hospital had molded a cast of his face and given him a choice of colors for his mask. Like John, he'd have to wear it twenty-three hours a day. He'd chosen a red one to match the rims of his rectangular glasses and the checks on his sneakers. Billy had his mask on while he waited in the hospital lobby for his ride to Sea-Tac International Airport.

He knew people would stare.

"Kids, they don't know better. They see me as kind of a monster," he said. "I can deal with that fine. I don't care." His leg shook up and down. "It's what I'm thinking about me that matters, not what they think." He repeated it like a mantra.

I caught my breath. It was as though he'd reached inside my brain and told me exactly what I needed to hear. The divide between how I felt inside and the way I appeared outside had less to do with how others saw me than with how I saw myself. The dissonance was in me.

His leg pumped faster. He clamped his arms hard across his chest. The shuttle arrived, and his future with it. Billy stepped outside and shivered at the unexpected chill.

By the time we arrived at the airport, it was clogged with Presidents' Day traffic. Billy hesitated, then waded into the mob of travelers. He put his head down. "Got burned. Got burned," he mumbled as he made his way through the crowd. He said it to keep people from staring, but the glances kept coming, frank and curious, sly and horrified.

I wanted to shoo the people away, shield Billy from their stares, the way I had with Christopher. I felt the fierceness stirring.

"We're halfway there," his mom said as the long line wound slowly to the ticket counter. At the front of the line, Billy abruptly peeled off his ambulance-red mask, releasing the pungent Band-Aid smell of hospital antiseptic mingled with sweat. "I'm not afraid," he said to no one in particular.

The woman at the counter asked for their photo IDs without looking up. Then she glanced at Billy and quickly down again. Their luggage bulged with the medical supplies the hospital had sent home with them. The woman motioned them toward baggage screening. Billy trudged forward, wheeling his overstuffed suitcase behind him. The woman had slapped a sticker on the side.

HEAVY, it read.

TWO MONTHS LATER, BILLY returned to Seattle for his first follow-up visit at the burn clinic, a routine he'd repeat once a month for most of the next year. I drove to Harborview to meet him, eager to see how he was doing.

When I walked into the exam room, he had his feet dangling over the edge of the table. A brush of new hair didn't yet hide the red bands on his scalp where his donor sites were healing. Bright red scars outlined the patchwork of new grafts on his face. A dozen members of the burn team squeezed into the room. "Are you looking forward to going back to school?" a nurse asked.

"Umm," he said, looking at his feet. He picked at the scabs on his hands. It had been three months since he'd flown from his home in Alaska to the burn unit at Harborview for graft surgery. His circle of friends back home had been supportive through his recovery. "They had prepared themselves for me to look all mutated and gross," he said. "I look better than they thought I was going to look." Strangers, though, presented a different challenge.

Melissa Christiansen, a therapeutic recreation specialist, was among those helping him develop a strategy for dealing with social situations. "The cool thing about scars is they tell a story," she said.

What if the scars are invisible? I ducked my head, momentarily ashamed to compare my situation to his. But the therapist's words remained with me long afterward. *The thing about scars is they tell a story.*

Billy said little while the adults discussed the logistics of his return to classes and how to handle questions. The burn team tinkered with his mask, adjusting it to distribute the pressure differently. He seemed relieved when they handed it back to him and all the palpating of his face was over. He slipped his red-rimmed glasses over the eyeholes of the mask.

"I look more like my old self with them," he said.

We took the elevator down from the burn floor. On the way, a slender young woman gave him a long, unflinching look. "When were you burned?" she asked. The tip of a ropelike scar clawed along her clavicle, just visible beneath her open collar.

"Three months ago," Billy said, his gaze trained on the elevator floor.

"Mine was a year ago," she said. "You should see my friend. Her face was just like yours. She had that mask and everything, and she looks so great."

Her voice was soft and insistent. The elevator was packed, but she spoke to Billy as though they were alone, as though she had a lot she wanted to say with only eight floors to go. "They just fixed her nose because one of her nostrils was crooked," she said.

"Mine is, too," he said. He glanced up at her now, oblivious to the rest of the people with their backs pressed against the elevator walls, trying not to stare.

"I think you look good," she said as the elevator doors slid open.

Billy held his head up and smiled.

IF THE GIRL IN the elevator was Billy's hopeful glimpse of what might lie ahead for him, John was mine. The thing I noticed most each time we met was his smile. He smiled a lot, even though he couldn't smile very well. He wanted people to see his face, he told me. Before his own accident, he'd never seen a burn survivor. He didn't want people to be afraid.

About a year after he got burned, he was running a boat up from the San Francisco Bay Area when the weather turned on him. "We couldn't make a bar crossing to come into port. We were bucking into it for days," he said. Hard green swells crashed over the boat, drenching it in salt water and drowning the generator. The bilge pump quit. "The boat would come up to the top of a twenty-foot wave and the wave would go out from underneath, and there'd be dead air. The whole boat would drop twenty-some feet and shake like it was going to bust apart." He got down in the hull with his Shop-Vac and bailed. "I just kept myself busy. There was nothing else you could do. And we got through."

He'd taken the same approach with his face. "When people say, 'I can't believe you're out in public,' I say, 'What did you want me to do?'"

I wondered whether John was just an unusually resilient person, so I called Amy Acton, the executive director of Phoenix Society for Burn Survivors. She told me that many burn survivors forge new, stronger identities as a result of the emotional and physical healing they go through. The mythological phoenix, rising from the ashes, was the perfect metaphor for this transformation.

"The people I meet, years down the road, who have done the work of emotional healing come to a place where they've identified strengths within themselves they didn't know they had," she said. "It gives them the tools to do things they might otherwise never have done."

Acton herself had been severely burned in an accident two decades earlier, when she was eighteen years old. The mast of a sailboat in the marina where she worked hit a high-tension power line, causing an electrical burn injury of her neck, torso, and legs. She went on to become a burn nurse.

She'd seen other changes in people's sense of self as well. "They often have more compassion for others, and a real zest for life," she said. "It allows people to connect deeply with others and to be more true to who they really are."

John's words came back to me: *I looked in the mirror, and I saw myself looking back at me.*

I'd gone to the burn unit to find out what it was like to be unrecognizable to yourself, and here was John saying the same thing Billy had, that they were still themselves beneath their scars. They'd given me the answer I'd been searching for: What I had to reconcile wasn't how others saw me. It was how I saw myself.

When Christopher was an infant, I'd fretted that my face would not be the first he'd know. Those early weeks in the NICU, he was surrounded daily by a parade of nurses and technicians, doctors and residents, all of them peering down at him to gauge the color of his skin and cadence of his breathing. A ventilator tube apparatus obscured his face. A sterile yellow mask covered mine.

For me to hold him, a nurse had to untangle his lines enough to place him, still attached to his vent, in my arms. His finger glowed red where they had taped a pulse oximeter. I rocked him while a hive of ICU worker bees swarmed around us, my fragile, alien child, his eyes mostly closed, mute except for the soft shuddering of the respirator. I watched the condensation gathering on the blue coils as the machine forced breaths into his inelastic lungs. And I waited.

Weeks went by, then months, until one day, while I was dripping formula into the tube that threaded through his nose into his stomach, he looked at me and smiled—an unmistakable smile, gummy and plump-cheeked, that claimed me for his own. I was his mother, and he knew it. I wanted to leap from the rocker and show everyone, but I was so tangled in his lines I couldn't. Instead, I pushed the call button.

A nurse hurried over to see what was wrong.

"He smiled. He smiled!" I said. She leaned over and gave me a big hug.

I was Christopher's mother and always would be. That was who I was in the world. Becoming his mother had altered my state, and those changes hadn't disappeared with his death. I didn't have to hide by pretending to strangers I'd never been a mom. I didn't have to hide it from myself.

IT'S A QUIRKY FACT of English that the word "person" derives from *persona*, the Latin word for an actor's mask. Masks conceal, but they also transform. Christopher loved the sign for "mask," essentially the same gesture you make when playing peekaboo with babies. At first the hands hide the face. Then they reveal it.

John had to wear a pressure mask for years after his injury, but he would not hide. "You can keep living, or you can dwindle away," he told me. "I chose to keep having a good time."

He and Jamie were married and had two sons by then. The boat charter he ran with his father and uncle was the realization of a dream. John grew up on boats. Now he was raising his boys around them.

On a warm, blue-water spring day, I met John and his family for my last interview with them, this one at the Seattle marina where *Discovery* was moored. John was getting ready to prep the vessel for the first run of the season. There was sanding and varnishing to do. He wasn't sure whether he'd have time to squeeze in another surgery before the charter season started.

"We do about four coats of everything," he said. In a few days, they'd be hauling the whole boat out of the water to change the zincs and caulk the seams.

On this day, though, he was playing with his two boys on the boat. Six-year-old Michael raced up and down the dock. Christopher would have done the same. He loved the water. I could see him cupping his hands and signing, "Fast boat. More fast." I smiled at the memory.

John's three-year-old son, Brandon, stayed close by. "I see you," Brandon said, poking his head around a door of the boat's mahogany-lined dining room in a game of peekaboo. He had John's old eyes—big and round, brown and deep. John held out his arms. Brandon giggled and ran toward his father.

"I see you, Daddy," he shouted. "I see you."

THAT EVENING I DUG a photo out of a box I kept in the back of a closet. It was a picture Christopher had taken of me from his eye level. We were at a park in Pasadena where I'd played as a child, a place

I'd gone for Halloween bonfires and Girl Scout camp growing up. I loved taking Christopher there to push him on the swings. "Higher," he'd sign, pointing to the sky. Pushing him was my meditation, the rhythm dissolving my worries about doctor's appointments and what the future held.

One day, as we sat side by side on the swings, he asked for my camera, an old thirty-five millimeter I hauled around with me. "Big picture," he called it in sign. I helped him lift the camera to his face and look through the lens. He swung around and pointed it at me.

In the picture, I'm leaning back in the swing, laughing. I see me through his eyes. I see me happy. I see me as his mother, still.

Having a child had changed me profoundly, as it does every parent. After Christopher died, I didn't know how to integrate the person I was inside with the childless person the world saw. It felt like living behind a facade.

This is something so many grieving people face—appearing recovered on the outside but feeling destroyed on the inside. "Fine," we say when people ask how we are doing. But it's a lie. John and Billy, too, had to wrestle with who they were when their inner and outer worlds no longer matched. I learned from them that the essence of who you are doesn't change when something in your outer circumstances changes. Indeed, those changes may reveal and enhance traits you hadn't known you had before. Becoming Christopher's mother had given me a new kind of strength. He'd taught me patience and acceptance. He'd shown me what endurance looked like. Now I needed those things, if I was going to make it without him.

In getting to know these burn patients, I began to see the ways I approached my life as a mother would, feeling protective of and wanting the best for young people I met and "mothering" others. Embracing that instead of denying it let me hold on to my identity as a mother in the world. No matter who else I might become in my life, I would always be Christopher's mom.

I balanced the photo on a shelf next to my bed. Then I went back to my study and dug out a wallet-size school picture. I slipped it into my purse, next to his library card and Band-Aids. The next time someone asked whether I had children, I would say, *Yes.*

This is my son, Christopher.

III.

THE CERTAINTY OF UNCERTAINTY

(THE GENERAL)

CHAPTER 8

Up until I got pregnant with Christopher, I'd led a pretty uncomplicated life. My parents were still married to each other after more than thirty years and supported my ambitions. I was a mediocre runner, an OK gymnast. I loved math and science, studied hard, and got good grades. It seemed a proportionate life, with outcomes directly related to the effort put in. I believed in cause and effect.

I met Frank, Christopher's father, my first year at the University of Washington. He played Bogie to my Bacall in a dorm skit version of *Casablanca* in our old brick residence hall. He was my first boyfriend, intense and wiry with dark wavy hair, a theatrical extrovert to my bookish introvert. I fell in love. The narrative matched my parents' perfectly—meeting young, falling hard, deciding he was "the one." We married the summer we graduated.

The turn of events seemed perfect. I wore my mother's wedding dress. The rustle of its ivory shantung silk and the bell of its skirt had captivated me since childhood. I was probably, at some level, trying to re-create my parents' life.

Frank and I began searching for a house of our own. On our way to look at a place one day, we drove by an ugly, two-story fixer-upper near Green Lake in Seattle. A bastardized bungalow, the house was covered with institutional-green asbestos siding. Its clunky front porch hung over a skinny cement stair with spindly, rusting metal rails.

We drove by without even slowing to read the fine print on the FOR SALE BY OWNER sign. When we got to the top of the hill, though, I glanced back over my shoulder and caught my breath. The whole view had changed. From two blocks up the hill, Green Lake spread out—an ancient glacial basin filled with rain—holding a silvery mirror to the late afternoon sun. Suddenly, I saw my future reflected there. It didn't occur to me then that reflections are illusions we project upon a surface. That water shifts in a storm. That survival requires being able to dive deep and rise back to the light.

We drove around the block and looked at the green box with new eyes. It was the house I wanted, newly transformed into the one of my dreams. We threw ourselves into fixing it up, imagination—if not money—on our side. Many of our friends had bought first houses around the same time. We'd been in sync for years, gotten married right out of college, embarked on first careers, held work parties, and consulted on each other's furniture choices. We played on softball teams together and hung out in each other's living rooms, listening to Talking Heads and Dire Straits, making plans for our lives.

Christopher was conceived on Mother's Day, six years after Frank and I got married. We were at the lighthouse at Montauk Point on the tip of Long Island, where my father had been stationed as a newlywed, when I first sensed I might be pregnant. Sitting on the lawn beneath the tower, I watched the clouds shape-shift the light across the water. Every cell of me felt different. I looked at my hands, turning them up to my face. *Are these the hands of a mother?* I traced my fingers across the flat of my stomach and felt a welling pride in my secret, felt a sea change.

After I discovered I was pregnant, the house went through its own gestation, expanding and changing along with my swelling belly to accommodate a new life. We were within walking distance of Woodland Park Zoo, where I imagined watching penguins and elephants with my child one day, and just a few blocks from the lake, which anchored a wooded city park encircled with paths for bikes and strollers. It was about as perfect a place to start a family as I could imagine.

All that fall, we worked to carve a space for a nursery out of the attic, tearing down plaster and putting up new drywall, inspired by the countless do-it-yourself exhortations of Martha Stewart. *This Old House* was our favorite show on public television. We were devotees of the notion that anything could be salvaged.

My pregnancy proceeded unremarkably. My best friend, Barbara, was due one week after me. We happily compared our growing bellies and shared notes from our close study of *What to Expect When You're Expecting.*

And then.

It started with a casual observation: My belly hadn't grown as big as expected by thirty-six weeks, two weeks shy of my due date. Ann, my doctor, measured and remeasured me.

"Hmm," she said. "Let's get an ultrasound."

Ultrasounds were not yet routine, especially for low-risk mothers. I was about as low risk as you could get—squarely of childbearing age, healthy, a nonsmoker, nondrinker who had no medical history of note.

I was nervous and excited to have the ultrasound, my first peek at this baby, whose vigorous kicking kept me up at night, whom I could lull to sleep by swimming laps in the community pool near my house. The technician squirted cool jelly on my stomach and ran the wand over my bulging belly. *Magic wand*, I thought as shadowy gray images shifted in and out of view until there, at last, was a perfectly curled spine, a baby shape. A boy. My heart fluttered. *Hello*, I thought. *It's you!*

The technician, who had been chatting with me through the procedure, went silent. He pressed the wand into the same spot again and again, clicking through different longitudes and latitudes on the screen. I could make no sense of what I was seeing. It looked like a lunar surface. He made a cryptic call for someone else to come in. Suddenly there were several people crammed into the dim room, staring at the images, their backs to me.

"Look at that," one of them said. "I've never seen them so large."

Dread crept over me, my first inkling that my old reality was about to collide with a new one. I began a barrage of questions, the only defense I knew. The technicians would not—could not—give me any answers. I kept asking anyway, with no success. They remained unmoved by my growing desperation. The radiologist would have to review the exam first. They would be in touch.

Ann called me that evening. She'd been my doctor for years, and we spent part of every exam catching up on where we were in life. I'd heard about her own family as it grew, and she was excited for me to start mine. When I heard her voice, I felt an immediate, irrational flood of relief. Ann wouldn't let anything bad happen to me.

I took the call in our upstairs bedroom. Frank and I had put up wallpaper, vined with plum blossoms, just months before. The nursery we'd prepared was empty next door, its yellow paint still fresh. A crib with blue and yellow bumpers sat against one wall, a black-and-white mobile dangling above it. A rocking chair I'd inherited and restored waited in the corner, overlooking Green Lake in the distance. The hall outside the room was newly covered with wallpaper I'd brought back from a barn sale in Amagansett on Long Island, where I'd learned I was pregnant. The stage was set.

"There's a problem," Ann said. She launched into a technical explanation, something about posterior urethral valves, a blockage between his bladder and urethra, enlarged ureters, damaged kidneys, the baby not making urine, not enough amniotic fluid. Severe case. Something about his lungs. Underdeveloped. Term. Healthy weight. The words rattled loose and unstrung in my brain. I couldn't make sense of what she was talking about.

"But will it be OK?" I kept asking for assurances, my heart starting to drum so loud I had to raise my voice to hear myself. My questions only brought more detailed descriptions.

She must have finally figured out she wasn't getting through. Maybe she needed all that time and explanation to prepare herself for the news she was about to deliver.

"Most babies with this severe a case die in utero," she said. Mine was on the borderline for survival. Neither his kidneys, damaged by the urine backed up by the blocked passages in his urinary tract, nor his lungs, which had failed to develop without the necessary amniotic fluid to push against, were sufficient to support his life without massive luck and technological help.

I went numb. I begged her to tell me it was a mistake.

"I can't do that," she said. She sounded sad.

I hung up the phone, a kind of scared I'd never been before.

CHAPTER 8

My carefully constructed life suddenly spun out of control. That small change—whatever had triggered Christopher's kidney development in utero to go awry—was beyond my control, or my illusion of it, and its impact was entirely disproportionate. The linear world I'd believed in—a world where specific actions had specific consequences—turned upside down. Overnight, I went from being a low-risk pregnancy case to a high-risk one. Doctors converged with plans. They would wait until beyond full term to induce labor and hope my water didn't break before then. More time was critical to give my baby's lungs the chance to develop as much capacity as possible before birth.

The wait felt endless—a month of wondering whether my baby would die upon birth, whether these would be my final weeks with him. I rocked and rocked in the corner of his room, watching Seattle's long gray winter drip down the windows, willing it not to be true. Wishing he could stay safe inside me.

His birth, when it happened, was fast. The drugs that induced it caused slamming contractions that made jagged tracks on the fetal monitor. I welcomed the pain; it was so consuming it left no room for fear.

THAT YEAR THE NOTION of chaos theory, which had been developing apace in scientific circles for decades, exploded in the public consciousness as a way to explain the predictable unpredictability of the physical world.

After Christopher's birth, chaos took on a new layer of meaning for me. Anything, at any time, the smallest, most inconsequential decision, the tiniest change inside me or my world that I might not even notice, could change the direction of my life, in ways and magnitudes I could never have imagined. Chaos meant I no longer had the comfort of statistical odds. Once you've been a statistic—one of those cases that happens one out of a hundred, a thousand, a million times—you never feel safe from chance again.

Years later, the accidental events that shape our lives became a running theme of my reporting. It was there in Seth's story.

Hutchinson-Gilford progeria, the type that Seth had, is caused by a random mutation—a single miscoded letter in the DNA that induces cells to break down and die sooner than they would otherwise.

The theme was there in John's and Billy's stories, too. Small events had set off chain reactions of larger ones. The strike of a match. The hanging of a light to work at night. Had one thing changed, their lives might have turned out quite differently.

In story after story, I tried to make peace with this paradox—how to live without fear when we can't foresee what will happen to us. How to maintain control when we have none.

ONE WINTER DAY, AS the tenth anniversary of Christopher's death approached, I got a call from my contact at Harborview about a high-profile patient who had had a massive stroke. I'd had a request out for a patient to follow for a story about advances in rehabilitative medicine, one of many standing requests I'd made to my various sources in the medical community. I was working my way through a punch list of stories that interested me, aware I might not get to them all. The *Seattle P-I* had been failing financially for years. We owed our continued operation to a complicated joint operating agreement with the *Seattle Times*. The JOA meant the *Seattle Times* handled the business operations of both papers. Revenues were split sixty-forty with the Hearst corporation, which owned the *P-I*.

Seattle was a two-newspaper town in spirit—the *P-I* and the *Times* were fiercely competitive with each other, though most of us had friends, or even in some cases, spouses, "on the other side." We hated being joined at the hip to our larger, better-staffed rival, but the agreement kept both papers going. There was an out for the *Times*, though. The owners of our partner/rival had triggered a clause that said if the joint operation lost money for three years running, the *Times* could pull out of the agreement. That clock was ticking now. I didn't like to think about what it might mean for the *P-I*, which was unlikely to survive. Or for me. Newspapers around the country were already spiraling as they scrambled to find ways to replace print ad revenue that had vanished to the maw of the internet. When Susan, my contact at Harborview, told me about the patient she'd found, I was intrigued. It kept my mind off my uncertain future.

This patient was willing to be shadowed, she said. But I'd have to be discreet, at least for the time being. My breath caught as soon as she said his name: General John Shalikashvili. He had been, until he retired, the highest-ranking military officer in the country. He'd stood at the sides of presidents. He'd led armies. He was chairman of the Joint Chiefs of Staff under President Clinton, the only immigrant and enlisted person to have risen to the pinnacle of the US military.

A few weeks earlier, the general had suffered a massive hemorrhage. I knew enough about strokes to recognize the implications. His body would no longer be taking marching orders from his brain. He would have to face no longer being in control. I arranged to meet him a few days later.

At the appointed hour, I drove to the hospital, cursing the traffic on the way. I didn't want to be late for a general. I dashed through the hospital's front entrance just under the wire and arrived at the physical therapy room out of breath.

The man I met upon entering was much less intimidating than I'd imagined. He seemed small, slumped in his wheelchair, unable to stand without assistance. His left side hung motionless as he waited in the hospital's busy, brightly lit gym for his daily PT to begin. He stuck out his good hand. "Call me Shali," he said. He didn't bother with small talk. He seemed to be conserving his strength for the ordeal to come.

The physical therapist breezed in just then, cheerful but all business. "Ready to work?" she asked. The general threw his right arm across her shoulders. "One, two, three, up." She hoisted his weight from the wheelchair and maneuvered him to stand between a set of parallel bars, not unlike the kind gymnasts used. "Let's do some walking."

The general white-knuckled his way into position for the long march down the mat. He still cut a trim figure in pressed green khakis, his salt-and-pepper hair closely cropped, gold-rimmed glasses spit-shine bright. His gaze, famously direct, drilled down on his objective—the end of the bars—but it didn't appear at all that he would be able to get there.

The therapist pulled at his stubborn left knee until his foot flopped forward.

"Now the other one," she said.

He hesitated, then dragged his right foot ahead of the left. His face flushed with the effort. He asked for water. They repeated the sequence for step two. And again, all the way to the end. When he was done, he collapsed back into the wheelchair, breathing hard. Sweat beaded his forehead.

"It's as bad as boot camp," he said dryly. I laughed. It was my first glimpse of what I would later learn was his wry sense of humor. He paddled his chair with his one good foot as we headed back to his hospital room to talk. His son, Brant, steered from behind and Joan, his wife of nearly forty years, walked alongside. Once he got settled in, I asked him to tell me about the stroke.

IN HINDSIGHT, THE SPELL he'd experienced a few months earlier should have seemed more ominous. He was driving home from his biweekly haircut to Steilacoom near Fort Lewis, an hour south of Seattle, when a numbing sensation crept through one side of his face and his left hand. Both his parents had died of strokes. He knew the signs. He about-faced his car and headed for Madigan Army Medical Center on the base.

Doctors at Madigan confirmed he'd had a transient ischemic attack—TIA—the temporary blockage of blood flow that sometimes preceded a stroke. They insisted on keeping him under observation. The general stuck to his agenda anyway. He borrowed a hospital desk and wrote a speech for the Democratic National Convention, which was a few days later.

As a high-profile military emeritus, Shali was a tightly scheduled man. For the next few weeks, he jetted around the country, speaking first at the convention in Boston in support of John Kerry and later at a leadership conference in Washington, DC. He had two more spells, but they were minor. "I was so busy I barely noticed," he said.

Then, just after midnight one August evening, he'd kissed Joan good night and was brushing his teeth when the sensation started again. Numbness flooded from his face down his arm to his leg. He staggered toward the bedroom to find Joan. In the space of nine minutes, his speech slurred, and the left side of his body went limp.

Joan called 911. But it wasn't just the stroke that frightened her.

"I'd never seen him so agitated," she said. Her normally unflappable husband, the general who had risen through the ranks on the strength of being calm in tense situations, was having a panic attack.

Shali had a secret. As a kid growing up in Warsaw, he and his friends used to play with bales of felt, making them into tunnels. One day, one of the tunnels collapsed. He lay there, entombed in wool, as the darkness caved in on him. He couldn't breathe. Shali had been severely claustrophobic since. The thought of having to undergo an MRI brain scan at the hospital, which would require lying still in the cocoon of the chamber, terrified him.

Christopher had been the same way whenever he'd had to get an MRI. He'd cry and struggle as he disappeared into the long white tube, its ceiling close against his face, his hands pinned to his sides. He'd grind his teeth and gulp for air, his breath coming in short panicky bursts, fat tears rolling across his face. He couldn't see me or hear my voice. I hated that I couldn't comfort him. All I could do was listen to the eerie metallic pulsing of the machine. When it was over, we would both be limp and sweating. I wondered now whether his dread was similar to Shali's. Maybe we are all programmed to fear closed spaces, to resist the loss of freedom they entail, a precursor of our own deaths.

For Shali, though, the MRI wouldn't be the worst thing he faced. The scan determined that a vessel in his brain had ruptured, flooding blood into his right front temporal lobe. Within hours, surgeons made a critical decision. They would have to drill through his skull to stanch the bleeding and remove the damaged tissue. Doctors told his family to prepare for the worst.

The bleeding had wiped out an area of the brain that controls the executive functions that plan and organize complex movement. The stroke's immediate signature was to paralyze his arm and leg on the opposite side from the brain injury. But the brain's wiring is rarely straightforward. A right-side stroke can also have subtle and profound effects in other areas—balance and regulation of speech and eating, as well as spatial perception and concentration. The general sensed early on that the enormity of the struggle ahead would test him in ways he'd never faced before. "I never knew," he told me, in his rolling Polish accent, "I had so little patience."

CHAPTER 9

My first meeting with the general highlighted once more how fragile our control over our lives is—how one event, a blood vessel giving way, a cell going rogue, an organ failing to form properly in utero, can set us on an entirely different path than we'd planned or expected.

Ten years after Christopher's death, I was still trying to regain my own sense of self-determination. There seemed no point anymore to charting out further than a day. I braced for worst possible outcomes, no matter their likelihood. I expected endings, and then they came.

The endings had started early.

The stress of Christopher's medical care was hard on my young marriage to Frank. For much of Christopher's first years, we were in and out of hospitals with him, dealing with one medical crisis after another, the fallout of his kidney failure. Conflicts surfaced. We handled interactions with medical staff differently, each of us trying our best to protect Christopher. Frank stood ready to question any decision, calling doctors and nurses to account, quick to anger when things went wrong. I tried desperately to make all the doctors like us best, thinking if they did, they would take better care of Christopher. I wanted them to love him so they would try harder.

The tension exposed other fault lines in our marriage. I was barely twenty-one when Frank and I had gotten married. I'd never lived anywhere on my own. In college, I'd always had roommates. Summers I lived at home to work and save money. We'd spent our twenties wanting each other to be people we weren't. A marriage counselor told us we had failed to "individuate." I had to look it up at home. It was true.

Frank left when Christopher was just two years and nine months old. I should have seen it coming. Things had been strained for so long, it seemed a normal state. It was hard to tell what tension was from the stress of having a chronically ill child and what was from the particular stress of us. Frank began a relationship with a woman in a support group we all attended for parents of young deaf children. She had three kids, two of whom were deaf, and was already fluent in sign. I worried my awkward language couldn't compete with hers.

Frank stayed involved in Christopher's life, but the split left me reeling. In the year that followed, I reached out to an old friend, looking for moral support.

I'D KNOWN JIM SINCE junior high. He and I had run cross-country together in high school, and though he didn't know it then, I'd had a crush on him since I was a teenager and would watch him and his buddies throwing Frisbees in the park near my parents' house. His lean, tan body and sun-bleached hair excited all kinds of new feelings in me back then, the first tugs of physical desire, a puppyish need to be near him all the time.

I'd asked him to our Tolo, a high school version of a Sadie Hawkins dance, and he'd given me a quick kiss on my parents' doorstep afterward. Nothing more developed, despite my wishing. I was a year ahead of him, which in high school was like a generation. He'd remained one of my best friends until I graduated. We'd lost touch after that.

When Jim and I reconnected, he was in his final year of medical school. This time the relationship took. I loved his dry sense of humor, the way he told a story. It seemed we could talk about anything, whether Czech art films or the latest brain science. He was an empathetic listener, even before it was his job to be one. Christopher's medical problems didn't intimidate him. Neither did the communication barrier. I'd often hear the two of them laughing conspiratorially over one prank or another. Christopher loved it when Jim would swoop a giant bubble maker through the air or toss him a Nerf football. He was thrilled when he got a set of toy golf clubs so they could putt together through the house. The next year, Jim started his residency in psychiatry in Los Angeles. A year after that, I joined him there. I knew his program meant he wouldn't be around much, but it still seemed a second shot at happiness. I wished we could all be together more, something the grind of residency and fellowship prevented. Nights and weekends on call, Jim tended to his patients. I stayed home and tended mine. Talking was what held us together.

The year after Christopher died, Jim and I moved back to Seattle and rented an old cottage under a spreading pink dogwood on the east side of Lake Washington. Jim spent his days wrangling the logistics of joining a small group practice and building a patient base. He was ready to put the "dark cloud," as he sometimes called it, of our previous lives behind us.

But that would mean moving on, and I wasn't sure I could. At dinner one night, he brought up a case study he knew about—a patient with severe obsessive-compulsive disorder. I'd heard of OCD and associated it with compulsive hand washing or checking the oven before leaving the house, but this patient was paralyzed by the thought that if he moved, he would shrink. It took him hours to go from one room to another. Passing through a doorway was agonizing. He spent most of his time hiding in a closet, wringing his hands.

As he detailed the case, my jaw tensed, the way it did when I tried not to cry. *That's me*, I thought. If I let myself go forward, even an inch, my life with Christopher would shrink away, disappear as though it had never existed. I fled the table so Jim wouldn't see my face begin to crumple.

I did my best to hide my grief from Jim, but it worked only so well. He asked if I was OK when I woke agitated from my nightmares. He noticed when I forgot to pick things up from the grocery store or when I wandered through the house, unable to settle down enough to work or read a book. I worried I would exhaust his sympathies. With a new practice and a stressful patient load, he increasingly had his own problems. We were growing further apart with each month, talking less and spending more time away from each other. The strain between us was like a small crack in a bone, a stress fracture that ached with pressure but could not be cast.

Both of us must have sensed we were on a course we might not recover from. Instinctively, we grasped at the one thing that might bring us back together and move us forward at the same time.

We decided to get married.

Technically, we'd been engaged for years. Three years earlier, I'd sat down for dinner in our bungalow in Pasadena and Jim had asked if I noticed anything unusual at the table. I looked around, puzzled. Christopher sat in his customary seat. I'd lit candles, as I often did in the evening to help ease us into a different space after the day. Candle therapy, I called it. A vase of pink tulips sat in the middle of the table, their stems beginning to bow, their petals folding open. Robert Plant's acoustic version of "If I Were a Carpenter" played on the stereo. I shook my head. Jim seemed pleased with himself.

"Look harder," he said. I was doing another spin around the room when I noticed a sparkle, like a droplet of water, on one of the tulip petals.

I caught my breath, my cheeks flushing. "Does this mean . . . ?" I asked. We'd sometimes spoken of getting married one day, but it always seemed like it would come after something. After he finished his residency. After his fellowship. After we settled down somewhere. After, after, after.

"Yes," he said. And so did I.

My fingers trembled as I plucked the loose diamond from the flower, careful not to drop it. Christopher whooped and clapped as we kissed and slow-danced around the room.

Jim had wanted me to have the chance to design my own ring, but we never got around to that, or to planning a wedding. The diamond stayed in its glassine envelope at the bottom of a drawer. Jim had medical boards to study for, and I was going in and out of hospitals with Christopher as his health slid toward a kidney transplant. A wedding was far down on our list of priorities. As the years passed, just the intent to get married was enough for both of us.

Now, though, marriage seemed the best way to put us back on track toward a future together. We could reset, draw a bright line between the past and present.

A YEAR AND TEN months after Christopher died, Jim and I stood before a justice of the peace in the town where we'd both grown up. We held a small reception in my parents' yard afterward, the light slanting through the golden leaves of the cottonwood trees. I wore an antique linen suit with Irish lace that I'd found at Goodwill and restored through a month of washing and gentle bleaching. I'd plunged my hands into the soapy water over and over, agitating the fabric, a repetitive, meditative task and the only kind of wedding preparation I could handle. I tried not to think about the after we now faced. After Christopher.

Jim and I bought our dream house together by the shore of Lake Washington, adjacent to a marshy wetland park. The house, a low brick rambler built in an L shape, had windows in every room to bring in light during Seattle's long, rainy winters. They looked out over paths lined with weeping willows, and tall stands of poplars in the distance. Eagles wheeled in the sky, their wings wide enough to cast shadows on sunny days.

I'm not even sure when it began, the seed of an idea. It lay buried through the winters after Christopher's death, waiting until the time seemed right. It cropped up in my sleep sometimes, dreams about infants and babies. Babies who were not Christopher. I fingered baby clothes in department stores and peeked under blankets at sleeping babies in parks. One day, I bought a tiny teddy bear on impulse. I hid it in my top dresser drawer and pulled it out sometimes to hold its soft fur to my cheek. Before Christopher died, Jim and I had talked about having a family together one day. The timing never worked. He was too busy with his residency and fellowship, and I was consumed with Christopher's care. After Christopher's death, we no longer spoke of having kids.

We were talking less and less. He'd stopped asking how I was doing. I'd stopped sharing. The void of my grief had sucked up all my words. We spent more time apart, him with friends and colleagues, me alone. His disappearances were a relief in a way. With the house and my head to myself, I didn't have to explain my moods or what I was thinking,

and neither did he. Our estrangement quietly metastasized, the L shape
of the house turning into separate wings where we could spend long
hours without crossing paths. Where the wings met, though, there was
a small empty room, a room that could be a nursery.

Sometimes we visited old friends of his, many of whom had young
kids by then. The children would drag me to their bedrooms to play.
They threw themselves at Jim, eager to wrestle or shoot hoops. I could
hear him chuckling as they shrieked around him. I wanted that for
him. For me. I wanted a family again.

One night, I told him I was ready.

"Are you sure?" He seemed taken aback. I thought I saw a moment
of doubt in his eyes, but I passed it off as nerves.

"I am." And I was, or so I thought.

Nothing happened, month after month. My periods came and went
until I stopped believing anything would. Jim was realistic about it. I
was about to turn forty. He knew my odds of conceiving had dwindled.
I secretly believed there was another reason. My body was willing a
baby not to happen. My sense of having failed Christopher was so
deep that I couldn't imagine putting another child through what he
had gone through.

Then one day I was late—not by a day or two, but by more than a
week. I'd teetered on the edge of this late before, but this time something
felt different. My breasts ached, and my morning orange juice tasted
funny. I bought a pregnancy test.

Alone the next morning, I perched over the toilet and peed on
the stick, an inelegant test for such a momentous occasion. I stared at
the paper strip. My head felt light. My heart was doing a little stutter
dance. There, unmistakably, was a pink band. For a long moment, I
just sat there, alone with the news. Here at last was the bright line we'd
been searching for.

Jim was in the family room when I found him. I don't remember
what I said, but in the next moment, he pulled me into his arms the
way he used to, the way it was before, when we'd been happy. We hung
on to each other, stunned and excited.

My dad choked up on the phone with the news, and my mother's voice took on a lilt of hope I hadn't heard in years. The next day, still on a high, I called my doctor's office. As soon as the nurse picked up the line, though, I started to cry. "I'm pregnant," I said, my voice wavering, my panic rising.

"That's wonderful." The nurse's voice was warm and excited. She knew that we'd been trying. "Congratulations!"

"You don't understand," I said. "I'm *pregnant.*" All my secret fears, the ones I'd managed to keep hidden, even from myself, came rushing to the surface. I was suddenly sure I couldn't be a mother, convinced I couldn't bring a new life safely into the world, keep a baby well and alive.

People had told me I was a good mother. I felt like a fraud. I'd asked my doctor: Had it been what I ate, or didn't eat, while I was pregnant with Christopher that had damaged his kidneys?

No. No. No. Over and over doctors insisted nothing I'd done had caused the random defect in my child's body. Still I carried my fears, my shame, gestating.

I was a bad mother. I'd left my baby with ICU nurses for five months. I spent the days there, worrying over the incubator, reading the charts, pestering nurses for answers. Most nights they sent me home to rest. "You'll need it for the long haul," they said.

I was a bad mother. I was the one who said, sure, his father could take him an extra weekend during the holidays to visit his grandparents. Because I was tired. Because I needed a break. I let him go that weekend. I wasn't there to see him start to fail. I wasn't there to see that, no, it wasn't the stomach flu—it was something more serious. And when they finally called the ambulance, when the doctors in the emergency room 110 miles away tried to save my son, I was not there.

All these old, tamped-down fears spilled out during the first few weeks of my new pregnancy. I escaped to the wetlands park near where we lived to walk and calm myself. It was the end of winter. Red-winged blackbirds swagged the sky with flashes of color. Cattails pushed up through the marshy water, and a pale haze of green buds draped the willow trees. With each passing day, the fears receded, and my excitement built for this baby. Everywhere I turned I saw new life rising out of the debris of past seasons. Little turtles lined up in rows on half-sunk logs, pointing their noses skyward like miniature sundials. Otters glided by in the distance, leaving whispers of wakes behind them. Bald eagles keened in their nests in the tall firs. Some days, I sat on the mossy planks at the end of the dock that pushed out through the marsh, and tossed pebbles into the water of Lake Washington, the way I had with Christopher. Back then, I'd thought how the ripples were like sound waves, a way for him to see the music of rocks splashing in the water. Now it felt almost as though Christopher were sitting next to me, excited for this baby, too. I thought how joy transmits in many mediums. I wanted to fold all his love into love for this new life.

I let myself begin to imagine a new child in all our lives, doing the things we had loved to do with Christopher—building with blocks, reading books, and "messing about in boats," as Rat famously said in *The Wind in the Willows*, one of our favorites. I imagined telling this new child about the brother they never knew. I thought, *If this baby is a girl, I will name her Grace.*

Fourteen weeks later, Jim and I went together to my prenatal appointment. The doctor was a former classmate of his from medical school, and the room filled with expectant chatter. They talked about their old classmates, internships, and new jobs while she hooked me to the fetal monitor. My heart surged with anticipation. It was all feeling true at last. We had a real baby and a real future to look forward to. I closed my eyes and pictured holding the baby. Wondered what it would feel like to nurse for the first time, something I'd been unable to do with Christopher. I could almost smell the milky sweetness of infant skin.

The doctor fussed with the monitor, positioning and repositioning it. I opened my eyes and watched her working over me. She seemed puzzled, embarrassed almost. The talk between her and Jim died until there was a long, awkward silence. Finally, she spoke. "I can't find the heartbeat."

Instinctively, I crossed my hands over my exposed belly. Maybe it was a mistake. I couldn't make myself look at Jim's face. I didn't want to see what I might read there. If I didn't see it, maybe it wouldn't be true. She sent me to another room for an ultrasound.

I lay there, holding my breath in the darkened exam room, while a different doctor slid a wand against my cervix. The radiologist had a small, pinched face and a mustache and kept his eyes fixed on a screen while he rotated the probe inside me. I could barely endure the wait.

He finally took the probe out and sat me up. "You were pregnant," he said. "But there is nothing there now consistent with life."

Consistent with life.

He said the words kindly, as though avoiding the phrase "your baby died" would ease the shock. "Is there anything I can do?" he asked. "Do you have any questions?"

I turned away. My mind went blank. I didn't want to get up from the table. If I got up, it would all be over—my dreams for the little nursery, my hopes of motherhood, my marriage. The doctor repeated his offer. But my questions were ones I already knew the answers to. I would never have a child again. I was a bad mother.

Doctors wanted me to let the miscarriage take its course. I couldn't bear the thought of it. I wanted this death out of me. I couldn't tolerate the idea of being conscious while the baby passed. They finally scheduled me for a D&C procedure to induce it.

The morning of the procedure, Jim called me at the hospital to tell me he wouldn't be there. He said he had a patient he needed to see and couldn't make it. His voice sounded disembodied and far away.

I held the phone for a long time after he hung up. I wasn't sure whether he was telling the truth or lying. I wasn't sure which was worse. No dream, however badly we might want it to, was going to save us. The nursery door had closed for good, locking us in our separate wings.

A few hours later, a nurse wheeled me into the operating room. I lay on the table in the OR and focused on a picture of panda bears taped to the ceiling. "Count backwards from one hundred," the anesthesiologist said. The last thing I remember thinking was *I don't want to wake up.*

My mother's face was the first thing I saw when I did. She stroked my hair while I sobbed, patting my arm in the hospital bed the way I had patted Christopher's so many times.

JIM AND I SPLIT up less than a few months later, after nearly ten years together. He moved out and we put our house beside the wetland park on the market. I lived like a stranger in my own home, staged for someone else's dreams. Magazines I never read lay in perfect fans on the coffee table. Glossy green plants replaced the ones I'd left unwatered in the aftermath of the separation. Realtors came and went, lugging clients with them. When we'd bought it, I'd thought this house would make me whole, fill my life with children, make my husband love me. The trouble with dream houses is when they're gone, the dream follows. I moved to a tiny house on the other side of town. I packed the little bear I'd bought for the new baby and put it in storage along with the rest of Christopher's things. I had no room anymore for fantasies and dreams. Sometimes it felt like all I had left were ashes.

The dark cloud, it turned out, was me.

In the years that followed, I turned my little cottage into a kind of safe house. I kept others out, avoided relationships of all kinds. I let fear make my choices for me, protected myself from chance by never taking any.

When I met the general, though, I saw that what I mistook for safety was my world growing smaller and smaller, the tunnel closing in on me.

CHAPTER 10

Shali was reluctant, even in the intensive care unit, to yield control of his situation. He asked Joan to post a schedule to help him keep track of visitors. When doctors removed his ventilator breathing tube, he commandeered the suctioning wand to clear his own lungs. Once he was stable, his doctors transferred him from Madigan to Harborview in Seattle, where he began the long process of reclaiming his autonomy. He arrived needing constant care. The stroke had short-circuited his inner clock, erasing his sense of day and night. Staff at Harborview tried posting his schedule using military time. It didn't help. He couldn't sleep at night. He lay in bed and thrashed around. His demon, claustrophobia, tormented him.

"What were you afraid of?" I asked. As soon as I said it, I realized it was really a question for me.

"My great fear is I'm lying in bed with a sheet over my face," he said. His answer landed on me like a punch. That was it exactly. Not just his fear, but mine. I watched the world from inside my private snow globe, but the longer I lived in it, the more suffocating it felt. The life I led wasn't really living. In some deep place, I knew that. The general, though, was determined not to abdicate control over the direction his life would take. I wanted to know how he did it, how to proceed with certainty in an uncertain world.

For Shali, the pace of progress was excruciating.

"My left side just ignores the world," he said. Doctors explained that a new part of his brain was having to learn how to move his body, almost like a baby's brain wiring itself for first steps. That was of no use to Shali. *Move, you stupid toes,* he wanted to shout.

He'd call his nurse at three A.M. on many mornings, complaining bitterly that his hand wouldn't move. "What exercises can I do to make it work?" he asked the nurse over and over.

"He told me, 'Only when your fingers understand they are a part of you will they work.' But I just don't know how to do it," Shali said. His frustration built. He tried entwining his right hand in his limp left one to help it do the movements his brain could not signal. "I hoped to God the doctors were right and the message would get through."

Eventually, he began to see little bits of progress. A team of physical and occupational therapists worked out a routine for him, and he threw himself into it. There was one ticking clock he did understand. Doctors had told him the first year was critical for recovery.

Strokes are one of the great levelers in life. A stroke strips you of control. It forces you to start over, relearn basic skills from how to chew and swallow to how to read, speak, and walk, depending on which area of the brain is damaged.

Grief, in some sense, had done the same to me. Everything required deliberate effort. Eating, sleeping, getting up in the morning. Nothing was by rote. I moved in slow motion, executing the daily mechanics of life against the weight of water. Grief had knocked me off balance. Forced me to rewire, reexamine my relationships, reconsider my future. It had removed the illusion of control.

But the nurse's words to Shali were strangely hopeful to me. Only *when* the body understands, he'd said. Not *if*. Parts of me had stopped functioning as well—the parts that loved to laugh and see movies, that cooked for friends and liked to travel. The part that wanted to share a life with someone. Those parts were paralyzed. It seemed a lifetime ago that they'd been working.

Maybe it was taking time for my brain to make the new pathways it needed, the way Shali's was having to. And maybe I had to start working at my own recovery, too, the way he was.

SHALI WENT HOME FROM the hospital a few months after I met him. He lived in Steilacoom, an enclave along the waters of Puget Sound that was popular with retired military officers. I drove there to check on how he was doing. A private, unassuming man, he had lived mostly under the radar since moving there after his retirement. But privacy now was scarce. His home was filled with aides and caregivers over whom he couldn't pull rank, even if he tried.

His internal clock had been repaired, for the most part. "For example," he deadpanned when I showed up at his door around noon, "I know that it's midnight right now."

I laughed. His expression was so stern that his wit always took me by surprise. He *had* to laugh. New aggravations had emerged. He couldn't dress himself, and the natural halt command in his brain was out of order. When he ate or signed his name, the motions of his hand didn't stop when the task ended, which drove him crazy.

Reading was also difficult. His brain neglected information from the left side of his environment. When he read, his eyes returned only to the middle of the page. He had to consciously make himself look all the way to the left to start the next line. Shali, however, kept head down at the task of recovery.

When I'd spoken with stroke doctors about what patients went through, this was the one thing they'd told me: You bring to the recovery the person you were before. *What has Shali brought with him?* I wrote the question in the margin of my notebook.

We sat in Shali's gracious living room, he in his favorite plaid wingback chair and me on the couch. Joan and Brant, who served as his aides-de-camp for this new phase of his life, hovered nearby, prepared to intervene when he got tired. The stroke had rewired family relationships as well. Because of his duties, Shali hadn't been around a lot when Brant was growing up. Now they were nearly inseparable. Brant had quit his job in the telecommunications industry to go to work managing his father's business and life affairs.

"It's amazing how many things in life require two good hands," Shali said, using his one good one to emphasize the point. "I can't even button a shirt or open an envelope with one hand." When they went out to dinner, Brant sat to his left to be his knife hand and cut his steak.

"This has definitely brought us closer," Brant said.

Joan, petite and blue-eyed, brought us tea, and I asked Shali about the events that had made him who he was. He seemed relieved to talk about something other than medical matters and warmed up as he went along.

SHALI WAS BORN IN Warsaw in 1936, a citizen of nowhere, his childhood forged in the chaos of war. His family survived the continual bombing of Warsaw by the Germans during the uprising of the Polish Underground in 1944. Shelling demolished the apartment building where they lived.

"People survived in basements," he said. "We traveled through sewer lines."

With Warsaw decimated, he was shipped along with his brother and sister to Germany in a cattle car with other refugees. They made it to Pappenheim, a small Bavarian town, where they lived with distant relatives.

"By the time the war was over, I understood what war was about," he said. He was nine years old. The fact stopped me. I imagined him as a young boy, little more than a year older than Christopher had been, already well aware of what death meant.

Shali's early experiences taught him about quicksilver shifts of circumstance, about destruction, about loss. They taught him the fine art of self-reliance at an early age. He deployed it when the Germans pulled out of Pappenheim.

"All of a sudden, the village was full of Americans," he said. Spying an opportunity, he went into business buying surplus American cigarettes and selling them to nicotine-needy villagers. "I would buy a carton for twenty marks and sell it for twenty-five or thirty, a considerable markup." He chuckled. Worried her son was turning into a "hoodlum," his mother packed him off to boarding school. "But I found out the wife of the principal smoked," he said. "So, I was back in business."

IN INTERVIEWS, I WAS always impressed with the peculiar turns people's lives took—how the events that would come to define a life didn't seem significant in the moment. It had been true in my life as well. My path to reporting hadn't been a straight one. My father was a scientist and my mother an English major. I grew up divided in my interests, getting degrees in chemistry and plant pathology. All along, I loved the stories behind the science more, the false starts and serendipitous discoveries. I was never a natural in the lab. I loved the discovery, but not the tedious process by which it happened. Instead, I began writing articles about the research going on around me at the University of Wisconsin in Madison, where Frank and I had moved when we were first married, and tried to sell them to science magazines.

My early efforts met a string of rejections. Then one day, I crunched my way through the snow outside married-student housing to my mailbox. Inside, there was a long, slim envelope marked "The New York Botanical Garden." I tore off my gloves and opened the letter right there. "We are pleased to inform you," the letter began. I ran back to our little apartment with my makeshift desk made of a plywood door, elated. My first published article—about ice-nucleating bacteria and frost damage in orchards—would be in the magazine *Garden*. I imagined a new path for myself, a whole different future. I could blend my interests and become a science writer.

Later that year, I got another break and received a fellowship that placed graduate science students in newsrooms. The fellowship, through the American Association for the Advancement of Science, was intended to raise science literacy in the media. I went to the *Charlotte Observer* in North Carolina—the first newsroom I'd ever stepped foot in—fully expecting to write stories about plant genomics and monoclonal antibodies, things I knew about. The city editor had other ideas. He needed someone to replace a general-assignment reporter for the summer, someone he could throw at everything from city council meetings to apartment fires. He sent me off on assignment every morning in a car borrowed from the police reporter, an old sedan, sticky with food wrappers and smelling of stale cigarette butts. I loved it. I loved the sense of urgency and camaraderie of the newsroom, so absent from the long, lonely hours I'd put in at lab benches. My first front-page newspaper story was about the ugliest dog at the pound. I never looked back.

Shali's path had been even more indirect. The man who would be chairman of the Joint Chiefs didn't set out to be in the army. Shali was sixteen years old when a man named George Luthy sponsored his family to come to the United States. Luthy was a banker in Peoria, Illinois, whose sister had once been married to a cousin of Shali's mother.

"He didn't know us from beans," Shali said, and laughed. But he brought the family over anyway. Shali was thrilled to discover the America he knew mainly from *Life* magazine. He taught himself English, in part, by watching John Wayne movies.

After finishing high school, he studied mechanical engineering at Bradley University. In May 1958, he was sworn in as an American citizen—the first citizenship he'd ever held—in a dusty courtroom in Peoria. In June he graduated from Bradley. In July he was drafted.

"The letter said, 'Your friends and neighbors have selected you,'" he said. He couldn't have been less pleased about it. He'd just bought a new green Chevy Impala and had gotten a job as a design engineer. The payments on his car were more than he'd be earning as a private.

His disappointment evaporated, however, with his first post to Alaska. He was put on one of the army's last ski units and sent to patrol the ice caps to keep American air bases secure from Russians during the Cold War. "I loved it. It was very physically demanding—forty degrees below," he said. "I thought, *If this is what army life is like, I want to be in it*. Of course, I never again had an assignment like that."

The army took him to Germany, where he met Joan in an officers' club, and later to Vietnam, one of the most difficult and formative junctures of his career. Morale—his along with the rest of the army's— sank in the quagmire of that war. The public was bitter and conflicted. Vietnam also was one of his first tests as an officer in combat, although not his first experience with death. "Seeing people killed had been part of my growing up," he said. "You deal with it by trying not to let it demolish you."

He rose steadily through the ranks. In 1992, he became supreme allied commander in Europe. The next year, he left that position to become Joint Chiefs chairman at President Clinton's request, an appointment he'd already turned down twice.

"I didn't want people to say, 'He's all right, but he's no Colin Powell,'" he said, only half joking. Eventually, Clinton prevailed on him to take the job. When he finally appointed him, he called Shali "a soldier's soldier."

A few months before his stroke, Shali had visited the wards at Walter Reed Army Medical Center. He thought often of one soldier he'd met there. "He had stepped on a mine in Iraq," he said. "I asked him, 'Are you mad at the world?' He said, 'No, I'm not bitter. I'm going to lead my life.'"

Shali spoke often of discipline—his and that of his troops. This, I realized, was what made him a soldier's soldier. It was what he'd brought forward from his prior life. It was what he now applied daily in his struggle to recover. He went to occupational and physical therapy nearly every day. When he wasn't in clinics, he worked on his exercises at home.

"Everything he does is therapy," Brant said. "Walking to the dining room. Every time he writes something. Stretching to keep limber."

Shali nodded. "It's a full-time job."

MY LAST VISIT WITH Shali was at his outpatient physical therapy, a few miles south of his home. His balance was still shaky. The stroke had knocked out his automatic equilibrium—the ability of his brain to relay and process sensory information from his ankles to his shoulders to keep him from toppling over. He struggled when he stood up. His center of gravity was so far behind him and to the right that he listed. Without someone standing behind him, he would crumple to the ground. To accomplish even the most rudimentary shift, he had to concentrate, consciously centering his weight.

Balance is crucial to almost everything we do. Even simple tasks, such as standing up from a chair and walking forward, require complex balancing skills, something I'd learned from doing years of physical therapy with Christopher.

Balance, in essence, is power.

On that morning, Shali worked with a therapist who was using technology developed under a NASA grant to help returning astronauts get their Earth legs back. The therapist steadied him on special force-sensing plates built into the floor of the therapy room. The plates were wired to a computer that detected Shali's center of gravity. A screen displayed a baseball-shaped cursor that moved as his center of gravity moved.

The approach appealed to the former engineer in Shali.

"OK, left. Left. More left. Now forward," the therapist said. Shali adjusted his body using feedback from the screen to align his center with a target. His face lit up like a kid's each time he nailed it.

"Good—you're nice and steady today," the therapist said.

"It's the decaf." Shali said. I laughed out loud from my corner.

After half an hour, Shali sank into a chair, drained. The therapist waited for him to regroup. But not for long.

"Ready to walk?" he asked.

Shali scooted forward in the seat as he'd been taught, then counted out loud to kick-start his brain. "One, two, three." He rapid-fired the order. His muscles snapped to, and he rose smoothly to a stand—straight up and at attention.

Watching Shali, a scene ran through my mind. I was back in high school. It was November, and I was running a muddy footpath under dripping cedars. I could see the backs of my teammates bobbing ahead of me, including Jim, who was on the team, too. My muscles cramped and twitched. I wanted to throw up. My coach shouted to me from the sidelines.

"You've got to run through the pain," he yelled. I could barely hear the words over my throbbing breath. A small, intense man, my coach, Mr. Weiser, was also my chemistry teacher. He'd recruited me and another young woman to run on the men's cross-country track team—less because we had any talent than because we were game. I was a terrible runner, mostly dragging up the rear.

You've got to run through the pain. He'd shout it each time I staggered by him, splattered with mud and sweat, sucking for air. He taught me how to keep going when my body said quit, how pounding on could quiet a wicked stitch in my side. That year, I ran through the pain; I finished every race.

It dawned on me then that this was what I had brought forward from my long-ago life, something I'd been drawing on all along without realizing it. It had gotten me through the years of fear and uncertainty when Christopher was sick. It would have to see me through now that he was gone.

I'd brought something else as well. The curiosity about people and life that had led me to be a journalist was serving me now in ways I hadn't anticipated. These people whose stories I was telling were helping me come to terms with my own.

Shali taught me that the one thing we do control is the discipline we bring to our lives, the discipline to strive for balance between what we can control and what we can't.

After Christopher's death, I catastrophized everything and assumed the worst would happen. The thought of taking risks paralyzed me, whether getting on an airplane or trying to find a new love. I'd lost two relationships in the course of Christopher's life and death. The first, my marriage to Frank, suffocated under the weight of our anxieties, each of us dealing differently with the uncertainty we felt through multiple medical crises. The second, my relationship with Jim, who was with me when Christopher died. His death proved more than we could handle. After Christopher's death, I was sure I'd never be able to love again.

But from Shali, I'd learned that to resume living requires the discipline to take risks. It meant being able to walk that tightrope between accepting the possibility of a bad outcome and reaching for a better one. If I was going to live a full and productive life, I had to find an equilibrium between taking action and accepting what I couldn't change. I had to work at managing my fear.

One other detail stuck with me from spending time with Shali: the image of the top general in the country cowering at the thought of being wheeled into the metal tube of an MRI machine, as frightened as Christopher had been when he'd had to do the same. How one of the biggest tests any of us face is being trapped in a confined space with our greatest fears, even, or especially, when that confined space is our own head.

CHAPTER 11

Ten years after Christopher's death, I still had not returned to Los Angeles. Every time I had an opportunity, I found a reason not to go. LA had held all my hopes for Christopher's childhood. It was the last place we'd read stories together, curled up on his little bed, the last place he'd come pelting off the school bus, signing, "Mama, home!" The last place he'd jumped into my arms so I could blow raspberries on his neck and make him giggle.

I'd grown up in the endless summer of LA when the Rose Parade was still a hometown spectacle and Orange County was still full of its namesake groves. To me, California was backyard lemon trees, the cooing of doves, the brightness of bougainvillea spilling over white adobe walls. It was mild, sunny weather, even in winter. I spent my youth breathing the sweet, sharp perfume of Coppertone and chlorine at outdoor public pools and chasing peacocks at Descanso Gardens. My brothers and I tracked sand home from the beaches that hugged the nearby coastline and built forts from tree limbs downed by the Santa Ana winds that blew in from the surrounding deserts each fall. I'd wanted Christopher to have that same kind of childhood.

By not going back, it was as though I could preserve the tiny magic bean of hope that Christopher wasn't really gone, that everything in my life since was a dark fairy tale I might wake from any minute.

I couldn't avoid it forever, though. One day, a new friend invited me to go with him on a trip to Southern California. I'd met Mike some months earlier. We were still in the shaky early stages of getting to know each other, but he knew about Christopher. When I explained why I couldn't go with him, he seemed puzzled.

"What are you running from?" he asked.

Mike relished danger—at least that was the way I viewed it. He viewed it as being willing to take smart, calculated risks. His passion when I'd met him was underwater cave diving. I couldn't imagine anything worse than that—being in the dark in a narrow, constricted space with limited air supply and no room to turn around. I started to hyperventilate just listening to him. Mike, though, lit up when he talked about pushing his limits and discovering worlds he didn't know existed. About mapping the unknown. So, when I said again that I didn't think I could go with him on his trip, he looked at me skeptically. "It might be good for you," he said. I took a breath. Shali's sense of impending doom when he'd had to confront the MRI flashed through my mind.

The children at Christopher's school had planted a tree in his honor in a garden behind his classroom. I hadn't seen it since the ceremony. It was the only memorial I had outside the cemetery in Seattle, which I'd stopped going to shortly after we'd buried some of his ashes there. The cemetery was a place where he'd only ever been dead. The school in Burbank had been the center of his life. He'd been so proud of being in first grade—"big school," as he called it.

Maybe it was time.

WE ARRIVED IN LOS Angeles in a pouring February rain, the kind that sends hillsides sliding and knocks homes off their foundations. I left Mike at his work conference and headed off on my own. I could barely see through my windshield as I forded up the Ventura freeway toward Burbank and George Washington Elementary School, a drive I'd been on hundreds of times before.

The route would take me through Pasadena, where I'd last lived with Christopher, past the hospital in Glendale where he'd taken his first steps out of a wheelchair after his transplant, through the scrubby hills where he'd learned to ride a horse, past Griffith Park, where we'd imagined journeys together on the old steam train at Travel Town—this road, the spine of his life.

My head started to pound. Christopher's life spooled forward in my mind as the road unwound in front of me. It felt like driving back in time, like I was heading for a collision. An image of Christopher floated into my vision above the wheel—the first impression I'd ever had of him—from a Polaroid the nurse had snapped right after his birth and taped to the rail of my hospital bed: Christopher's solemn gray eyes taking in the world, his tiny pink lips pursed like he was blowing me a kiss.

CHRISTOPHER WAS BORN AT the old Group Health Hospital on top of Seattle's Capitol Hill just east of downtown, one of the steepest of the many hills that define the geography of the city. Doctors told us his odds of survival were slim to none. The blockage in utero had grossly damaged his kidneys, which also meant he had stiff, underdeveloped lungs that, like new toy balloons, refused to inflate. His chart noted his diagnosis—"post-urethral valves with severe bilateral hydronephrosis." Next to it, a doctor had written, "incompatible with life," a medical euphemism as unsubtle as it was terrifying.

He arrived, utterly beautiful and strangely silent. My first glimpse of him showed a shock of dark hair and long, slender fingers. *A future pianist!* Within minutes, neonatologists swept him away, but I didn't know enough to see it as an omen. I lay there in my euphoric brew of postnatal hormones, ecstatic he had come into the world at last—alive.

A few hours later, a dour-looking doctor woke me. A blur of words. Christopher was turning blue. He had to be transferred to Seattle Children's Hospital a few miles away. I signed some forms. They were bagging air into his lungs as he was wheeled from the nursery past my recovery room to a waiting ambulance. I touched the glass of the transport incubator as he went by. He seemed so small.

He seemed smaller still in the brightly lit neonatal intensive care unit, surrounded by other stations, other infants, each at the center of their own island of machinery. A nurse blocked me at the door of the unit. She spun me around and tied a yellow gown behind my neck, then taught me how to wash my hands up to my forearms with foaming disinfectant. Finally, trembling, the cuffs of my gown soaking wet, I approached the center of the NICU.

Christopher stood out in his incubator, a clear plastic box set in a thicket of IV poles hung with pumps and monitors. At full term and more than seven pounds, he dwarfed the nearby preemies, babies no bigger than a hand. His lungs, though, were like theirs, underdeveloped and incapable of supporting him without mechanical help.

The first time I saw him connected to his ventilator, he was gray, the color of newspaper, despite the heave and shudder of his mechanical breaths. He lay splayed on his back, medically paralyzed to keep him from fighting the vent, his skin streaked orange with Betadine where surgeons had inserted tubes to drain his lungs and kidneys. A bubble of panic rose in my throat, choking off my air. Frank and I hung over him, buttonholing any staff we could for information about what was happening. A urology resident, not known for his bedside manner, finally said to us, "If I were a betting man, I wouldn't bet on him." The words are burned into my memory.

Christopher, though, bet on himself. Frank and I rotated our time at the hospital so one of us would always be there. In the beginning, doctors wouldn't let me hold Christopher in his nest of tubes and wires. I stood beside his isolette for hours, patting his silky back, the bleating of machine alarms and the rhythmic suck and hiss of the ICU our only lullaby.

I doubted everything in those early months—my ability to be a good wife, a good mother. I pumped my breasts on a floor above the neonatal unit, fumbling with an industrial breast pump to extract a few milliliters of milk, while below me teams of experts kept my son alive. Thin curtains divided the pumping cubicles. On either side of me, other ICU moms did the same. Sometimes I heard them crying. My milk dried up quickly.

I lost my faith in intuition, obsessed instead over numbers: his weight and blood urea nitrogen, creatinine levels and oxygen saturations. I learned the language of the doctors, mimicking a cool detachment so they would share information without censor to spare my feelings. This was the mode I knew best—reporter. Making lists. Taking notes. Keeping a record. Packs of doctors would round his bed in their white coats, and I'd be ready with my notebook. My inventory of unanswered questions.

Christopher spent the next five months in the hospital, struggling to breathe, to eat, to grow. Doctors murmured about a "failure to thrive." We didn't see it that way. We saw a baby who had declared himself, unequivocally, *compatible* with life.

At last, Christopher was stable enough to come home. Frank and I had absorbed enough of the hospital nursery routine that staff felt confident we could manage him, even though he was still tethered to an oxygen tank and gastric feeding pump. I knew how to mix his medications, crushing pills and squeezing capsules into the slurry of a liquid diet that pumped through a tube into his stomach overnight. I knew how to hold a needle upside down and flick it to release the bubbles before plunging a dose of erythropoietin into the soft baby squish of his arm—a drug that helped him produce the red blood cells his failing kidneys couldn't. I knew when to turn the oxygen up to keep his pink cheeks from turning gray. How to clap his back with a cup to keep secretions from accumulating in his lungs. How to clean his ureterostomies—the open holes in his back that drained urine—and keep them clear of infection.

What I didn't know was how to take care of a baby. My hands shook that first afternoon as I put him in the old enamel tub of our Green Lake house, a few miles from the hospital. I'd dreamed of raising a child in this house, but now that he was actually home, I wasn't sure I was cut out for it. In the bathtub, Christopher waved his hands and reached for the little yellow ducky I'd been saving for this day. I tried to wash the hospital smell off him with a squirt of baby shampoo, but he was so slippery. My heart raced. I was terrified of dropping him, of being on my own without a medical team a call button away.

Worse, like many long-term ICU babies, he was averse to touch. He'd arch his back away from me and turn his cheek from my kiss. I'd devoured all the parenting literature about the importance of putting a baby on a mother's chest right after birth, how the skin-to-skin contact was critical for healthy development. Christopher had never felt more than the brush of my fingertips, never latched onto my breast. At night I lay awake, sure that proper bonding had been another casualty of his illness.

Then one afternoon when he was six months old, I propped Christopher on the floor with pillows against our old blue sofa for one of his weekly physical therapy sessions. He looked like Humpty Dumpty, his middle fattened with a bulky layer of cloth diapers wrapped around his back to soak up urine. I hovered above him on the couch, watching intently as the therapist, a young woman barely older than the students at nearby University of Washington, worked with his small, slack muscles, trying to catch his body up to his correct developmental age.

"You go like this," she said, tucking his foot into the palm of her hand and bending his knee against his chest. I took notes so I could repeat the exercises when she wasn't there. She tickled him to make him kick against the pressure of her hand. He giggled. His legs straightened, poking like sticks out of his summer onesie. I was concentrating so hard it didn't register at first—a gentle tap, tap, tap—his little hand on my leg, patting me as I had patted him to sleep all those months in the ICU. I wanted to smother him with kisses. We had bonded after all.

THE IMAGES IN MY head tumbled faster as I headed north along the freeway. Glendale Adventist Medical Center loomed up on my passenger side, one of the many hospitals where Christopher had received various kinds of care.

Until you lose the use of them, you don't realize all the ways your kidneys affect your body. They do so much more than clear waste from your system. They control blood pressure and appetite, help lay down bone. They make red blood cells, regulate fluids and electrolytes, affect the function of our hearts. They make children grow. We're born with all the kidney function we will ever have. It's one reason we're usually born with two, so we have one to spare in case of injury or illness. Christopher had less than 10 percent total kidney function between both of his, barely enough to sustain a baby. His kidneys would be less and less able to keep him going, the balance of his body's systems becoming more precarious as he grew. A transplant could save him, but we were in a race against time. For him to receive a kidney transplant, he had to get big enough for his body to accept an adult organ. With his kidneys on the verge of failure, every pound gained was a struggle.

Our lives hovered in limbo between emergencies. His first year, he developed severe seizures. The first time it happened, he was on my lap, his back pressed against my chest, poking his fingers through the pages of *The Very Hungry Caterpillar*. I rested my chin on top of his head, dozy with his post-bath scent of apricots and honey. Suddenly, he went rigid, the way a fawn might freeze in the light. He let out a high, thin cry. The book fell to the floor. His eyes rolled back, and his face turned blue. I ran into the street, screaming for a neighbor to call 911, too afraid to put him down to make the call myself. I stood shrieking in the middle of the street, turning in a circle while his body jerked in my arms, sure that he was dying. Sirens seemed to come from very far away, Dopplering toward me until I collapsed with him into the safe womb of the ambulance, into the hands of people who knew what they were doing.

After the seizures started, one of the medications that controlled them damaged his pancreas and he needed insulin as well. The house and hospital began to blur. At home, we stocked his nursery shelves with gauze and extra tubing, pumps and monitors, needles and gloves. In the hospital, we lined his crib with his favorite toys—a soft, square-shaped elephant that rattled, a little terry-cloth bear, a striped dinosaur—and papered the room with crayoned "get well" cards from family and friends. It felt, almost, like home. Frank and I took shifts. Sometimes he would sleep on the hospital window bench, eye level with Christopher in a crib across from him, and pretend they were camping. I'd bring breakfast. Then we'd switch.

For his part, Christopher charmed the doctors and nurses who stopped by to attend to him, crowing with delight when they offered stickers or crayons. He laughed when they let him hold their penlights or use the reflex hammer. He held court, a tiny Ben-Hur in the chariot of his bed, sitting straight up, tented in a small yellow hospital gown that drooped over his hands and puddled around his toes. When the same phlebotomists appeared day after day to draw his blood, he didn't appear to hold grudges. Sometimes at the end of the day, I'd find a pile of watches in his crib, left by various doctors who'd lent them for him to play with.

THE WINDSHIELD WIPERS ON my rented car beat a frantic rhythm back and forth, unable to keep up with the downpour, the flickering lights on the hillsides I passed barely visible through a gray curtain of rain. I hung on to the wheel as though it were a life preserver, but it didn't help. The deluge had already swept me to another rainstorm in another time.

The year Christopher turned three, I'd set off for my parents' house in Seattle one dark, wet night with him in his seat behind me. Christmas lights made wavery watercolors on the pavement as we passed. Rain pounded on the windshield and "Little Drummer Boy," one of my favorites, played on the radio. I sang along, drumming my fingers on the steering wheel. A movement in my rearview mirror caught my eye. Christopher had started to sway. A notion darted through my mind—one I almost couldn't bear to let myself think. *Maybe he can hear me singing after all.* For an instant, I pictured myself bursting into my parents' living room, the tree lit, a fire going, to announce the news. What an amazing gift that would be for them. I lowered the volume of the radio and held my breath, waiting to see what would happen. Christopher kept rocking. A beat later, I realized he was keeping time to the windshield wipers. My fantasy disappeared. At the same time, I wanted to stop the car and hug him. I turned the radio back up; the wipers scraped and squeaked, and each of us kept dancing to our own music. By the time I arrived at my parents' house, I was happy in a way I couldn't quite explain. A way I would never have anticipated.

We'd found out Christopher was deaf the spring he was fourteen months old. The tulip magnolia tree that hung over the back fence of our Green Lake house was in full bloom, its pink petals shining in the sun. Christopher and I sat facing each other on the lawn beneath it, playing with a working plastic stethoscope one of his doctors had let him take home. These simple rituals still felt surreal to me after so many months in ICUs. Sometimes I just stared at my baby, drunk with his aliveness.

Christopher put the earpieces in his ears and pretended to listen to my heart, then grabbed the chest piece of the instrument and tried to chew on it. When I took the medallion from his mouth, he started hitting it on the ground. He kept banging the stethoscope and laughing. He never flinched. There are moments you realize everything you know about your world is about to change. Moments that feel like they're happening to someone else. Moments you can't un-see. A sense of déjà vu, of foreboding, washed over me like nausea.

Time seemed to slow way down as I wrestled the earpieces out of his ears and fit them in my own. I tapped the chest piece on my hand. *Thump, thump*—it was working. I didn't need the stethoscope to hear my heart racing. I held my breath and hit the end of it on the ground. The bang was so loud it made me jump. My heart tremored in my chest, the elevator dropping out from under me.

A round of hearing tests confirmed my fears. Christopher was profoundly deaf. Doctors couldn't tell us whether he'd been born deaf or if he'd lost his hearing from hospitalizations, or medications, or a combination of both. It made no difference. He couldn't hear the sound of wind blowing, or distant thunder, or music. He couldn't hear the sound of my voice.

Through all his medical crises, I'd held myself together on faith there would come a day when our life would be the way I'd imagined when I first found out I was pregnant. My child would be strong and healthy. We'd fill his world with songs and stories. I clutched Christopher to my chest, sure the dream was gone. "I love you, I love you." I pressed the words against his throat, his cheek, his forehead, terrified that if he'd never heard me say them, it meant he didn't know.

Walking out of the doctor's office that day, the world was filled with so much sound it hurt. The lap of waves, the tinkle of wind chimes, all of it scraped my nerves, the way touch feels on feverish skin. I pressed my fingers into my ears, trying to imagine his world without sound, but heard only the thunder of my heart. I sat at the piano in my parents' home with the cover closed, my hands in my lap, and cried. I'd practiced on it endless hours growing up and had hoped that, one day, my own child would, too. I could hear my mother's voice in my memory, reading me *Charlotte's Web* when I was little. And later, my father's, reading *The Hobbit* and *The Lord of the Rings*. This silence swallowed all my hope. I didn't want Christopher to grow up in a world without the joy of music and words.

During my pregnancy, I'd sung lullabies to my belly, and for the first few months in intensive care, Frank and I had put a cassette player in Christopher's isolette. The tape played our voices and Vivaldi's *Four Seasons*. I'd hoped Vivaldi would soothe and lift my baby as it had always lifted me. Now I prayed Christopher carried the memory of my voice in his cells, the way a shell holds the song of the ocean. I held him tighter, wanting him to feel the current of my voice against his skin, willing it to enter him. I worried his deafness would drag him away from me, that he would know there was a world out there that I belonged to and he didn't.

For Christopher, of course, nothing had changed. He still experienced the world as before, joyfully and without reservation. Though he couldn't hear, he was never silent. One day, not long after we'd found out he was deaf, I put him down for a nap and went back to the living room. A few minutes later, I heard an unmistakable sound coming from upstairs, a sweet, small voice, singing: "Ma-ma-ma-ma-ma." I rushed up the stairs before he could stop, so excited to hear his speech for the first time. He could say "Mama" a million different ways, an exclamation of delight, a statement of surprise, a beseeching, a lament. He chortled and whooped and tried to form his mouth around the words he saw us make at him.

"Ahh, uhhh, oooh," he would say. I love you.

A STRANGE GUTTURAL SOUND filled the car, a low feral moan I didn't at first recognize as my own. *Ahh, uhhh, oooh, ahh, uhhh, oooh.* An invocation, a plea, a prayer. I blinked hard, damming back tears, and made myself keep going.

After we learned Christopher was deaf, Frank and I began taking sign language classes. When I had imagined becoming a mother, I'd looked forward to teaching my child the language I loved. Now we were having to learn to communicate side by side. Christopher picked up signs quickly, far faster than I did. He was my teacher as often as the other way around.

In February, just before his second birthday, Seattle had a big snowstorm—his first. All that morning, we watched out the windows as the soft flakes swirled by. We practiced the sign for snow, making a game of tearing paper into bits and tossing handfuls into the air, then letting them drift down around our shoulders. By afternoon, the snow had robed the yard in white. I bundled him into a little gray snowsuit and tucked his ears into a baby-blue knit hat with reindeer on it. We pushed the back door open, scraping the snow away. His cheeks pinked up as soon as the cold air hit him, and he let out a little yelp of surprise. Gently, I sat him in the snow, lay down next to him, and scissored my arms and legs to make a snow angel. He watched me intently. Then I laid him on his back and moved his arms and legs so he could make his own. When we were done, we both lay there, looking at the gray sky. He fluttered his hands like snow coming down.

Later that night, he waved his arms in his crib like he was making an angel and patted his head, asking for a hat. It took a moment for it to sink in. *He was talking to me.* I could hardly stand to turn the light out. When I checked from the doorway a few minutes later, he was still babbling with his hands in the semi-dark.

By that spring he was starting to "read." *The Three Bears* was a favorite. He'd open to the first page and sign, "Birds fly," pointing to tiny bluebirds in the background of the picture that no one else would have noticed. He'd flip a few pages forward. "Bear cold," he signed for porridge, shivering dramatically. Flip, flip to the back. "Bed sleep," he'd sign. He'd draw his hand closed in front of his eyes, then sweep his hands apart with a flourish. "The end." The sign left his tummy momentarily exposed. I'd dive in and tickle him until we were both breathless with laughter.

If we didn't know a sign, we made it up, a language between us, finding combinations of signs to express what we were trying to say.

"Expensive" equaled the sign for "money" plus the sign for "to throw away."

"Peaceful" was the sign "to become" plus the sign for "quiet."

"Earthquake" was "dinosaurs" plus "walking."

Frank and I had planted a quaking aspen outside the Green Lake house the year we bought it. Every fall the tree blazed a honey yellow that shimmered in the sun. "Shiver leaf," Christopher called it.

Besides learning to sign, we'd also fitted Christopher with hearing aids and begun speech therapy to help him use his residual hearing. The hearing aids let him detect very low frequencies outside his damaged range. Each week, his speech therapist, Jill, came over with her "bag of sounds" full of bells and buzzers. He'd rush over to pull out his favorite, a toy microphone, and hold it to his lips. "Mmmm, mmmm," he'd say, his hand against its little speaker. The vibrations of his own voice made him giggle. Soon, the whole house became an extension of her bag of sounds. When I turned on the vacuum cleaner, he'd put his hands against it and point to his ears. The same with the garbage disposal. When it ran, he'd startle.

"Ears on," he signed.

His sign vocabulary grew steadily. "Where are Mom's keys?" I signed automatically to myself one morning while rushing around, late for work, not expecting him to understand.

Christopher scooted over on his seat to the heat register and pointed inside. "Keys," he signed proudly, turning the knuckle of his index finger into the palm of his other hand like a lock to show where he had dropped them under the grate next to the living room fireplace. I swept him up, so excited he'd understood me I forgot to be mad.

Gradually, he put together more complex sentences. "Water mix wait," he signed to me one evening while we were drawing a bath. By the time Christopher was in kindergarten, we'd cobbled together a working sign vocabulary. If I stopped to rest or turn the page as we read books together, he'd pick up my hands and form them into shapes to make me keep going. When it was time for bed, he'd make the sign—palms together, cheek resting on them like a pillow—except he'd use my cheek instead of his, our private joke.

On kindergarten graduation day, Christopher pulled me over to introduce me to one of his friends. We stood together under the hot sun, the smell of tar wafting off the playground, waiting for his teachers to pass out diplomas spangled with glitter stars. "Mama, my," Christopher signed to his friend, pressing his hand to his heart, then pointing at me. "Hearing closed"—the sign for deaf. "Me. Same."

Translation: *My mother, deaf, like me.* I nearly danced on the pavement. He didn't see our worlds as separate after all.

I WAS LAUGHING NOW, and crying, and something that was both and neither, my whole emotional wiring short-circuited and scrambled. The corner of Griffith Park appeared out my driver's side window. Christopher had loved playing at Travel Town there, bouncing on the conductor's seat of the old parked train. I could picture him signing vigorously that he was taking us home. But nothing could reverse where we were headed. No train could bring him back to me now.

In Pasadena, Christopher grew with the aid of his stomach feeding tube. With each pound gained, though, his damaged kidneys became progressively less sufficient to keep him alive. His body began to bloat. His bones turned brittle. When he was five, he went into end-stage kidney failure. He still was not big enough to qualify to receive an adult kidney transplant, so his doctors at UCLA started him on peritoneal dialysis at home to buy time.

Every evening, I checkmarked my way through a sterile procedure to hook him to a device the size of a washing machine. I'd set a timer to scrub my hands with antibacterial soap for three minutes, put on a mask and gloves, calculate how much glucose to put in his dialysate solution, and soak every surface that connected the machine to his body with iodine for four minutes before beginning.

A port went straight into his peritoneum, the lining of the stomach. The machine flushed fluids through his peritoneal cavity all night, ridding his body of its daily buildup of toxins. Any contamination could result in a deadly case of peritonitis. I taped a set of clamps and sterile scissors next to his bed in case I had to cut him free of the machine in an earthquake or fire.

Days, I kept track of his fluid weight, temperature, and blood pressure, alert to any sign of infection or that his condition was turning critical. Nights, I lay in an edge state, not quite sleep, listening for machine alarms. The prospect of a power outage terrified me. We were on life support.

He needed a kidney soon. Dialysis was an imperfect substitute and he was growing weaker by the day. After a few months, he could no longer walk, his wasted legs unable to bear his weight. With his complicated medical history, Christopher had been considered too high risk to go on a regular donor wait list for a kidney. Our best shot was from a living, related donor.

Our families volunteered to be tested along with Frank and me. The morning we got tested, I threw up in the corridor of the hospital, pressing my forehead against the cool wall and heaving up years of worry about this moment.

The transplant had hung over us for so long, enormous in its implications and terrifying in its finality. It could mean a normal life for Christopher. Or it could mean the end of our hope for one. One of us had to match. Without a match, Christopher would be yoked indefinitely to a regimen of clinic visits and regular blood cleansings, his growth permanently stunted.

I barely ate the morning we were to get the test results. The doctor parsed through the complicated language of the antigens and what our options were. I don't remember exactly what he said, only my stomach flip-flopping as I absorbed the meaning of it. Frank's kidney was the better match. In August, the year he turned six, Christopher finally got his kidney transplant from his dad at UCLA Medical Center.

Even a good match, though, couldn't guarantee success. Another image, this one seared in my memory like a tableau: Christopher just rolled out of transplant surgery, his face puffy with fluids, his body tangled in monitors and drains. The new kidney we'd pinned all our hopes on wasn't working. Doctors had set up an emergency bypass of it, and now Christopher's blood circulated outside his body through a machine. All his blood—his *lifeblood*—hung in bags off the side of his bed. I grabbed Christopher's hand, pale and stabbed with an IV line, and held on for dear life, the way I would when we went to cross a street. My father, standing beside me in the ICU, held mine the same way.

The transplant surgery set off a new round of frightening complications. Our hospital stays began to run together. I wandered the fluorescent corridors at night, long connectors between places of illness and recovery, bad news and good, fear and prayer. I paced, hoping to get from one place to another, one moment to the next. Hospital time kept its own clock, measured in intervals of beeping alarms, the appearance and disappearance of strangers at the bedside, people taking vitals, taking blood, taking a measure of the situation. Outside, time proceeded. Inside, the season of the sick never turned.

We moved Christopher's bed by the window when we could. It perked him up to see outside. He'd lie on the white hospital sheets, his skin pale, blue shadows under his eyes, and watch the birds go by. "Fly," he'd sign.

Other patients in other beds came and went. Once, a little baby appeared one curtain over, a speck in a large metal crib. A pink, hospital-issued bear was the only clue she was a girl. No parents came to visit her. She twitched and shook, raising her tiny fist in the air, the one not weighed down by an IV. She cried the maddened, rasping cry of a wasp, barely loud enough to summon the nurses. She vanished as quickly as she came.

A sixteen-year-old boy named David arrived in her wake. He came with a loud extended family. They brought chicken-salad sandwiches and argued with the nurses over David's dinner.

"He only eats pureed food," his mother said, sending the nurse scrambling to find a blender. They argued over parking and other minutiae necessitated by moving into the hospital, however briefly.

"He has a very bad heart," his father said to me, as though by explanation. David, with a thick neck and low, little baby ears, waved to Christopher.

"Sick," Christopher signed to him. "Same."

THEN, THE MIRACLE. AFTER several nerve-racking months, Christopher's stubborn new kidney at last kicked into gear. His body began to restore to a natural balance. The curve of muscles reappeared along his limbs. His eyes brightened and his cheeks flushed.

By Thanksgiving, he took his first steps after more than a year in a wheelchair. The day he did it, his physical therapist and I burst into tears and hugged. By spring, he'd relearned to run. He gained an appetite for the first time in his life, allowing doctors to at last remove the stomach tube he'd been fed through since he was an infant. No more changing tape and gauze multiple times a day. No more attracting the stares of strangers whenever we stopped to eat and pulled out a funnel and tube. Each morning, he helped me pack his lunch box—once reserved for medical supplies—with peanut butter and jelly sandwiches. "Delicious for school," he'd sign, patting the lunch box approvingly and smacking his lips for emphasis.

He took to ordering hamburgers, something he'd seen other children do for years, as though making up for lost time, although he rarely ate more than a bite or two. We'd go to the McDonald's near us—his choice—to order a Happy Meal, and when the employees saw him coming, they'd have his ready, along with a free ice cream cone for being such an enthusiastic customer. He stashed the little windup Happy Meal toys beneath his bed like treasure.

He played so hard he barely stopped to sleep. Sometimes he threw in a skip when he walked. We called them his "happy hops." He rode horses in a special therapy program, showing off like a small circus performer. "Mama, watch," he'd sign as he whirled by, riding hands-free and whooping to get my attention. He joined a Little League team and learned to hit a baseball on a tee.

One day, after his regular physical therapy appointment at Glendale Adventist, we scavenged an iron gate from the hospital's thrift store, where I often shopped to find things for an antiques booth I kept in Pasadena. Christopher clapped while I wrestled it to the street, thrilled as a pirate hunting for loot. I thought it would make a fine coffee table, set on a base with a piece of glass on top. In the center of the gate, forged in iron, was a star.

We talked about the stars that night as we sat on the front steps of our bungalow in Pasadena.

"How many?" he signed, pointing up. A warm evening breeze ruffled his hair. I smoothed it down.

"Many, many. Big number," I signed, holding my hands apart to show him.

"More big," he corrected me, pulling my hands farther and farther apart until I'd thrown my arms wide open. He squealed with glee and climbed into the infinity of my embrace.

A YEAR AFTER HIS transplant, Christopher went to spend part of the summer with Frank's new family, including his stepbrother and step-sisters. When he came home that September, he signed so fast the words seemed to spill from his fingers—about fishing and fast horses, a big hit and a baseball trophy.

Then the sign that always made me melt. "Miss you," he signed, pressing his index finger into his chin as though he were making a dimple, the sweetest gesture.

His body seemed even sturdier than the month he'd left, the indentations of his muscles still a wonder. In the bath that evening, I admired his little back, so straight through it all. His spine seemed much more knit into him somehow, not loose and bony, his scapulas no longer the sharp chicken wings he used to have. Such a fine little boy had at last emerged.

"Same," he signed, pointing to himself, when we drove past fields of children playing. A few weeks before he died, he was Santa Claus in his school play. I remember his eyes were shining.

I NEARLY MISSED THE turn I'd taken so often to get Christopher to school on time. Whether it was accidental or intentional I didn't know anymore. I just knew I didn't want to go where I was going, but also that I had to. My breath was coming in hard inverted gulps, my chest squeezing down as I breathed in, my stomach pulling up hard against my lungs. I started to panic, unable to get enough air. The closer I got to the school, the slower I went, dreading the moment my past and present would collide and I might stop breathing altogether.

The school was tucked up near the foothills hugging the city of Burbank. As I pulled up, a row of cheerful yellow buses lined the front as usual. I almost turned around at the sight of them. *What are you running from?* Mike's question stopped me. No matter how fast I ran, I could not outrun my grief.

I sat in the car for a few minutes to calm myself before walking up the cement path, past the flagpole toward the red front doors. The school was still painted its namesake colonial blue with white-trim windows set under a roof of red clay tiles. I'd called ahead to let the principal know I was coming to see Christopher's tree. The ladies at the front desk were expecting me. They nodded me through, their expressions kind, but their glances slid past mine, as though to afford me some privacy. I walked the long school hallways, a gauntlet of colorful bulletin boards and busy classrooms, maneuvering through the maze of corridors the way you find your path in a dark house, by shape memories in the blackness. I scanned children's faces as I passed them, searching by reflex for familiar ones, but I recognized none of them. The kids I'd known had long since graduated. At last, I pushed open the doors to the playground.

Kids zigzagged in their raincoats, playing tag and chasing kickballs. I dodged through them until I reached Christopher's old classroom, in a portable building at the far end of the playground. With its scattering of desks and tidy row of cubbyholes, it looked exactly as it always had when I picked Christopher up from school. For an instant, I thought if I looked hard enough, I might still find him hiding behind a row of coats.

The day of the tree ceremony, one of his teachers—Julie Lambert or Nancy Parker, I'm no longer sure which one, but he had loved them both—laid a small pile of his belongings in my arms: a sheaf of penciled homework, his extra jacket. On top was a calendar he'd colored for the coming year. Neither of us could speak.

Here my memory flickers in and out.

I have no recall of the tree ceremony itself, though pictures show me there, standing next to Carl Kirchner, the director from the preschool. Tall and affable, Carl had been one of Christopher's favorite people. When Carl had visited him at the hospital, Christopher had eagerly introduced him to his doctors as his "papa." In the photos, we're surrounded by little girls and boys with sunny faces, hanging cards they'd made for Christopher from the peach tree sapling they had chosen.

Arthur, a sturdy deaf boy with a cap of dark curls and brown eyes, ran up right after the ceremony and pulled on my sleeve. Like many of the kids that day, he laid claim to being Christopher's best friend. A bull-in-the-china-shop kind of kid, his perception of the space around him lagged his size. But he'd always been extra cautious around Christopher, taking care not to knock him over. I had a soft spot for him because of it.

Arthur made Christopher's name sign, cupping his hand in the shape of a C and circling it over his heart.

"Box for Christopher, how big?" he signed, and pointed to the sky. He looked at me expectantly, waiting for an answer.

I knelt to hug him so he wouldn't see my face begin to shatter. I had no words to answer him. The funeral director in Seattle had asked us much the same thing. Nobody should have to answer such questions.

He tugged on my sleeve a second time. "School Christopher again, when?" he signed.

I squeezed my eyes shut at the memory. How I wished I could see death as a child did, as a place from which you could return. I couldn't move my legs. They felt heavy, paralyzed, the way they did when I surfaced from a bad dream unable to scream or run. I was trapped there on the playground between my sleep and waking nightmares. I thought again of Shali, how he'd had to will each step forward. I made myself do the same.

The path to the garden was shaded like a tunnel, but as soon as I stepped through, I recognized the tree right away. A sudden surge of memories I hadn't thought of in years washed over me. A few months after Christopher's death, I'd shown up at the school and asked if I could volunteer there. Kreigh (pronounced like Craig) Hampel, the sun-beaten man who ran the garden, didn't seem surprised to see me.

We'd stood together before the spring planting, surveying the tumble of overgrowth and scraggly march of dead sunflower stalks. He didn't see the carcass of a garden, the ugliness of it, only a lovely learning laboratory, a place where kids from the Los Angeles basin—children who had grown up surrounded by cement—could learn to make things grow. The children called him "Dr. Rot," for his abiding love of compost.

"Everything here is a lesson," he told me. "It all teaches something important. Plant succession, native plant dominance, insect food, weeds." Kreigh handed me several lengths of old hose and told me to form them into hoops. Then he took the circles and placed them around the garden. When the kids came piling out of their classrooms later that afternoon, I saw why. As each child tromped through the garden, Kreigh directed them to a different spot.

"Weed your own circle," he told them.

I put my circle around Christopher's tree. Over the next few months, I dug alone while the children were in class, pounding my hands against the soil until they bled, hauling rocks to make a low retaining wall around the tree to protect its roots. Each rock felt heavy, like his sleepy head in my lap, like his body curled against my chest.

One day, Kreigh handed me something different—a pruning saw.

He explained how to shape the trees to receive more light. There was a rhythm to making the cuts. If I stopped or thought too hard, or tried to analyze where to go next, the whole process withered. If I let the tree tell me where to cut, the right form emerged. I pruned Christopher's peach tree to the recommended funnel shape, heading back the one-year-old growth by a third to strengthen the next year's peaches. The apple next to it, determinedly upright in growth habit, I pruned to a more open form, releasing the center to the light. Next to the apple was a sickly plum, its bark bleeding and swollen in places, the leaves burnt at the edges. I trimmed the dead and dying growth, sawing back to the first buds, where new growth seemed headed in a promising direction.

I cut the trees back hard that year.

After I returned to Seattle, I received a letter from Kreigh. Christopher's tree had developed a sturdy growth habit, he wrote. "It has outproduced all the others. It's blessed with a strong spirit."

As I stood there in the garden, the rain began to lift and lighten. I could still see the remnants of the stone wall I'd built, and the marker with his name on it that the children had made. The tree itself had grown high and wide. The principal told me it bore buckets of peaches each summer. But there was something else that drew me to it. *A strong spirit.* I stood beneath its branches and a kind of quiet settled over me.

When I finally got back to the hotel late that afternoon, I was exhausted. I threw myself on the bed. Mike sat on the edge beside me.

"How was it? Did you see the tree?"

I nodded.

"And?"

"I'm glad I went," I said. "It was like Christopher wanted me to visit."

IV.

THE CRUCIBLE OF GRIEF

(GERRI)

CHAPTER 12

When grown-ups die, there are so many affairs to put in order. Wills to read and estates to settle, busywork to occupy the living and put the loss on hold. After Christopher's death, there was little to do. My parents returned his final library books, a task that nearly crushed them. We donated leftover medical supplies. Final medical bills trickled in.

A woman from California Children's Services called to check on the status of some physical therapy the agency had been providing. I'd spent months going back and forth with the state, forwarding records, being denied eligibility, forwarding different records, finally getting Christopher approved for the therapy. By the end of the ordeal, I was on a first-name basis with the person assigned to my case. When I picked up the phone and heard her voice, I realized she didn't know. I wanted to stay in that instant, the instant where if you didn't know, then Christopher was still alive somewhere in some parallel universe. I wanted to rewind to the instant before I knew.

"I'm so sorry to tell you this." My words came out flat. "Christopher died."

There wasn't even a pause. She kept talking, about how the last time we'd chatted, he was doing great. How she couldn't believe how big he'd gotten. The news hardly seemed to register. I knew it had, though. I knew the sound of the voice in your head that said, *If I keep talking, I won't have to face this awful realization.*

I disconnected and sat there in the dining room nook, the exact spot where I'd received the news of his death. I stared out the window for a long time, listening to the drone of the dial tone, until a sudden noise, the lilting *coo-ahh, coo coo* of a mourning dove, startled me from my trance. The bird lit on the air conditioner just outside my window. I watched it preen its soft, tan feathers. For a split second, it seemed to peer at me with Christopher's eyes. I blinked, and it was gone.

"Fly," I signed.

There were other bills to settle. At Glendale Adventist, a woman in the hospital's finance office told me she had written off Christopher's final balance. She was trying to be kind. When she hung up, I kept holding the phone. I couldn't breathe.

Written off, and just like that, it was as though he'd never existed.

THE SIGN FOR GRIEF is made by wringing the hands over the heart— "crushed heart." The word itself is a hand-me-down from *grever*, Old French for "burden," which in turn comes from the more ancient root, *gwere*, meaning "heavy." It seems even our early ancestors could not explain a state of mental anguish except through its physical analog, the sense of a great weight. And it was true. It felt as though I were buried to my neck in sand, a long-standing nightmare from my childhood, my body pinned beneath the surface of my sadness, unable to move. But what is the word for the weight of absence?

Days, I drove through Los Angeles, through the tawny hills to Griffith Park, where we'd climbed the observatory, to the Santa Monica Pier, where we'd ridden the antique carousel, up the dusty, pine-scented arroyos where he'd learned to ride horses. I drove up and down Lake Street, the Pasadena boulevard that connected me to my childhood and to his. I drove along Mulholland, high above the LA basin, under the denim blue of a Southern California sky at dusk, a pale moon rising like an oncoming headlight, and watched the carpet of lights bloom below me. I parked in front of his school in Burbank and watched children pour from buses in their red-and-blue uniforms. Sometimes I'd arrive somewhere with no memory of how I got there, as though the grid underneath me had tilted to a different axis, cast me off with no bearings.

I drove to find him. I drove to get lost. I drove with the windows up and the radio off, running the loop of Christopher's life over and over in my head, a daisy chain of *if only*s. If only we had found out about his original birth defect sooner, before it had damaged his kidneys so severely. If only I hadn't let him go with his father that last weekend. If only we'd known it wasn't the flu he was coming down with—it was something worse. I kept searching for the magic moment when, had I acted differently, there would have been a different outcome. In the car, I could pretend his life had taken a different course, that he was still here, that I was just about to pick him up from school, or his physical therapy, or his father's house. Alone in the car, I could refuse to believe he was dead. If I refused to believe it, it would not be true. In the car, I was still his mother. In a car, I didn't have to see people, talk to people, answer unanswerable questions about how I was doing. I didn't have to respond when people asked what they could do to help or what I needed.

You can't help me, I wanted to scream. *No one can help me*. What I needed was for Christopher to come running toward me, waving his Batman lunch box, signing, "School finished," flinging his hands apart. What I needed was for him to curl against me after a bad dream until our breathing synchronized like fireflies. What I needed was to see him grow up.

I passed a sign in a parking lot: FIVE MINUTES' GRACE ALLOWED, it said.

Five minutes' grace. That was what I pleaded for.

THE FIRST YEAR, I was numb. The second year was worse. The shock had worn off by then. By the third year, people were ready for me to be done with my mourning. To move on with my life.

But you're never done.

Triggers were everywhere. The yellow school bus driving by, the sound of an ambulance, the smell of Magic Markers. They left me shaking.

Soon after Christopher and I had moved to Los Angeles, an earthquake jolted me out of bed before dawn. The shock wave from a 7.4 quake, one hundred miles to the east in the desert town of Landers, nearly knocked our little bungalow off its moorings. I remember the peculiar sense of the house swinging, as though we were suspended a moment, waiting for the floor to drop out from under us. I ran to Christopher's room while the floor bucked beneath me. He was still sleeping when I got to him. I couldn't go back to sleep.

Waiting for aftershocks. Grief is like that.

The Oklahoma City bombing happened. The news flashed images over and over of a firefighter carrying a limp child's body from the wreckage. Then 9/11. Then Sandy Hook. Then Syrian children washing up on distant shores. Each mass grief plunged me back into the tunnel of my own.

IN THE YEARS THAT followed Christopher's death, I was afraid I'd wear out whatever reserves my friends and family had for my grieving. Reporting stories became my surrogate for hashing through my sorrow. Sometimes I realized right away what drew me to a particular story. Sometimes the realization would come many years later in a flash of recognition. Most of the people I reported on passed through my life, and I theirs.

Once in a while, though, I met someone whose life would weave into my own. That was true of Gerri Haynes, though I wouldn't have guessed it when I met her.

One of the first pieces I did after going back to work at the newspaper was about pediatric palliative care, a field then in its infancy. Hospice for children was a Hobson's choice. To qualify required ceasing medical treatment that focused on a cure and redirecting it toward quality of life and relief of pain. But families and medical staff alike seldom wanted to give up any possibility of saving a child's life. Acknowledging that children die was a taboo. It meant that, even though their children were dying, families didn't have access to the kinds of services and support adult hospice patients received. Families were left to deal with their fear and sadness on their own.

Christopher had once shared a hospital room at UCLA Medical Center with a little girl shrouded in an oxygen tent, a drowning victim.

She looked like a doll, with blank eyes and splinted hands. Her father stood by her crib.

"Good girl, good girl," he repeated like an incantation. The mother sagged against the wall, silent, staring. Occasionally, staff drew a drape around the bed and suctioned the little girl's lungs, a horrible gasping sound, to clear the airways. Only a thin curtain separated the world of the living and the world of the dying.

It wasn't something we could talk about.

Some in the medical community were working to change that. They wanted to find a way to support parents as they faced their children's illnesses and likely deaths, which was how I met Gerri. Slender and athletic, with lively hazel-brown eyes, she'd worked as a critical care nurse and also as an administrator who focused on hospice and palliative care. At the time, she was helping put together one of the first palliative care units in the country for children. During our interview, she told me about a group she ran for bereaved mothers out of her home, in a quiet, wooded suburb of Seattle. She invited me to come.

I hesitated at first, not wanting to cross source-reporter lines, but I kept thinking about the group after putting the story to bed. I rarely spoke of Christopher's death. I expended a great deal of energy trying not to appear "damaged." I didn't want to be "that sad lady who lost her kid" that people whispered about. I made sure that—to the outside world—I appeared to have moved on. It protected me, too. Distancing myself from my feelings let me function normally, even laugh. Inside, though, I felt like I fit nowhere. I decided to go.

THE DOZEN OR SO mothers that gathered in Gerri's living room could have been any group of women assembled to get out the vote, or orchestrate a garage sale, or plan a school fundraiser. Some chatted and laughed together like old friends. Others sat alone or milled about uncertainly, clutching mugs of tea. Eventually, we settled on couches and pillows on the floor facing Gerri, who sat on the hearth in front of her fireplace. She had us introduce ourselves, say the names of our children and something about their lives. Details about their deaths spilled out, too—cancers, suicides, car accidents, murders, all the hard, hard luck of life.

As my turn neared, I grew more and more tense. Flickering lights floated like confetti at the edges of my vision, the shimmering aurora of an oncoming migraine. I pressed my hands to my temples, trying to keep the walls from closing in.

I said little that first meeting, unable to find the words to recount the story of Christopher's life and death, a story I'd kept buried so deeply I could barely tell it to myself. In an odd way, the group made me feel lonelier. The mothers there were more like me than most others I knew, and yet they still did not know Christopher, could never know him. Nor could I know their children. I couldn't see past the ways we were all different. Some had lost adult children. Others, babies. Some had had a chance to say goodbye. Others had gotten the terrible news from a police officer at the door. I could not imagine the particular horrors of their grief. I had only my own. I left that first meeting unsettled, convinced I wouldn't go back.

But I did go back. The ritual repeated each time we met. Gerri opened a space for each mom to talk about whatever she wanted. Some talked about their lost children. Others about the siblings left behind. They talked about the unwitting ways that friends, family, and partners hurt or helped. Gerri listened intently to each mom, zeroing in on what she wasn't saying as much as what she was. Anger poured out. And tears. And also laughter. Guilt and shame lurked like noxious weeds.

"All the pain and guilt inside, you have to decide what you're going to do with it," she said. "If you don't turn it into compassion and wisdom for yourself and then for others, what is the point?" She talked about how anger masked sorrow, and sorrow was mourning what we couldn't control. She talked about how crying was necessary and good. And not crying was all right, too.

"Bless the dam," she said after a mom said she was too numb to cry. "The dam is what protects us."

I sat there, listening to the others, and at the same time wanting to push them away. The vortex started sucking me back in, threatening my fragile purchase on happiness. I didn't want to be near their pain. Eventually, I stopped going.

Gerri, though, stayed with it, month after month, year after year. She let these women into her house, into her heart. She held their pain. I couldn't imagine how she was able to do that. So many had fled me by then. Two love relationships—first Christopher's father, then Jim. Friends had moved on in their lives. I had run, too, trying to put distance between myself and my feelings by pretending they didn't exist.

When Christopher was a baby in intensive care, a minister had come to speak to some of the ICU parents about life and loss. His baby had rolled off a table and died while his wife was changing her. His wife had thrown herself off a ferry a few weeks later. His manner was kind, but he had a sadness in his eyes so deep it was hard to look at him. He said it was his mission now to reach out to others in pain.

How did someone stand and face down that kind of grief, let the tsunami wash over them? I'd wondered then. I wondered now. Gerri taught me, though not in the way I expected.

I'D KNOWN GERRI FOR two years before learning she'd been diagnosed with breast cancer. I heard through a mutual friend, who also worked at the paper. The news shocked and worried me. I called her up. She sounded unfazed about her diagnosis. I hung up, thinking maybe her work had something to do with her lack of apparent distress.

By then I was on a newly formed team at the paper we sometimes jokingly referred to as the "Ordinary People" team. As the JOA clock counted down on the *P-I*'s financial future, management had tried an ambitious newsroom reorganization we nicknamed "Tornado." Tornado was a Hail Mary that was supposed to save us from the relentless encroachment of the internet, make us more responsive to our audience, nimbler, more efficient, "digital-first." We reorganized ourselves into interdepartmental reporting teams. Mine was dedicated to writing profiles. The Tornado reinvention was an effort to help more people see themselves reflected in the paper. You didn't have to be famous or running for office or accused of a crime to warrant a story. But that also meant our choices were virtually endless. The dilemma was how to choose.

I loved the idea that every person had a story worth telling and quickly developed my own metric for choosing people to profile. I looked for stories where there was tension between the extraordinary and the ordinary. The more "extraordinary" a person was, the more ordinary a situation it took to find the tension. General Shali had fit that scenario—a person of uncommon status facing a stroke, an exceedingly common medical calamity. In contrast, an "ordinary" person facing an extraordinary situation also created a good foundation for a story. Seth fit that profile, a regular little boy coping with an unimaginable illness.

But I also had another metric for finding stories. I looked for people facing unexpected situations that mirrored something else about their lives. Years earlier, I'd read a story by *Milwaukee Journal Sentinel* writer Crocker Stephenson about a history professor with Alzheimer's. As a medical reporter, I'd run across plenty of stories about patients with Alzheimer's and their families, but this one was different. Stephenson's choice to profile a man whose life was devoted to history as he lost his own personal history gave the story a powerful resonance. When I heard Gerri had breast cancer, I thought of Stephenson's article. How would someone who had made death her life's work face the possibility of her own?

I called Gerri back and asked if I could profile her as she went through her treatment. Breast cancer is the second-most-common kind of cancer in women. Almost every woman I knew had either dealt with it herself or knew someone who had. I thought Gerri's experience as a hospice nurse could be helpful to others facing the disorienting aftermath of a diagnosis. I wanted to write about how she approached having cancer, but also what having cancer might show her about her own life. She said yes right away, which didn't surprise me. If I knew anything about Gerri by then, it was that she believed in the power of sharing stories. She had no problem revealing her situation in the hopes it might help someone else.

That was how I found myself in July, three months after she'd discovered the lump, watching her disrobe unselfconsciously for her final round of treatment. There was a deep scar under her arm where her lymph nodes had been taken out. Her breast tissue was slightly darkened where the previous radiation had burned through the skin. A pale crescent of a scar remained from the operation that removed the lump.

She lay on a platform suspended beneath the sleek metal body of a linear accelerator. Pen marks outlined a target on her breast to help direct the beam of electrons. Alone in the chamber under a dome of painted stars, she imagined the radiation as the sun, recast it as a healing force instead of a destructive one. "Recharging my solar battery," she said when the session was over. "That's how I think of it."

GERRI FOUND THE LUMP on a Good Friday. High up on her chest wall, this one felt different from other lumps she'd had. It had connections, almost like webbed feet, within her breast. It was as though a tenacious invader had embedded in her tissue. She knew instantly what it was. She turned to her husband, Bob, a physician. He felt the lump.

"That's got to come out," he said. Matter-of-fact. They both believed, even then, it was malignant. Neither panicked.

"If this is my terminal event, I need you to know I'm at peace with that," she told her husband. Then she went to sleep.

At fifty-eight, she already knew more about dying than most people. Her mother had died of breast cancer when Gerri was six years old. Her father had died of a heart attack when she was thirteen. As an adult, she'd become a cardiac critical care nurse, working in the intensive care unit, where thin green lines on beeping monitors daily wavered between life and death. Partly because of her ICU experiences, she'd helped found a hospice at Evergreen Hospital, near where she lived, and later one at Seattle Children's. She was passionate about the work. Just a few years earlier, she'd lost her stepmother, the woman who'd raised her, with whom she was very close. "Everyone dies, and if you're going to, you should be able to die a dignified death," Gerri said.

All of which is to say, what Gerri knew about dying informed her living.

A biopsy of the tumor proved her intuition correct. Not only was the tumor malignant, but on the spectrum of severity, it measured a "three out of three, and nine out of nine," she said. "It was as aggressive and malignant as they get."

As news filtered out that the tumor was malignant, friends and family deluged her with emails, calls, and well wishes. It pressed a role reversal on Gerri. "I had to turn my head around," she said. "I'm not somebody used to all this love and prayer coming to me. I had to make room to receive this. I envisioned my chest as a sponge to receive it all, receive this gift."

A week after Gerri found the lump, a surgeon friend of hers took it out, along with her lymph nodes. Based on the initial pathology reports, she and her doctor assumed the cancer was likely to have spread. Doctors recommended six weeks of radiation. She knew she was lucky to have medical colleagues running interference for her. She knew not everyone had that luxury. Still, events had happened so quickly; she could barely think about her options. She felt pressure to make decisions about treatment choices, about what to do next. Her life felt out of balance. She needed time to think.

"When you have a diagnosis like this, you get shepherded along," she said. "It creates chaos in your decision-making. You need to take time to evaluate what treatments are appropriate for you and your body."

Chaos. I circled the word in my notebook.

Eight days after her surgery, Gerri and her husband headed for their vacation home on a beach along the southern coast of Oregon, a place they often went to reconnect and weed their garden while listening to the waves. "Weeding is where we come together," Bob told me. Sometimes, they'd even put their camping headlamps on and work in the dark. Gerri had often spoken to the moms group about how there was something healing about connecting hand to earth. She advised anyone having a tough conversation with someone they loved to get seated on the ground. "Trust me, it will help," she'd said.

I pictured Gerri weeding in the circle cast by her headlamp, a cancer growing in her body, trying to glean the right next move at her home by the sea.

On that visit to the beach, though, something happened that took the decision out of her hands. Gerri slipped and banged her incision. The bleed was slow at first, into the tissue beneath her scar. Soon she had a bulging sack of blood pressing on her nerves, a grapefruit-size hematoma, making her arm numb and her head dizzy.

Bob had brought large syringes along in case he needed to draw off lymphatic fluid, a normal part of healing after removal of the lymph nodes. Instead, he began drawing off blood.

"It wouldn't stop," he said. "I knew it was bad. We looked at each other and said maybe this is it. This was one of those moments where we're facing something bigger than we are." Then they both threw all their weight into pressure on the incision. Pain seared through the surgery site. She nearly fainted.

I thought of something else she'd often told the moms in her group: Pain is part of life. And pain is part of healing.

"It's emotionally healthy to move pain instead of store pain," Gerri said. "If you store pain, it begins to do mischievous things to your body or psyche. Cry. Laugh. Go to the beach and move. It's all part of restoring the soul to health."

IN FOLLOWING GERRI FOR the story, I realized the group for mothers that I'd attended at her home years earlier had to be a part of it. She continued to host the group, even during her own treatment. It was, she said, a source of her strength.

On a warm Tuesday that July, I went again to the group. By then, some of the women had been meeting continually in her home for more than a decade. She sat cross-legged in front of her fireplace, surrounded by about a dozen of us. Some, like me, mourned children lost years earlier. For others, the wound was only weeks old and still raw. Even though I was there as a reporter, my brain began its familiar, unwelcome calculus—who there had suffered most like me?

This time, though, I really listened to the other mothers' stories, and this time I heard not how we were different, but how we were alike. I saw that I *did* know their children. They were a presence there in the room. I felt the force of their spirits in the will to survive of their mothers. I saw, too, how Gerri's living room was one of the few safe places mothers like us had to grieve, to share our stories, without making others uncomfortable.

A week after Christopher died, the hospital had sent a first-year social work student to my house as a "grief counselor." She could not look at me and say the word "death." She focused instead on the drooping Christmas tree with the electric train I'd given Christopher two weeks earlier still wrapped around its base. She asked me to talk about my family's holiday traditions. She squirmed throughout. She seemed relieved when our session was over. She never came back.

In Gerri's living room, though, no one turned away. Sometimes the pain in the room was so palpable I could hardly breathe.

"How can you keep doing these meetings? Doesn't it wear you down?" I asked her later. Gerri seemed genuinely surprised by my question. She shook her head no.

"Lord, I've learned a lot from them," she said. "About survival and unconditional love. Continuing to breathe even when you don't want to breathe. These women are a gift to my life. Part of my gratitude is to be present without fear."

How to be present in my own life without fear was what I had yet to learn. How to face into the pain and not let it overwhelm me. When I'd spoken with psychologists, they talked about how fear was one of the first emotions associated with a life-altering diagnosis, loss of a loved one, or any other traumatic loss. But there was a fearlessness at the heart of how Gerri faced her cancer.

"Why are we afraid of dying? We're afraid of being out of control," she'd once told me. But embedded in that was a deeper fear, the fear of losing control over the meaning of our lives. She'd seen that over and over in her work with critically ill patients. People who had neared death and survived often later said that the greatest gifts of being alive—and what they would have missed most—were their relationships and the responsibilities that came with them.

"If you look at responsibility as a gift, and not a burden, it changes your life," she said. "You revel in being able to be responsible."

Gerri had a lot of responsibilities—a family with six grown children and seven grandchildren, her work, her gardens, her mothers group, and her activism for children's welfare in the Middle East. She'd joked with one of the moms once that her epitaph should read: *She got a lot done.*

The day after she found out she had cancer, Gerri came home from the doctor and learned Bob's daughter had gone into labor. A healthy baby girl followed a few hours later, the second of what would eventually be three new granddaughters in four months.

"So many babies. So much living to do," she said. "Being busy is a blessing," she said. "Death is one of those things we have precious little control over," she said. "We have to be grateful for every moment we have, the moment we're in."

GRATITUDE WAS A THEME I heard often in my interviews with Gerri.

"There will always be things to rattle you," she said. "It's a matter of getting quiet in your core and opening up your heart, being grateful wherever you are."

Maintaining calm in the face of uncertainty hadn't always been easy for her. "Unless you're Buddha, you don't get to peace and stay there," she said. More than twenty years earlier, she'd left a destructive marriage in Hawaii with four young children in tow and moved back to Seattle to rebuild her life.

Gerri searched through her purse and retrieved a small burnished red rock, shaped like a baby shoe, to show me. She cradled it in her palm before passing it to me. When her son was eight years old, he'd found it on the beach and come running back to give it to her during a time he knew she was hurting. She'd kept it with her ever since.

I reached for the little star of my necklace, a reflex to reassure myself it was still there. Christopher had given me so many similar gifts, totems that comforted me: a picture of him framed in popsicle sticks I kept posted on my refrigerator, a thumb bowl made of kindergarten clay, a print of his small hand on burlap.

When he was four years old, I'd tried forcing some paperwhite bulbs in a shallow bowl of pebbles. They'd sat on my coffee table in Pasadena for weeks, nothing happening, until suddenly, overnight, one of them sent up a single stalk of flowers, just in time for the holidays. I was so pleased; their sweet, peppery perfume mingled with the balsam of the Christmas tree, filling the living room with the pungent scent of Christmas.

That morning Christopher found me in the kitchen, his hands behind his back. "Mom, surprise," he signed, presenting me with the lone blossom I'd managed to grow, now drooping from his small fist. He circled his other hand in front of his face, the sign for "beautiful," and wriggled with delight at his present. A little ripple of warmth ran through me at the memory.

I handed the rock back to Gerri.

"When I fell and was bleeding, I thought something must come of this that will ultimately benefit me," she said. "What it bought me was time."

Doctors couldn't begin radiation until the hematoma had healed, so she took a trip with her daughter instead, time that helped her re-center herself. A gift.

"In a way, falling and bleeding slowed things down for me," she said. "It satisfied my need for more time."

Gerri's gratitude came through when she spoke of her own early losses as well. Leaving a clinic appointment one day, I asked her about her mother, who had died of the same cancer she was facing now. She paused. "I'm so lucky to have had her. When I was very small, I had rheumatic fever. She would wrap my legs in warm blankets and sleep next to me, holding my hand. That's one of the memories I have. After she was gone, I would still sometimes put my hand out and talk to her and feel she was there."

Just before she started treatment, Gerri was invited to a healing drumming ceremony. The ceremony gave her a vision of herself as a bear emerging from a dark cave into a full sunrise, her arms outstretched. "I hadn't felt my mother's presence in a long time," she said. "Both my mothers were there, and they were so happy. They were happy to be together, and they were happy to see me."

Gerri believed in all kinds of ceremonies, especially those drawing on the power of nature to ease and heal. Family, the earth, her gardens, the sea. These were her touchstones. She'd incorporated that philosophy into the hospice she helped build at Evergreen. "I love organic building and development of spaces that support a spiritual connection," she said. At Evergreen, she helped plan where the rooms would be and how they'd be organized. The final building had windows that opened to let in as much light as possible. Every room had a door that led outside. The hospice itself was built around a center courtyard with play equipment for visiting children. "One evening, I remember seeing a gray-haired woman swinging on the tire swing," she said. "That's one of my favorite memories."

TWICE A YEAR, GERRI invited the mothers group to her house by the ocean to hold a ceremony to honor their children. I went the year of her cancer. It was a long drive south through Oregon, then a cut over the mountains on Route 38 to the coast. The road wound through tunnels of mossy, reaching trees, their branches templed like a child's hands, spilling green-gold light on the floor below. It crisscrossed ever-widening streams as they gathered toward the Umpqua River on its run to the sea.

The farther I got from Seattle, the more anxious I was to get to this place she'd spoken of so often. Being close to the ocean, the origin of life, the coming and going of the waves, calmed her. "After you're here a while it's akin to your heartbeat," she'd told me. "You incorporate the rhythm into your breathing."

Finally, eight hours after leaving Seattle, I pulled into Bob and Gerri's driveway. She came out barefoot on her front porch to greet me, enveloping me in a hug that felt so much bigger than her tiny frame. She pulled back. "How are you?" she said, in a way that demanded a real answer. It was what she said to each mom in turn as they arrived. If someone answered, "Fine," and didn't really mean it, she'd cock her head quizzically. We knew there would be follow-up questions later.

She and Bob had built the house after more than a decade of camping on the land. "We built this place to honor the passage of life and death," she said as she showed me around. Light danced through the high-ceilinged space with its wide ocean views. A jar of rocks gathered from the beach sat on the mantel, a large bowl of shells on the table.

That evening, I slipped away to the beach by myself for a ritual of my own. I'd loved taking Christopher to the beach at Santa Monica. We'd ride the merry-go-round out on the pier, then go down to sit on the sand. We built sandcastles in all seasons, patting them into shapes until the waves carried them away. "Mama, waves," he'd sign and I'd hold him in the surf to let the ocean crash against him, let him feel the pull beneath our feet as the wave ran back to sea. Sometimes, if the conditions were right, I skipped rocks for him and he'd clap, as though I were a magician who could make stones leap like flying fish.

It was chilly that evening as the sun set at Gerri's house. I drew my sweater and my memories around me as I stood facing the ocean. The wind had died for the day. I picked up a smooth stone and sailed it across the water, the way I used to. The wet stone caught the last light, a wink before it disappeared into the deep.

Early the next morning, the ringing of a phone rose like the call of a seabird over the sound of the surf. The voice on the other end of the line bore news of a baby's death. The parents had been referred to Gerri, who would be their safe harbor in the storm of grief to come. She nestled her two-year-old grandson in her lap after the call. His head rested against her scar.

I walked with her later. Behind the house was a clearing, a natural circle in the woods where deer grazed and the moms gathered each year to remember their children. Along the edge of the clearing, a giant old-growth Sitka spruce spread its heavy limbs out in every direction. "The mother tree," Gerri said, pointing to the saplings that sprouted from the base, where some of its limbs had fallen. She and Bob had scattered his father's ashes here, and it was where she and family members had gathered to bless the building of the house.

She walked through the wild grasses surrounding the clearing, bending to yank out a stalk of tansy ragwort. "It's a toxic plant," she said. "If you don't root it out, it will take over everything." She kept walking, her hands full of ragwort, making room for new growth.

AS A SOCIETY, WE'RE obsessed with closure. People want their own pain to end, as well as the pain of others. The well-known stages of grief—denial, anger, bargaining, depression, and acceptance—have formed the basis for how we think about getting through. Noted psychiatrist Elisabeth Kübler-Ross was among the first to suggest these as stages that people who are dying face, as well as those who are losing them. But most people who have encountered a severe trauma can tell you the stages don't end there, and they don't necessarily come in the prescribed order. Indeed, Kübler-Ross herself later said her model had been misconstrued as a linear progression. Still, it has taken root in our collective psyche as the way things are supposed to go, and it fuels the concept of "closure" as the final goal. But how do you survive grief when it's more like the infinite loop of a Möbius strip, when there is no end in sight?

Gerri helped me see that grief never fully disappears. It's constantly retriggered. I had to find a way to make room for it without letting it take over. The goal was not to "get over" Christopher's death, but to somehow integrate it into my life. Her words rose in my mind often over the years: *Endless what that pain has to teach.*

Gerri also showed me that destruction contains the possibility of rebirth. It is the god Shiva, the seed in the fire. It is the trees cut back hard to let in the light. Grief can transform you in ways you might not imagine if you open yourself to the gifts it can bring with it— compassion, empathy, wisdom, and gratitude.

In the darkest early days after Christopher died, I was sure I was the only one in the whole world who could possibly know so much pain. Now I see this pain everywhere. I see it in the stoop of an old man, in the crossed arms of a teen at the back of the room. I see it in waiting rooms at doctors' offices and in line at the grocery store. Grief doesn't look the way I thought it did. It's not all keening or rending of garments. It's also vacant stares and nervous energy, anxiety and drifting focus. It's drinking too much and eating too little, or vice versa. It wears many colors, not just black or white. The fingerprint of grief is unique for each of us.

In the beginning, well-meaning people would tell me they knew how I felt because their grandmother had just died, or their best friend or their dog. I would seethe at their clumsy attempts to comfort me. *You have no idea*, I wanted to scream at them. But grief can't be compared. My grief was not bigger than theirs. It took me many years not to bristle, especially, when people compared my loss to the death of their favorite pets. And then one day I realized we were mourning for the same reasons—the loss of companionship, of trust, of unconditional love. The comfort of a future. We have this need to compare our grief, to show how much we suffer, but one cannot be understood in terms of another. There is no "proof of suffering" and no award.

By holding on to my status of having suffered the worst grief imaginable—the loss of a child—I had walled myself off from the losses of others. And that made me feel worse. Entombed in my own grief. How could they understand my pain if I didn't understand theirs? Now when people minimize their sadness by suggesting it's nothing compared with losing a child, I say it's hard to lose anybody we love. Opening my heart to the suffering of others also meant opening myself to their compassion and empathy for me.

Gerri helped me stop fearing that each time I plunged back into the tunnel of grief, it would take me to my darkest place. I learned to trust that when something happened to trigger me, I could work through it and come back more quickly toward the light. I learned to accept that the gift of grief is that you never again take your joy for granted. That pain is part of healing and healing wounds still hurt.

Grief was a force as powerful as the ocean. It could build things if I let it. But it would take a kind of courage I was not yet sure I had.

V.

THE QUESTION OF WHOLENESS

(ROSE)

CHAPTER 13

In the years after Christopher died, all the things I'd ever said to other people in condolence came back to haunt me.

When I was twenty-seven, not yet a mother myself, neighbors I hardly knew lost their grown son in a car accident. I felt sad for them and awkward. I'd had little experience with grieving people at that point and didn't know what to say in person. Instead, I bought a card and wrote them a note to tell them how their loss made me appreciate my life more. How it reminded me to be grateful every day. My intent was to let them know their son's life had had an impact on me, even though I hadn't known him. I cringe now thinking how selfish that must have sounded. How horrible it must have been to hear from a stranger across the street, going about her daily business, feeling more alive because of their loss.

When I was twenty-eight, I told a close friend whose newborn daughter had died a few days after birth, "I can't imagine what you're going through." Later, when people said the same thing to me, I felt desperately alone.

Yes, you can imagine it, I wanted to say. *Imagine your worst nightmare*. Every person has one. It will be like that.

Over and over, I deployed the fallback condolence for when you don't know what else to say: "I am so sorry for your loss." I said it to friends who lost grandparents and siblings and beloved pets. Mirrored back to me, I heard its terrible impotence. "Loss" is such a weak word, the soft sibilance of its final *s*'s vanishing wisp-like into the ether. Its definition is "a failure to hold," as though loss were like letting go of a balloon, a gentle disappearance. But the word itself derives from the ancient root *leu*, meaning "to cut apart." This was what loss felt like to me. A butchering.

I once told my uncle, who was diagnosed with an aggressive form of multiple sclerosis in his thirties, when he had a new wife and a new career abroad, that he must have been given this challenge because he was strong. Because he could handle it.

I heard so many variations on this throughout Christopher's life and after his death. You are so fill-in-the-blank: strong, wise, brave. You're given only as much as you can handle. None of it comforted me.

My secret was that I was not brave.

One of the first words Christopher learned was the sign for "courage"—two hands clenched in front of his chest. It was a sign he taught me and later taught his doctors. When he was five, I tripped on a curb once while carrying him. We both went flying to the pavement. I was petrified I'd crushed him, but he was fine. He laughed and kissed my cheek. "Mama hurt," he signed, poking the tips of his index fingers together as I limped the rest of the way home on a sprained ankle. "Be brave."

The following year, I watched him sitting straight up on a gurney, making the sign for courage to himself as he was wheeled into the green abyss of the pre-op area before his transplant.

And yet courage failed me after he died.

People whispered that those who have lost children never recover. That in the hierarchy of horrible losses, it was the worst imaginable. That I would be driven mad with grief. I was terrified, imagining my future bereft of relationships, of joy, of purpose. The question of wholeness consumed me. How to put a life back together around the missing pieces and empty places. How to be brave.

I WAS ALONE IN the newsroom on a Sunday, covering a weekend shift on the desk, when the first reports about the shelling of Baghdad that launched the US invasion of Iraq came in. A police scanner squawked softly in the background as I watched the bombs make eerie green traces on a small television set at the empty night city editor's desk. Anchors spoke in urgent tones about shock and awe. Months later, soldiers started coming home from the Iraq War with damaged brains and missing limbs. They'd been brave in battle. But I wondered what it would take for them to confront the life that lay ahead.

The question haunted me. Christopher's death was, in some sense, an amputation. I marked birthdays and milestones as they came and went, my child growing older alongside me. I noted when he would have started second grade, then third. The year he would have gotten his learner's permit, graduated high school.

But my phantom child only made the hole of his absence in my life even wider. Few people knew my history, and fewer still spoke to me about him. I didn't bring him up, either. Even talking to my family was hard. My parents had taken hundreds of photos of Christopher over his life. My mother had put them in fat green albums that lined her study walls. Sometimes she'd take one out and sit on the porch swing of their house and pore over its pages.

"Remember when he gave them feeding tubes?" she asked me one summer evening. We'd just finished clearing the picnic table on the porch after supper and had sat down to talk. She pointed to a picture of his Bert doll, propped on the couch, its cotton stomach covered carefully with paper tape the way his own had been when he'd had his gastrostomy feeding tube. She rotated the album and leaned it toward me so I could look, but I couldn't. My throat seized up, and I fought back tears. I bolted into the house, not because of the picture but because of the empty spot beside her on the swing where Christopher had loved to sit and turn the pages of his picture books with her.

One of the hardest parts of losing Christopher was bearing my parents' loss of him as well. My mother called each year when she and my dad took pots of daffodils to his grave site on his birthday. "You can come with us," she'd say, a hopeful note in her voice. Her gentle urging did no good. I couldn't go, couldn't face the spot only yards from where I'd had to view his body during his memorial service.

Eventually, my family developed their own rituals for honoring Christopher. My dad planted a fir tree in the yard one Christmas and draped it with lights each December. We could see it from the living room window and referred to it as Christopher's tree. My mother sent me cards on his birthday with remembrances or poems tucked inside. My father and brothers seldom spoke of him, but they slipped me

Mother's Day cards each year. For my part, I stayed behind the wall of my grief.

In many ways, I had yet to embrace the realities of my life without him. I couldn't deal with selling the house I'd lived in when Christopher was a baby. I hung on to it even when I couldn't live there anymore. I couldn't dispose of his things, moving them from storage place to storage place. I couldn't handle scattering his ashes. Each time I contemplated such an action, I immediately abandoned it, paralyzed by fear that I could not face the finality of his absence.

I needed someone to show me how to be brave.

SEVERAL YEARS AFTER THE start of the war, I got permission from Harborview Medical Center to report on a support group for amputees. I planned to do a story about advances in prosthetics research. Between the University of Washington and our VA hospital, we had an active nexus of researchers working on the next generation of artificial limbs. What I really wanted to understand, though, was how people who had suffered such a profound loss became whole again in a new way.

I walked into the small meeting room at the hospital, expecting to find the support group packed with veterans who'd been injured by roadside bombs. But war is not the only way people lose pieces of themselves. People of all ages in the group had lost limbs to disease or accidents. Out of the corner of my eye, I noticed a young woman sitting silently in the back, slouched in a wheelchair. The stumps of her legs dangled above the floor. Her arms were crossed over her middle. She looked as though she couldn't wait to get out of there, which, I later learned, turned out to be true. She really wanted a smoke.

Her name was Rose Bard. My first impression was that she was a tough girl. She projected a sense of not needing anyone and not caring about people's rules or expectations. She especially didn't seem happy to be in the group, talking with a bunch of other amputees.

I wasn't sure whether to approach. When I finally did, she agreed to talk to me. She actually *was* a veteran, having enlisted in the army a few years after high school. She'd worked for a year as a Patriot missile radar technician in South Korea before getting pregnant with her daughter, Karma, then nine. She hadn't lost her legs during her time in the military, though. The accident had happened on a fishing boat during a record-breaking storm on the Bering Sea in Alaska. Losing her legs wasn't the only thing that had changed the course of her life that day. The morning of the accident, she'd gotten some news she didn't expect.

By the time I got back to the office, I knew I wanted to follow Rose for the next six months as she worked to gain her balance while her world shifted under her. If anyone could show me how to be brave, it had to be her. My editor at that point was Scott Sunde, another of the newsroom's cadre of proud and taciturn Norwegians. He also happened to be married to a photographer who'd shot many seasons of wildlife in Alaska. He knew the treachery of the Bering Sea. When I described what had happened to Rose, he immediately got the power of her story. Gruff by nature, he waged war on any overuse of adjectives in my stories. But on this one we agreed: Rose's rescue qualified as epic.

TO TELL ROSE'S STORY, first I had to piece it together. With her permission, I went after her medical records, along with the accident reports and transcripts of first responders. I interviewed the Coast Guard pilots, rescue swimmers, and the rest of the cast of players responsible for her survival. Reconstructing what had happened to her was strangely reassuring for reasons I didn't want to admit. Christopher had been gone eleven years by then. Sometimes it seemed like he was fading in my memory, like I was losing him all over again. I'd paid a price for my vigilance in not talking about him, for being what a counselor once told me was "well defended." I feared that in my effort to keep from missing him, I had turned down the flame of my memory so far it would sputter out, that I would forget the way his body felt curled against mine in the early morning when he'd had a bad dream, that I wouldn't be able to recall the sound of his voice when he said "Mama."

Working on Rose's story, I wanted to believe a life could be reconstructed—no, *relived*, almost—with the right records, my defense against the limits of memory. I'd spent much of Christopher's life running on adrenaline and cortisol. Many things never made it past my short-term memory, blocked by fight-or-flight responses. Now that he was gone, I struggled to remember. The story of Christopher's life floated up here and there in my conscious mind, images surfacing in arbitrary order—as though all the slides for his View-Master had spilled out and been restacked. My brain tried to make sense of things that didn't make sense.

I'd kept a journal, but the entries were sporadic. I'd written about Christopher in tattered notebooks and on the backs of envelopes. Fragments and snatches in no particular order. What I did have, though, were boxes of records. Physical, occupational, and speech therapy reports, lab slips, chart notes, an autopsy report. These were silent witnesses to the things I'd forgotten or could not face remembering. I kept the cardboard boxes stacked in storage areas, out of sight: three-ring notebooks full of pages on sign language, on speech therapy exercises, on managing symptoms in transplant patients; tests I'd had to pass to qualify to do home dialysis and special education reports from his schools; lists of medications and the instructions I'd leave for nurses when they came to spell me at home. I had notes on caring for a diabetic patient and how to give CPR to infants. A how-to on emergency tracheotomies. I needed none of the records anymore but couldn't part with them. They were my last tangible link to the life we'd lived together. They moved with me from place to place. Each time, the stacks of boxes seemed to settle more under their own weight, giving way to gravity and time.

Rose's story thrust me back into the world of medical records and reports. It reminded me how much I missed the doctors and nurses, lab techs, physical and speech therapists, teachers, tutors, and parents I used to interact with on a weekly basis, all of us focused on keeping Christopher healthy, communicating, learning, alive. Unraveling the mechanics of Rose's rescue made me appreciate anew all the heroics that had gone into saving Christopher during his first hours, the doctors and others who put aside their own feelings and fears to save me from my worst ones, who could operate on a baby without flinching, who could make split-second decisions that would paralyze them if it were their own child.

Except this time, it was Rose whose life medics were trying to save.

CHAPTER 14

It was still dark when Rose climbed out of her upper bunk on the C-deck of the *Excellence* on that October morning, feeling uneasy. A question had been dogging her for days. The Bering Sea, sixty miles off the coast of Russia, had been calmer than usual for most of the fish processor's fall season. Now gale-force winds were building from the west. The hulking factory ship, stretching longer than a football field, still held steady, but the mercury was plunging. To Rose, something seemed off.

She reached for her bag on the shelf over her berth and fished for the spare pregnancy test she kept there, just in case—a leftover from a two-pack she'd bought for a friend. She squeezed through the narrow corridor toward the head.

Then, as she did most mornings, she went in search of her boyfriend, Alex Laigo, so they could eat breakfast together before they started their twelve-hour shifts. Usually, Rose would grab an orange from the galley, and the two would go sit on one of the giant cleats on deck to stare out over the swelling seas, share a cigarette, and watch the orcas play. Sometimes the whales came so close it was crazy. Once, they'd seen an ice field on top of a mountain cleave off and plunge into the sea.

For Rose, who'd knocked around the Midwest and racked up her share of hard times—the death of her mother, a divorce, and bankruptcy before her twenties were up—there was solace in the stark and restless scenery. At age twenty-eight, she'd come to work on the boat to start her life over, even though it meant leaving her young daughter with relatives for long stretches. It was better than dancing in bars or managing convenience stores, which she'd also done. In her first fourteen days fishing, she'd hauled in twenty-three hundred dollars. She'd worked just about every job on board—been a freezer rat, and slung roe at the gut table. What had kept her at the dirty, numbing work for two years now, though, wasn't just the money, but the camaraderie she'd found.

Rose and Alex had met working aboard the *Excellence*. Alex, dark-eyed and soft-spoken, had briefly been her supervisor. He was attracted to Rose, who had a fresh-faced beauty, even caked with salt and slime. The two shared a quirky, dark sense of humor. They talked for hours—about techno-metal music, their scattered families, and their dreams. Few secrets kept aboard the mother ship. If you hooked up with someone, even the proverbial cat in the wheelhouse would know about it. Rose and Alex, though, kept each other's secrets.

That October morning, Rose rolled Alex out of his bunk to talk. With only a few days left in the two-month season, they were both looking forward to a week of shore leave. They planned to discuss their future when they got to land.

Rose headed to the processing deck. The factory was the guts of the ship, sandwiched between sleeping decks above and engine rooms below. Low-ceilinged and reeking of fish, it wasn't a place for "pukers." A few portholes let in light. Workers waded, occasionally ankle deep, on a green grated floor that drained salt water and fish scales. A constant stream of silver-bellied fish slid by on long metal conveyors. The hammering of metal on metal—screeching and thumping—forced the factory workers to wear earmuffs when the line was running. Rose went to find her friend Ruby and relieve her of her shift. Ruby was one of the few other women on the boat. Rose pulled her aside, eager for some private conversation before starting her own shift.

By eight thirty P.M., the boat began to pitch and roll. The storm that had been only a suggestion that morning had descended in force. Below deck, the jolting felt like bad turbulence. The chop didn't bother the seasoned crew. Many had already logged months at sea.

One of Rose's routine tasks as a quality-control technician was to scour equipment with pressure hoses. She donned her rain gear and XtraTuf boots, then checked with her supervisor to make sure a large hopper funnel she was about to climb into was shut down for cleaning. A waist-high, stainless-steel vat with two fat screws at the bottom of it, the funnel churned pollock into paste and extruded it into pans for freezing. She climbed into the bowl-shaped machine and scrubbed away, chatting with a fellow worker, who was cleaning the machine next to hers.

Suddenly, a massive wave slammed the side of the boat. The impact sent a deckhand reeling against the switch that turned on Rose's machine. Something grabbed her feet from behind, yanking her to her knees. Pain seared up her legs. Above her, the orange emergency stop cord hung just out of her reach.

"Help me!" she screamed. "Get me out."

Crew members raced toward her and turned off the machine. Fifty feet down the line, Alex heard Rose's wail above the storm, despite his ear protectors. He tore in her direction. "What the hell is happening?" he shouted. The factory manager, one of Rose's closest friends, lunged for her, shouting for plasma torches to cut her out. Someone scrambled to wake Ruby, who was a nurse by training.

The boat's electrician climbed beside her to hold her hand. Other crew members corralled Alex to try to calm him down. Two more blasted away at the metal encasing her. The stream of superheated ionized gas from the plasma cutters sliced through the steel, scattering bits of molten metal slag. The heat was so intense the crew had to spray Rose with water to keep the rubber of her rain gear from melting to her skin. Despite the heat, the warmth was already draining from her body. Her legs were going numb. She started to panic.

Ruby ran up, still in her pajamas. "Oh my God," she said when she saw Rose's legs trapped in the machine.

"Please, Ruby," Rose said. Ruby knew immediately what she had to do. She rushed to the boat's infirmary, where the phone had a hotline to the George Washington University Medical Center in Washington, DC. The boat's purser was already on the line talking to medics when Ruby burst through the door. "There's something else you need to know," Ruby said. "Rose is pregnant."

AT 9:55 P.M., THE Coast Guard command center in Juneau, seventeen hundred miles away, caught the first wind of trouble on the Bering Sea. "Initial Notification," reads the Coast Guard log. "The F/V *Excellence* reports a female crew member has her foot stuck in an auger. He is requesting a Medevac."

Injuries on the Bering Sea can turn critical in moments. Time, weather, and distance conspire to transform even minor injuries into life-threatening ones. This one wasn't minor. The Juneau crew patched the boat through to Dr. Russell Bowman, the flight surgeon on duty in Sitka. Bowman had handled plenty of accidents aboard vessels, but this was one of the worst he'd encountered. Even if they freed Rose from the machine, she could bleed to death. With no blood on the boat to give her transfusions, he feared the worst.

Bowman got on the line to the bridge crew of the *Excellence* and delivered the first of what would be a long night's worth of orders.

In Seattle, the phone Joe Bersch kept with him, even when he slept, rang at about midnight, Seattle time. Bersch's years as a maritime lawyer had made him steady under pressure, but this time he had a bad feeling. Night calls in the fishing business were never good. Bersch, president of the company that owned the boat, listened for a few seconds, trying to take in what the frantic caller was saying. He made out that the crew from the *Excellence* was worried about saving a worker's legs.

"Make sure you save her *life*," he barked into the phone. "Do whatever it takes. Just save her life."

The question was how. Getting Rose to a hospital was critical, but the boat's bearing put it 265 nautical miles northwest of remote St. Paul Island—one of the small wild islands in the Pribilof chain in the middle of the Bering Sea. St. Paul was the closest spot for fuel and had a small emergency medical clinic. The problem: At the moment, even if the Coast Guard refueled its powerful Jayhawk helicopter in St. Paul, the *Excellence* was still beyond its range.

The Coast Guard called the boat: The *Excellence* would have to head as fast as it could to rendezvous with the rescuers, no farther than 140 nautical miles out from St. Paul. As soon as he heard the order, Capt. Lee Vestal radioed the fleet of catcher boats feeding his processor to cut loose. It wasn't an order he took lightly. Casting his fleet adrift meant sending their nets—and financial lifelines—to the bottom of the sea. But if he didn't, they would surely lose Rose.

The *Excellence* had to leave, he told them. Now.

Trauma medics refer to the first hour after an accident as the "golden hour," the critical time window for maximizing chance of survival. Rose would have to count on the steady nerves of a host of people over the next forty-eight hours as they made decisions that would dictate not only the trajectory of her own life, but also the fate of her baby's.

Captain Vestal amped the engines and headed into the Arctic storm. Winds out of the north at fifty knots whipped the waves two stories tall. Even going at the boat's top speed of twelve knots, they wouldn't make the rendezvous point until ten A.M. the following day. Vestal, with his blue eyes and bushy red mustache, looked the part of a sea captain from central casting. He'd worked aboard this ship for sixteen years. Ugly storms didn't faze him, but he'd never had an injury like this on board before. He chewed through a fistful of Tums as he plowed the ship through the pummeling waves.

In Cold Bay, Alaska, the Coast Guard's forward deployment crew picked up orders from Kodiak to ready for a launch at first light. The dispatch triggered an elaborate choreography that sent multiple rescue aircraft from different locations to converge on the *Excellence* for a series of complicated handoffs, all timed to maximize the chances of picking up Rose—alive.

EVEN UNDER THE BEST circumstances, helicopter hoists in the Bering Sea put lives in danger. Lt. Kerry Blount, flying directly into fifty-knot headwinds, knew this one could turn disastrous. Blount, who had flown Black Hawks for nine years in the army before joining the Coast Guard, was concerned first about time. Flying into the wind, he'd already burned through more than half his fuel. He wasn't sure what shape the patient, Rose Bard, was in—just that it was bad. He worried whether he could make it there and back to the handoff vessel without running out of fuel and ditching them both.

Now, looking down at the *Excellence*, he had the added worry of getting his rescue swimmer to the deck safely. Trained to execute missions in heavy seas for thirty minutes at a time, rescue swimmers were steel-nerved enough not to panic under extreme circumstances. They could detangle a downed pilot from a parachute underwater. But a swimmer could do little good if the helicopter cables themselves snagged the boat's rigging, crashing the helicopter into the ship.

The ship below them bucked around like a toy boat in a washing machine. Blount hovered over the bow, trying to anticipate the direction it would roll so he could maneuver the Jayhawk to avoid "aircraft vessel contact." Things, he knew, "could get pretty bad in a hurry."

BELOW THEM AT THE helm of the *Excellence*, Captain Vestal struggled to control his ship. For a normal helicopter rendezvous, he would head upwind to give the helicopter a stable target. But upwind in this storm would have put the whole bow of the ship underwater, so he headed down sea and did the best he could to give the helicopter crew its shot. They had to land the swimmer between two huge cargo beams that normally towered over the bow and were now laid forward on the deck. Winds were so stiff that the helicopter flying headlong into them appeared to be blowing backward.

Finally, the pilot and medic on board the helicopter spied their moment and gave rescue swimmer Ben Cournia the "go" sign. Cournia aced the landing, dropping 170 feet to the deck with a litter and hitting square between the beams.

This was Cournia's first real rescue, and he concentrated on what he might find below the deck. His would be the first outside eyes on the scene. He was most anxious about the bleeding. The body has only about five liters of blood, and the patient had already lost a considerable amount—no one was sure how much.

Working quickly, Cournia splinted the broken bones in Rose's lower legs and bundled her in blankets against the freezing wind. Eight crew members carried her up several steep flights of stairs to the rain-slick deck. Cournia attached four steel cables to the litter and a trail line to keep her from twirling, then signaled for the hoist.

At last, Rose spun slowly toward the belly of the helicopter as Alex and the rest of the crew watched from below.

Twenty hours after the accident and after a series of harrowing handoffs, Rose finally arrived at the emergency room of Providence Alaska Medical Center in Anchorage. She was pale, her pulse rapid, but she was still conscious.

Orthopedic surgeon George Rhyneer tried to be gentle as he talked to her. "We will do everything we can to save your legs, but you've sustained a substantial injury," she remembered him saying. He handed her a consent form to sign.

"Please," she begged. "Please don't cut off my legs."

Hours later, Rose, still groggy from surgery, looked down the length of her bed to where her feet should have been. The sheets were flat. She turned her head in shock. Then a second, worse fear hit her.

The doctor who was tracking her hormone levels came into the room. He was blunt. With the amount of blood she'd lost, and the trauma, there was only a 5 percent chance her unborn baby would survive to term. Rose, who had been keeping her emotions checked, started to sob.

Joe Bersch, who had flown in to be by Rose's side, rushed the doctor into the hall. "You can't do that to her," he shouted. "Don't take her hope away."

HOPE IS THE MOST critical and elusive tool in a doctor's tool kit. Knowing how to deploy it is something they can't teach in medical school.

When Christopher was twenty-two months old, I took him to a reunion of babies from the neonatal ICU at Seattle Children's. We'd joined the other giddy parents, holding balloons while staff members all around us greeted the babies they'd taken care of. It was the first time

I'd seen some of Christopher's earliest doctors since we'd gone home. One of them, a neonatologist I recall only as Dr. P., approached us. He'd buoyed me with his confidence in Christopher from the beginning. He made me hopeful.

"Look at you," he said to Christopher, pinching his chubby cheeks in amazement. He told me he'd been talking about Christopher just a few days earlier with another family whose baby had been admitted with kidney damage. He'd told that family how Christopher had survived, despite being sicker. It occurred to me that in all those early weeks, he'd never once told us about a baby sicker than Christopher. Hope in the absence of evidence is the very hardest kind. That was what Rose needed now.

CHAPTER 15

On a gray day in early March, I drove up to meet Rose at the small rambler she and Alex had rented in Edmonds, twenty minutes north of Seattle.

My plan for the story was to check in with her regularly to see how she adapted both physically and psychologically to her new reality, a process all amputees had to face. Rose, though, would have the added challenge of doing it while bringing a new life into the world.

Following someone for a story amounted to temporarily embedding myself in their life. I'd show up for doctor's appointments, for family occasions, for trips to school and the park. I'd go along when they went shopping or had meetings, hang out when they cooked. When people agreed to a story, few probably realized how much they'd have to put up with me. A few no doubt regretted saying yes. I usually worked with photographers, who put in many hours of their own time with the subjects as well.

No matter how much the photographer and I aimed to be invisible, at the end of the day, we were strangers in the midst of a story our subjects were living. I tried to be around enough that my presence no longer registered much, until people would let their guard down and say what they felt, not what they thought I wanted to hear or what they thought made them sound good. But if my presence changed their behavior, theirs also changed mine.

Years later, Rose told me that my showing up along with Dan, the photographer, was what got her out of bed on many mornings. What she didn't know was that reporting her story did the same for me.

THAT FIRST DAY, I found Rose sitting in a wheelchair at her sliding glass door, staring at her backyard. Wearing gym shorts, with her dark brown hair pulled back in a ponytail and a stud in her tongue, she looked like she could still get carded at a bar. She crossed and uncrossed her legs—legs that men used to say nice things about. Now they ended abruptly below the knee.

Though she was six months pregnant, her belly barely showed. She had a scorpion tattooed along one side of it, a reminder of her old army platoon. "I used to have a really cool tattoo on my ankle," she said. Then stopped.

Her prosthetic legs, with their bulbous purple sockets and spindly metal shafts, sat plunked into unused white tennis shoes on the bench of the picnic table they'd set up in the dining room. She eyed them as we spoke, as though sizing up an enemy. "They're not me. They're plastic. I don't want to wear them," she said. When she'd first tried standing with them, her physical therapist had had her close her eyes to test her equilibrium. "At first, I thought, *Ah, this will be easy*. I knew how to walk." But when she closed her eyes, she panicked. "I was telling my leg to move, pick up and go forward, and my brain's going, *Are you smoking crack? I'm not doin' it*. I thought, *Oh my God, I'm gonna fall*. My heartbeat goes up. My body's just like—*no*."

These days, she mostly lay around the house, feeling tired and sluggish. Sleep didn't help. "Oh, God," she said. "The dreams are pretty bad." In them, she was still trapped in the machine on the boat.

Doctors and therapists had been pushing her to get on her new feet. The sooner she started, they told her, the more independent she'd be by the time the baby came.

"I get really worried," she told me. "How am I going to do anything for the baby if I can't get out of this chair? I remember when my daughter was little—she wanted to be carried all the time. How am I going to go to the grocery store? Push a stroller and carry a diaper bag?"

When she tried to wear the legs, though, her muscles spasmed. Nerve flashes bolted up her legs. Her bones ached. Her brain, still wired to receive information from her missing limbs, sent her signals that her feet throbbed. The phantom pain felt real.

I nodded as she spoke. There was little about Rose's experience that resembled my own. But phantom pain was something I could understand. At night, I sometimes woke hurting to hold Christopher so badly it was like an ache all over my body, a wrenching pain that made me sweat and cry. After he died, I'd developed pain in my hands—a cramp that curled them into fists, as though my hands, which could no longer smooth his hair, or brush away his tears, or make words for him, were grieving. I developed pain in my left breast, a throbbing ache that wouldn't go away. Doctors found nothing wrong. "Referred pain," they called it—the sensation moved from one place to another.

Rose had stopped going to the support group for amputees. If there was one thing she would rather *not* do, it was cry in front of others. She'd rather tell a funny story about how she practically fell into the toilet bowl early one morning when she was half-asleep and not wearing her legs. Or the time she told a gawking bystander that she'd lost her legs "in 'Nam." Or how after her first baby was born, the doctor had looked at the tattoo of a scorpion on her stomach and said, "Nice backhoe."

She'd like to just focus on her pregnancy. "We go to stores to buy baby stuff and people say, 'Who's having a baby?'"

"I am," she'd say.

"Oh." There'd be a long pause. "You are?" She imitated their responses—scrunching her face into a look both incredulous and disgusted.

"I'm like, 'Yeaaaahhhhh.'"

"I'm kind of a smart-ass," she said. "Always have been. Didn't work out too good for me in the military."

There was another reason she was feeling on edge these days. Though the baby's odds of survival had improved since the accident, her latest ultrasound had shown some suspicious spots, possibly cysts, on the baby's brain.

"Sometimes I think it would be so much easier to either be an amputee and go through physical therapy and then get pregnant," she said. "Or be pregnant, have the baby, and then be an amputee. It's hard having to deal with both things at once."

Negotiating wasn't possible, though. There are all kinds of amputations—physical and otherwise—that can abruptly cut you off from the life you wanted. We don't always get to choose.

IN APRIL, I DROVE up to Edmonds again, this time to meet Rose's new physical therapist, Bernice Kegel. I hung out in Rose's living room, waiting for Bernice to arrive. Rose lounged on the couch, her prosthetic legs parked in another room. Karma's toys were strewn about and there were cartoons on the television. Rose started in on some funny story about Karma's day. Then she paused.

"So, do you have kids?" she asked. The question threw me for a moment. I considered saying no, the way I usually did. But something stopped me.

"Yes," I said. "I had a son. He died years ago." She got quiet.

"I'm sorry," she said. Exactly the right thing, the only thing you can say, the thing she had probably learned the hard way from all the wrong things people had said to her. I changed the topic, but I was glad she knew, grateful, for a moment, that Christopher was there in the room between us.

There was a rap on the door and Bernice poked her head in. A no-nonsense woman with a lilting South African accent, she had a client base of amputees that ranged from land-mine victims to geriatric patients. She was not intimidated by heartbreak, and she was accustomed to ignoring excuses. She coaxed Rose into her pros-thetics and then up from her wheelchair, having her use a walker for support.

"OK, now I'm going to take this away," Bernice said. She moved the walker a few feet out of reach. Rose stood frozen.

"How's that?" Bernice's voice was calm.

"A little weird," Rose said. "Like standing on air." She started to tip forward. "Whoa."

"I'm pushing you," Bernice said. "I know you're not ready for this." It was her way of saying they were going at it anyway.

And so it had gone, inch by inch, week by week.

THE NEXT TIME I saw Rose, she was having new prosthetics fitted. She arrived at the clinic with Alex, wearing her old pair. Made of plastic, these limbs were heavy—more than four pounds each. Her feet dragged when she tried to go farther than a few paces with her walker. The prosthetics gave her blisters, even when she didn't bear weight on them or try to walk. She sat down and stripped the legs off carefully, one layer at a time. First the prosthetic itself. Then the socket liner that fit over her stump and into the artificial leg. Then the three socks that kept it wedged in place. Then "shrinkers," a tight layer that helped mold her stump to fit the prosthetic. Finally, the silicon layer that lay next to her skin for protection.

Gingerly, Rose massaged lubricant into her scars where the tissue had started adhering to the bone. On that day, she was getting fitted with lighter legs made of carbon fiber. Her new legs would weigh less than half as much. Her mood, too, was lighter. She'd chosen fabric decorated with fairies for laminating the sockets. Karma had helped her pick it out.

Ryan Blanck, the director of the prosthetics clinic, examined Rose, then took both her new and old sets of prosthetics to the garage-like shop at the back of the office and tinkered with them. Her pregnancy made Rose a moving target. As her weight and shape changed, so did her center of gravity and the volume of her residual limbs. It kept her constantly off balance. The changes made it hard to keep her prosthetics aligned and fitted correctly, which was essential for teaching her to walk.

Recovering from amputation surgery can be a long, painful process. Patients have to put enormous loads on tissues that were never designed to take them. Some of the pain was good, indicating healing and progress as the remaining limb took on its new role. Some indicated poor fit, which could cause pressure sores, bruising, blisters, and nerve problems. Striking that balance was critical for success.

While she waited for technicians to finish adjusting her new prosthetics, Rose chatted about her old life aboard the *Excellence*. "One season, we went to the Aleutians, and we couldn't find any fish," she said. To amuse themselves while they waited for fish to show up, the crew had a mini movie festival in the break room.

"We'd already watched *The Perfect Storm*, *Titanic*, and *Storm of the Century*," she said. "So, I went and got *Finding Nemo*." She chuckled. "It was crazy. Kind of like being in the army. We joked around all the time. I miss it sometimes. Me and Alex, we both do."

Ryan came back with her new legs just then. She turned them over on her lap, admiring how the white wings of the fairies spread against the deep purple background. She put them on and started to stand. Aboard the boat, she'd slung fifty-pound sacks of sugar and hoisted hundred-pound stacks of cases of fish, but now her arms shook as she pushed her weight up out of the chair. She braced herself on the walker and repeated what Ryan had told her: "There's good pain and there's bad pain."

Later that day, I went home with Rose. Bernice would be coming over to test the new legs. Rose rested on the couch in preparation. The baby had been kicking steadily, jabbing her ribs and bladder. Karma hopped onto the couch next to her mom and picked up a prosthetic leg. "Will you wear pants over these?" she asked.

"I will unless it's summer, and I'm wearing shorts," Rose said.

"I saw one lady, and I didn't know she had them," Karma said.

This was Rose's secret dream, too. She spent some nights scrolling the internet for information about leg transplants or other futuristic solutions. "I just haven't accepted that this is it for me," she said. "I'm waiting for prosthetics that are implanted, all blend in, and look like skin and you don't take off. Star Wars stuff. That's what I'm waiting for."

THE WAITING WAS WHAT worried the rehab team at Harborview. They didn't want to waste any time that could help her be on her feet by the time the baby came. Rose, though, could be hard to push. Early on, she missed her therapy appointments and blamed her morning sickness. When the morning sickness went away, she dodged her sessions because she didn't like wearing her legs, or because it was such an ordeal to get herself and her wheelchair to Seattle, or so she told herself. But Bernice wouldn't let her slide.

By April, Rose could use her walker to make it halfway down her street. Each step required a huge effort. She had to will every motion and use different muscles to walk, ones unaccustomed to lifting her feet or correcting for balance. She'd had to relearn where her center of gravity was, the same way General Shali had. Bernice and I walked beside her to make sure she didn't fall. We stopped to rest by the side of the road so she could catch her breath.

"It's like climbing a mountain," Rose said, panting. Even minor unevenness on the ground took major effort to navigate. "I'll be walking along, and then it's *Holy crap—it's a twig!*" She laughed. Something I'd come to appreciate most about Rose in the months I'd been visiting her was her grasp of the ridiculous and her sense of humor. At the end of the session, she sank back into her wheelchair. She put her hand to her neck to register her pulse. "I feel like I just ran a marathon."

By May, nature was gaining on her. Her belly had grown so big she couldn't see her new feet. She was scared of falling and hurting the baby. Her stumps were so swollen that putting any pressure on them made her wince. Trying to walk made her nauseated. She told Bernice to stop coming over.

There had been some good news. An ultrasound showed that the apparent cysts in the baby's brain had disappeared. It was one weight lifted, but another still hung heavy—the worry about walking before the baby.

A few weeks before her due date, Rose made an appointment to see her obstetrician for an exam. Alex wheeled her to the nurse's station. The nurse nodded to the scale.

"Can we skip it this time?" Alex asked. The nurse said they couldn't, so Alex helped hoist her to the scale and steadied her. He let go for an instant. Rose's face blanched. She nearly collapsed as pain shot up her legs into her belly.

There's good pain and there's bad pain. It had been her mantra for months. Sometimes it felt like there was only bad.

I repeated it to myself. *Good pain and bad pain*. Christopher's death seemed like an endless pit of bad pain. It was hard to see beyond the edge to a place that held anything good. People asked how I was doing. I'd say, "Fine," and even believe it. But the body expresses what the mind cannot.

Pain is sometimes called the "fifth vital sign." Assessing Christopher's had been one of my main hospital preoccupations. Doctors brought pain scales with faces in various stages of distress for him to point at to describe how he was feeling. Or they'd ask me, on a scale of one to ten, how bad I thought it was. The scales were never very helpful. A ten on the pain scale wasn't ten times harder to endure than a one—it seemed a thousand times or more as hard—and watching someone you love in any kind of pain is a ten. No scale could measure the pain of his absence.

Over those months with Rose, though, I began to think about pain in a new way. Pain was how I felt my edges, boundaries. Pain was how I knew I was alive, and staying alive was how I kept Christopher's memory alive.

ROSE WENT INTO LABOR early in the morning of the summer solstice. The pain had been building steadily, the contractions rolling through every five minutes. Rose sucked in her breath as they crashed against her.

Earlier that week, she'd gone on a cleaning spree, crawling around Karma's room on her hands and knees to straighten it up. She did load after load of laundry, including all the dog's toys. Her body had retained so much fluid her fingers were as big as cigars. She hadn't been able to wear her new legs for weeks, let alone try to walk. People had been asking her what this journey had been like.

"It's like being reborn into a completely different life," she told them. "I'm still the same person. I just know bad stuff happens, and you've got to hang in there."

The pain rocked through her again. Alex helped her into the car and tried to stay calm at the wheel as they headed for the University of Washington Medical Center, a half hour away in Seattle. The black night faded to gauzy gray, the first light of the longest day of the year, a tipping point.

I rushed to the hospital to meet her. This delivery would be different. With Karma, she'd walked through some of her labor to manage the pain. She wouldn't be able to squat or kneel to let gravity do some of the work, either. For this birth, she'd be trapped in bed.

By the time I arrived, her contractions had intensified. She pounded her fists against the rails of her bed to get through the worst of them. An anesthesiologist finally gave her an epidural, and all of us in the room—Alex and Karma, two friends from the boat, and Dan, the photographer—breathed a little easier. The contractions seemed to ebb away. In the lull, Rose sat up like her old self and regaled her little audience with tales of the sea.

Then, just after ten in the morning, nature took charge again. "Push!" the doctor said.

Rose blew out hard and bore down. Baby boy Aries rushed into the world, slick as a seal pup. Alex beamed. "Look at his little hands and feet," he said. "Look at his toes."

Aries will have his own sea tale to tell one day, a story about the dozens of people whose actions, linked by a precarious chain of events, ensured his arrival. There was Rose's friend Ruby, who alerted emergency workers. The crew members who cut her out of the machine and stabilized her. The captain who steered the boat through heavy seas to rendezvous with rescuers. The pilots and medics in the air who, through white-knuckle, acrobatic flying, got her off the boat during one of the most difficult trauma rescues on record. The surgical team in Alaska that managed to do a clean amputation on a devastating, highly contaminated wound, keeping her and the baby safe from infection. The rehabilitation teams that worked to get her back on her new feet, the boat company that supported her, and Alex, who had been there every step of the way.

Rose leaned back on the delivery bed. She cradled baby Aries in her arms and offered him her breast. He drank in his mother's scent, his new world.

"Oh, God, look at him," Rose said. "He's perfect."

He was. And for the briefest instant, when I looked at him, I saw Christopher—his dark hair and rosy face in the moments right after he came into the world. I could almost feel his fingers grasping mine, the instant before I had to let go. All the hope and all the wonder. My joy for Rose mingled with gratitude to her for giving me back that moment.

A SEA CHANGE. THAT was what the accident had been for Rose's life, and what this baby now brought.

For many years, I thought "sea change" was a sailing term, one that captured the moment the wind shifted and a sailor's fortunes with it. But the term belongs more deeply to literature, borrowed from "Ariel's song" in Shakespeare's *The Tempest*. Ariel sings to Ferdinand, a prince of Naples, about the shipwreck of his father:

> *Full fathom five, thy father lies;*
> *Of his bones are coral made;*
> *Those are pearls that were his eyes;*
> *Nothing of him that doth fade,*
> *But doth suffer a sea-change*
> *Into something rich and strange.*

A sea change was what Christopher's birth and death had brought to my life, too. I'd felt the first tug of one that day at the lighthouse on Montauk Point when I realized I was pregnant. His death had left me drowning.

Following Rose had shown me something, though. Wholeness could look richer and stranger than I could ever have imagined. The path toward it meant I had to embrace both the good pain and the bad, and to learn to tell the difference. Good pain was the pain of growth and new beginnings. As a child, I sometimes woke up with my legs aching. "Growing pains," my mother called them when she'd bring me a heating pad to wrap around my knees, and I would drift to sleep, picturing myself emerging into my new body, my new life.

Bad pain was the pain of rupture and isolation that came from cutting myself off from people. Bad pain came from not allowing myself to experience the good. And courage meant taking that next step forward even though the last one was painful.

It's like being born into a completely different life. Rose's words stayed with me. My life would never be as I'd imagined it as a young woman. It would have to be something different.

Be brave, Christopher had signed to me. It was my turn to try.

CHAPTER 16

In the first few years after I'd rejoined the staff, the *P-I* had added new people. I straddled both newspaper worlds. I was part of the old guard, but I'd also rejoined around the same time as a bunch of new reporters. They took me in as one of theirs as well. Slowly, I began to crawl out of my self-imposed exile to join my colleagues for coffee or happy hours or walks along the waterfront.

I hung out over drinks with a reporter named Mike Lewis, who had joined the *P-I* from a paper in Northern California and made me laugh with his sly wit and keen observations, or Claudia Rowe, who'd arrived at the *P-I*'s doorstep from New York, with the intensity and writing chops of a young Joan Didion, or Mary Lynn, whose nuanced profiles raised the bar for all of us. We shared a love of stories, critiqued each other's writing, deconstructed pieces we admired from outside the paper. The conversations would start over our work, but as the evenings wore on, we'd slide into stories from our own lives.

Years later, I realized that the people I grew closest to after Christopher's death were all at various crossroads when we found each other. And they had something else in common that wasn't apparent at first. Most had faced grave losses of their own, losses we seldom spoke of but that formed an invisible scaffolding for our friendship. We shared a certain understanding of the pain and urgency of needing to move on, recognized the unspoken anniversaries. We stood in as each other's families.

My longtime newsroom friends drew me out of my small orbit as well.

One day, Rita and I decided on a whim to go salsa dancing, something neither of us had tried before. We'd been taking a screenwriting class together and considered it research for a scene we envisioned.

Century Ballroom, tucked into the second floor of an old Odd Fellows temple on Seattle's Capitol Hill, had a certain retro glamour, with its crystal chandelier and gilded balcony overlooking a worn wooden dance floor. Something happened to me the moment I walked in. The music with its cheerful cowbell clave and the bodies swirling in the dark mesmerized me. I was hooked. It was as though I'd come back into my body after a long absence. I'd dwelled so long in my head, in my memories and my thoughts. In the ballroom, I could stop thinking and just move, turn myself over to the beat, the heat of other people. After the first night, I went home and cried. Cried because I'd let myself hear the music. Cried because it felt good. Cried because I was scared, because I wanted something else, something more in my life. I wanted to love again. I wanted to live in the moment, not in the past. *Be brave.* I thought how Christopher would have wanted me to be happy.

After that, Rita, Merry, and I began taking trips together, first to New York, then to France and Italy. One evening in Florence, I walked alone, awed and overwhelmed by the lit Duomo against the dusky purple of the night sky. As I stood in the shadow of the ancient building with its deep ties to this place, a sudden wave of sorrow slammed over me. There was no one waiting for me in my darkened house back in Seattle. No partner. No child. I had nothing binding me to my past or future. I swam in my private sea of pity for a few minutes until I saw Rita and Merry coming toward me, laughing, hands full with cups of gelato, their steps echoing on the stones of the plaza. The mood lifted as fast as it had descended. I was with people who mattered to me. In the years our friendship had built outside the newsroom, we'd grown as close as sisters.

After work, I'd sometimes head to Rita's place for dinner. She'd call ahead to remind her sons to pick up the house for company, with mixed results. Once, by the time I got there, her fourteen-year-old had neatly folded all the dirty towels strewn around his bathroom and put them back in the linen closet. It felt good to at last be able to laugh with someone over the crazy things kids did.

That same son later went with us on a trip through Italy. Thereafter we were known in his circle of friends as "the ladies," a title that always made me smile. Her boys treated me like an aunt, describing their latest adventures and keeping me abreast of pop culture.

I TRAVELED WITH ANOTHER longtime *P-I* friend as well.

I'd met Jim Erickson when we were both young reporters on the business desk. We'd sat next to each other when Christopher was little, in the years before I'd quit the paper and moved to LA. He'd covered Microsoft, while I covered Boeing. I used to joke it was me who gained ten pounds the year he tried to quit smoking. He'd plopped a giant jar of Tootsie Pops on top of our shared computer terminal, and I devoured them on deadline. We'd become fast friends through the eras of each other's divorces, hanging out on the paper's steps while he smoked and I talked, sorting out our lives. He generally saw right through my various defenses and prevarications. We'd stayed in touch after I moved to California with Christopher. He was the one who had stepped forward without my asking to write Christopher's obituary when I could not summon words.

He'd since moved to Hong Kong to report for *Asiaweek*, and we made a travel pact, meeting up in various places around the world when we could. We hiked in Patagonia, sailed inside the Great Barrier Reef, and explored the hutong villages in the heart of Beijing before they were torn down.

One rainy day in Beijing, we took a taxi out to the Great Wall. Our driver careened through traffic, singing along in an unexpected tenor to *Madame Butterfly* on the radio as he zoomed up on tuk tuks and pedicabs. Pedestrians scattered like billiard balls in front of us. Whole fruit stands, lashed to bicycles, veered away as he barreled by. I was a nervous wreck by the time we got to the wall. The driver dropped us, and I climbed out, my stomach still in knots. The throng of usual tourists had vanished. A lonely postcard hawker waved a few cards at us while a nearby T-shirt vendor napped on a pile of blankets in his stand. Jim and I climbed up and walked along the stones paving the wall. A shroud of mist obscured our view, but we kept going. The rain muffled even our footsteps, the silence a relief after the din and blare of Beijing's city streets. After about a mile, the mist lifted, and suddenly the wall unwound as far as we could see, far into the past, far into the future, its steep green banks dropping away on either side. The sheer enormity and undulating beauty of it took my breath away. We stood there, side by side, a dot in time.

How rich it felt, how strange.

VI.

SEASONS
(DARBI)

CHAPTER 17

"Is it a gift?" the lady at the grocery store flower counter asked. She took the small pot of paperwhites and swaddled it in tissue paper on the day Christopher would have turned twenty-six. I put the pot on the seat next to me and drove to the cemetery. I hadn't gone there in many years.

We'd held Christopher's memorial service on a rainy winter morning in Seattle, the kind that smears all the colors to shades of gray. My family had to push me to view Christopher's body, laid out in a simple casket, before the service. They were concerned if I didn't see him, I wouldn't accept his death as real. There is nothing simple about grief, but there are known complications, and that was one of them. They probably had good cause to worry.

I wasn't there to say goodbye.

I repeated the phrase to myself, over and over. I said it to whoever would listen. It would become the one fixed detail in the recounting of his death down through the years. The rational part of me knew it would have made no difference, but delusion is a powerful defense. We believe what we need to believe. Somewhere deep inside, I'd developed a fixation about his death that defied reality. If I'd been there, maybe it wouldn't have happened after all.

My heart stumbled as I stepped into the small chapel on the day of the service. There was a body that looked like his, wearing his school uniform—a red sweatshirt, white polo shirt, and blue pants—clothes I'd picked because he was so proud of being in first grade. His hair was neatly combed, his lashes a dark fringe against pale, waxy skin. I touched his cheek. It was cold. I ran from the room, filled with the frantic, familiar panic of a mother whose child gets lost and separated in a crowd. That wasn't Christopher in there. Christopher was somewhere else.

I've blocked out much of the service. I know from the register that people from every corner of his life came—his family, my colleagues, his doctors and nurses, his teachers, his friends. Children signed the song "Circle of Life" from *The Lion King*. My friend Barbara, whose oldest daughter was born a week after Christopher and who had talked me through countless anxiety-ridden nights, spoke of Christopher's love of merry-go-rounds.

"Every day of his life, that boy went forward, always eager to play, to learn, to grab life's brass ring," she said.

Frank took the podium and read "O Captain! My Captain!" by Walt Whitman. He told the people gathered that he and his wife were expecting a baby—one who would be Christopher's half brother.

I could not speak at the service. I sat mute and shivering in my pew. Outside afterward, a dot of purple in the grass caught my eye—a tiny, early blooming pansy—almost as though Christopher had pointed it out to me. I picked the flower and pressed it between the pages of my copy of *The Little Prince*.

IN THE FALL AFTER Christopher's death, my parents and I visited Nova Scotia, a trip to search out family roots. The forced break from my routine seemed a good idea. I was barely functioning at the time, sleepwalking through my days with little memory of each one. I dreaded going to bed at night, afraid of my unrelenting nightmares. My journal is littered with fragments of dreams, as though writing them down could exorcise them:

"Dreamed was on a ferry on the ocean, looking and looking for something under the water."

"Dreamed Christopher's scarf got caught in the elevator doors and it started to go down. No one could hear me scream."

"Dreamed was trying to 'run a code' to resuscitate a patient. Except, I wasn't a doctor, and didn't know what to do."

I'd wake up sweating. My heart racing. My breath shallow. The code, I think, was for me.

My father's family had arrived in Nova Scotia from Scotland generations earlier. We busied ourselves with the minutiae of genealogical research, tourists looking for landmarks along the family tree. We held up each fact we unearthed as though it were the most delicate relic. I was grateful for the distraction.

A week into the trip, we took a ferry from Pictou, on the northeastern coast of Nova Scotia, up to Prince Edward Island. My grandmother's parents had once lived on the island, and it was where they'd buried a baby boy. I wasn't sure I could face a baby's grave, the memory of Christopher's so fresh, but I had no choice. I had to go along.

We landed at Wood Islands with its ruddy banks of sand. Low, late afternoon sun lit up the wheatgrass as we drove the island's country roads, watching for signs to pioneer cemeteries. After many false starts down dead-end lanes, we finally found a small graveyard in a clearing bordered by white birches. I hung back while my parents poked among the graves until they found it—a stone etched "In Memory of Willie. Aged 15 months and 18 days."

I hesitated at first, but something drew me toward it. The grave marker, bleached white, stood like a miniature lighthouse in its sea of grass. I recognized the marker right away by the little lamb carved into it. My grandmother had mentioned the lamb whenever she told the story about how her parents had lost a baby boy in a faraway place before she was born. She'd never been to Nova Scotia, never seen this grave, yet it had been as real to her in her imagination as it was to me in the cemetery that day. I knelt beside the marker and cleared debris from its base. The wording on the headstone struck me—every day recorded, the measure of a lifetime, poignant in its exactness. The image of that little grave in a sunlit cemetery, a lullaby of crickets playing around it, a foghorn bleating in the distance, lingered with me long after we left. There was something startling about the actual count of the baby's days, so few of them, stacked up against the years since.

It was a reassurance, too, that time doesn't forget what memory won't let it. After Christopher died, one of my greatest fears was that he would be forgotten. That there would one day be no one left to remember his laughter or talk about his love of trains and cowboys. When he was little, he was invited to be an extra in the movie *Mr. Holland's Opus*. People tell me they've glimpsed him there. I've never watched it, a superstition that somehow if I don't, some piece of him still lives in the world for me to find, one last memory not yet pinned to a board.

Yet here, more than a hundred years after the fact, Willie's death had the power to move me. It had left a mark on his parents that my grandmother could sense, the sadness of it passed down through the generations. A link.

I felt linked to my great-grandparents another way as well. When they'd first stood here, cloaked in their own grief, they could not know the joy the future held for them. They could not know that someday, someone from the future would come to share their loss for a moment and honor the life of their son. They could not know if not for them, I wouldn't be here. The glimpse of hope for my own future was as fleeting as the breeze in the cemetery, but I reached for it.

During the two weeks we were in Nova Scotia, the trees started to turn. They brushed bright strokes against the sky, staining the landscape the last colors of a fire going out, their pigment signaling the moment between living and dying that is letting go. There is no death without notice, even in nature.

Traveling back along the skeleton of my family tree, I saw how small each of our individual tracks really was. Christopher's death loomed so large for me, the brevity of his life so overwhelming, but he had made his mark. His place on the tree was the same, no more, no less than any other life.

I PARKED AND CARRIED the pot of paperwhites up the hill toward Christopher's gravestone. Beneath my feet, the flat green of the lower lawn gave way to the gentle undulations of grass grown over small caskets, a distinct wave pattern found only here in the children's part of the cemetery. Muscle memory guided me to his marker. Some of his ashes were there, some still with me. We'd placed his stone by a tree and hung a feeder so there would always be birds nearby.

"Chris-7," the stone read, our nod to his custom of adding his age whenever he'd introduce himself to someone new.

There's that line from Emily Dickinson's Poem 372: "After great pain, a formal feeling comes." Not here in the children's cemetery. Balloons bobbed in the breeze. Pinwheels spun. A green plastic lizard lay on a grave marked with one date—June 14, 1958. Before I was born. Who were these children with long names and single dates, children who did not live to be even one day old? For the first time in many years, I thought of that long-ago day in Nova Scotia at Willie's grave.

I sat on the bench beside the tree, the paperwhites on my lap, and stared out over the waters of Lake Washington. The traffic on Lake City Way just outside the cemetery gates flowed by, its dull roar like the sound of a river. In the distance, the peaks of the Cascade Range revealed themselves in layers, like one of Christopher's construction-paper dioramas, growing blue in the distance. My memories, too, had faded, folded one beyond the other, just out of reach, like the distant flanks of retreating mountains. I wished for some way to find the colors on their slopes again.

Wind tangled the branches above me, the way I used to run my fingers through Christopher's hair. I closed my eyes for a moment and thought I heard his voice. But it was the chatter of black-capped chickadees lifting off the tree in sudden unison. I shook the feeling off and left the flowers on Christopher's grave. Back at my car, I sat for a while, slumped against the wheel. When I looked up, two cars full of young people had parked near his marker. There were five of them, standing under the tree next to his stone. Two of the young people signed animatedly to the others.

One hoisted a baby to her hip. Another held balloons. It dawned on me these could be Christopher's stepbrother and stepsisters from his other family, his other life. Or perhaps the half brother, whose impending birth I'd learned about at Christopher's funeral. They appeared to be celebrating Christopher's birthday, maybe there to tell the baby about him. Watching them remembering Christopher made me happy.

There was a time I wouldn't have been able to feel any joy in that. When Frank and I split up after almost ten years of marriage, it was devastating for all concerned. Christopher, though, showed us he could love us all. When he brought me stick drawings he'd made of his family, I'd be represented there, along with his dad, stepsiblings, his dad's new wife, and Jim. I recognized myself by the two yellow lines for my long hair around the circle of my face. The way he signed "family" came back to me—the thumb and index finger of each hand forming a small circle at his chest, his palms facing out. Then his hands drawing forward around a big horizontal circle like he was folding a group of people into a hug. To him, we were one big family.

Frank and I may have failed at being good partners to each other, but the one thing we always shared was our love for Christopher. The divorce was bitter at the time. We've since forgiven each other for being young.

I'd lost track of those other children, but watching the young people at Christopher's grave reminded me that it was possible to do both— mourn and celebrate. Hope and loss can coexist. Grace and grief. Joy and sorrow. They have to.

I'd learned that from a story about a young mother who carried twins.

CHAPTER 18

The young man from the paper's computer support staff who approached me looked anxious. I seldom saw Paul out in the newsroom. Mostly he and the other technical staff labored out of sight, keeping the paper's servers humming. But that day, he had something he wanted to ask me. His sister, Darbi Johnson, and her husband, Mike, were having twins, and there had been a problem with the pregnancy. She'd had to undergo a highly unusual fetal surgery. It hadn't worked. He was worried for her, and he thought it could help not just his sister but others in her situation to share her story.

"Would you tell it?" he asked. Whenever a fellow staff member approached me with a story idea, especially a personal one, I took it as a sign of trust. This time, though, I hesitated. He had no way of knowing why. Still, he persisted out of concern for his sister.

Finally, I said yes.

I met Darbi for the first time on a hot July day at a clinic where she was having an ultrasound. We chatted in the waiting room. She had a girlish voice and, though she was twenty-six, looked little older than a teen. She wanted, more than anything, to be a mom.

After a few minutes, a nurse called her name, and we entered the darkened ultrasound room together. She held her belly and leaned back in the exam chair. The nurse took her blood pressure. It was a little high.

Probably anxiety, the nurse assured her. "That's normal."

I could already feel my heart beating faster and wondered what my own was. The panic started to well, small bubbles usually kept down by the weight of years. This room—the semi-dark, the cool jelly and glide of the ultrasound wand—was so like the ones long ago where a technician had detected Christopher's blockage in utero and where I'd learned my second baby's fate. These shadowy, shifting images, like a map of the bottom of the ocean.

I made myself concentrate on Darbi.

The technician's ultrasound wand skimmed her stomach. A figure swam into view—a head and miniature hand, fingers clutched. The room filled with the galloping echo of the baby's heartbeat—*wow, wow, wow*—as though someone were waving a sheet of tin into a microphone.

"I just love the sound," Darbi said. "I wish I could have it on all the time."

Her husband, Mike, a firefighter, walked in just then after an overnight shift. He wore jeans and a fleece, his close-cropped hair hidden under a baseball cap marked FIRE DISTRICT #9. He looked young and a little anxious.

"The head is big!" he said, his gaze fixed on the screen. "Good!"

He drummed his fingers to the heartbeat.

The two of them stared at the line the baby's pulse traced on the chart trailing slowly out of the ultrasound machine. A look passed between them. There used to be two hearts beating there. Now there was one.

DARBI AND MIKE HAD met as first-year students at a college in Portland, Oregon. They'd been instantly attracted to each other. Darbi was bubbly and warm. Mike, plainspoken with a dry sense of humor. When they'd married, they talked of having children. They settled on three.

The first time Darbi suspected she was pregnant, she was at a Krispy Kreme with relatives. It was Christmastime. She'd ordered two glasses of milk.

"I hate milk." Her laugh was high, musical. "But I figured that's what you should do."

In the car, she'd leaned over to Mike and whispered, "I'm *late*."

He'd nodded.

"No," she said. "I'm *late*."

A huge grin spread across his face. He squeezed her hand.

They had waited until New Year's Day to take the test. They sat side by side in their living room, their eyes shut as it developed. Then they counted to three and looked together.

"There was a pink line," she said. "We cried. We jumped. We hugged." They didn't sleep that night they were so excited. They prepared to be parents.

Mike read children's stories and prayers to her growing belly. One day, she noticed the baby seemed quiet. They went for a heartbeat check. For ten minutes, two ultrasound technicians watched the screen in silence. They left the room without saying anything. A doctor came back to deliver the news. The baby's heart had stopped in the night. He sent her next door to give birth.

A sharp pain torqued through my belly as I imagined what she must have felt. It flashed me back to the hospital room where I'd labored with Christopher. A friend had given me a vase of white tulips. I placed them on a narrow ledge where I could see them. Beside them, I put a card my mother had given me with a Carl Larsson painting of a girl in a nursery that she'd said reminded her of me. Between contractions, I stared at the card, limp and panting, trying to will the strength of my mother into my own body. Frank brought me ice chips while nurses slow-dripped oxytocin into my IV. We watched, with a rapid-cycling mix of terror and excitement, as the trace of my contractions morphed from the shape of a hill to a cliff, my body thrown against it over and over. Occasionally, the thin wail of a newborn would break through the haze of my pain. I prayed my baby would be born alive. I was lucky. Darbi didn't have that chance.

Darbi lay in shock in her room at the end of the obstetrics wing. All night long, she saw flashes from other new parents' cameras going off. "It was a horrible feeling," she said. "Then it just came to me. You have to choose to have hope, no matter what happens to you. I knew someday I'd need a reminder of that. I told Mike, if it's a girl, I want to name her Hope."

Hope arrived, stillborn, four pounds, one ounce, with thick, dark curly hair. "She was absolutely perfect," Darbi said. Their pastor came and prayed with them, then Mike took the baby to another room to rock her as their families came to pay their respects.

"He was holding her," Darbi said of Mike. "He was immediately, instantly a dad. Bouncing and patting her. Even though it was only a half hour that we got to be parents, I feel proud I still got the amazing feeling of being a mom and that Mike and I created something so beautiful and perfect."

WHEN DARBI GOT PREGNANT a second time, they went for a checkup at eight weeks. Again, the ultrasound technician was silent. "It made us nervous," she said. "Then she said, 'There's two heartbeats.' We could not believe it. We were thrilled." The babies were identical twins. It seemed almost too lucky to be true. For eight more blissful weeks, the couple imagined the future for the two boys they'd already named Carter and Blake. Then, at sixteen weeks, doctors made a discovery. The boys shared a placenta and key blood vessels, a condition called twin-to-twin transfusion syndrome.

When an embryo divides within four days of conception, it usually results in two identical babies with two placentas. If the embryo divides between four and eight days, it creates two embryos that share a placenta, separated by a thin membrane. In these cases, the plumbing for the two babies' circulatory systems can get mixed up.

In Darbi's case, blood flowed from the smaller "donor" twin to his brother, the larger "recipient" twin. The flow was uneven. Carter, half the size of his brother, was getting too little circulation, and Blake, too much. Doctors told them that in more than 80 percent of cases, the donor twin died of severe anemia, while the recipient died of heart failure. Although it affects only about forty-five hundred pregnancies a year, it accounts for a disproportionately large percentage of fetal deaths. Doctors suggested they terminate.

Mike and Darbi were stunned. They couldn't imagine doing that. Darbi had named their first baby Hope, and now hope was what they clung to.

CHAPTER 18

In past cases, doctors had tried serial amnioreduction, or periodically withdrawing a large amount of fluid from the uterus, a procedure that seemed to increase survival rates in milder cases, though doctors weren't sure why.

They'd also tried something called a septostomy, which involved punching a hole in the membrane separating the babies to try to distribute an equal amount of amniotic fluid on each baby's side. Again, the mechanism was mysterious, but somehow it seemed to improve survival. With both approaches, however, the babies were still at risk for brain damage caused by inadequate oxygen. And neither approach helped in the most severe cases, like Darbi's.

There was one other thing they could try, though. If doctors could find a way to separate the "communicating vessels" so each baby could receive its oxygenated blood directly from the placenta and not from each other, they could save both twins. The field of fetal therapy—operating on a fetus—was still new, however, and laced with ethical quandaries.

This was something I already knew. The first fetal surgery had been performed at the University of California, San Francisco, only a few years before Christopher had been born. Ironically, in that case, it was done to correct the same congenital birth defect he'd been born with. Doctors had placed a catheter in the baby in utero to let urine drain and keep it from backing up and damaging the kidneys. That allowed the kidneys and lungs to develop normally. The blockage itself was corrected after birth. Had I been able to have such a procedure, it might have prevented Christopher's many complex medical problems.

But when I was pregnant with Christopher, such surgeries were considered highly experimental. Also, because ultrasounds themselves were uncommon, we hadn't discovered Christopher's birth defect until the damage to his developing systems was already done. Fetal surgery was never an option for us.

For Darbi, it was. But twin-to-twin transfusion syndrome was among the most delicate and complicated cases for fetal surgery.

Surgeons would have to sever blood vessels the size of threads, and any breach of the uterus carried the risk of bleeding or sending the mother into premature labor. If that happened, it wouldn't be just her two babies' lives on the line, but hers as well.

Darbi and Mike sought a second opinion from Dr. Martin Walker of Evergreen Hospital Medical Center in Kirkland, a suburb across Lake Washington from Seattle. Soft-spoken with a trace of a British accent, Dr. Walker handled high-risk mothers with a combination of gentle humor and candor. Decisions in high-risk prenatal cases were often tough. The intricacies of those situations were partly what had attracted him to obstetrics. That and the extraordinary journey to birth. "I love the complexity of it," he said when I went to visit him. "Seeing something come from nothing."

Dr. Walker was one of a handful of clinicians in the United States trained to do a technique called fetoscopic laser photocoagulation, which used lasers to separate the vessels of twins in the womb. Pioneered ten years earlier, the procedure was still relatively uncommon. He'd learned the technique in England and apprenticed under the originator in Florida before coming to Evergreen. Only a few places in the country were equipped to do the surgery. Dr. Walker had yet to have a case. As soon as he saw Darbi's ultrasound, he knew she was a candidate.

Her case was severe, he told me. One baby's heart was already stressed. The other, smaller twin was struggling to hang on. If the smaller baby died while there was still a connection between the two twins, it would cause a sudden plunge in blood pressure for the surviving one. Within an hour of the first fetal death, the drop could cause brain damage or the death of the other baby. By separating the two, at a minimum, they hoped to protect one baby from the death of the other. They had to move fast, though; the procedure could be done only before the pregnancy reached twenty-six weeks. If successful, about two-thirds of pregnancies resulted in two live births. In three-quarters of cases, it saved at least one of the twins.

On the day of the surgery, Dr. Walker threaded a flexible tube not much wider than a piece of spaghetti through a three-millimeter incision in Darbi's belly. For forty minutes, he guided the laser over the placenta by watching its path on an overhead screen. He needed steady hands for the work, and good map-reading skills.

"You need to be able to recognize landmarks and think in three dimensions," he said. By the end, he'd separated the dozen veins and arteries that linked the twins.

Then the waiting began.

For the next few weeks, Darbi lived from ultrasound to ultrasound, the sonar images their one window into their babies' world. At first both twins gained weight. Blake weighed one pound. His brother was half that, and he didn't seem to be catching up. More worrisome—the portion of placenta nourishing Carter was much smaller than Blake's.

Three weeks later, as Dr. Walker scanned the ultrasound, he saw only stillness in the shadows where the smaller baby's heart had beat. Breaking this kind of news was difficult.

Softly, he said to Darbi and Mike: "The little baby died."

When Darbi got to this part of her story, I bowed my head, remembering the words the radiologist had said to me: *There is nothing there consistent with life.* My heart sank for her.

Darbi prepared to notify their friends and family. "We've grieved and we've rejoiced," she wrote. "Now we are forced to do both at the same time."

A FEW WEEKS AFTER first meeting Darbi, I went to visit her at her home. A hard summer rain doused us as we stood in the backyard of the modest beige house she shared with her husband in Olympia, about an hour-and-a-half drive south of Seattle. She wanted to show me a garden she was planting. Pieces of reflective tape flew like Tibetan prayer flags across the grass to keep out the deer. Their next-door neighbor's garden was already lush with towering dahlias and roses. Darbi's was barren. One stubborn patch of rhubarb anchored a corner. Still, it was a start

Blake had grown strong and active. Darbi was doing "kick counts" every day, checking to make sure the baby kicked at least ten times in two hours. "He does it in under four minutes every time," she said, beaming. She went for stress tests twice a week. Her scheduled delivery date, a planned cesarean, was two weeks away.

In the meantime, she and her stepmother were busy preparing the nursery. She waded into the room, which was already covered knee deep in gift bags and boxes from three recent showers, and began sorting through the bibs and crib toys, stuffed animals and onesies.

"When we brought them all home and put them into the nursery, Mike said, 'How's Blake going to fit in here?'" She laughed. Children's books were strewn about the room. She picked up a Dr. Seuss book. "We think *Green Eggs and Ham* is Blake's favorite," she said. "We got to the part where he talks about the fox and Blake kicked. Mike said 'fox' again, and he kicked again."

A book of secrets for dads, with instructions on everything from skipping stones to finding the North Star, lay on a table in the living room. I felt for the star around my neck and closed my hand around it. There were no books on how to celebrate one baby while losing another. That part they were making up as they went along.

Darbi picked up two tiny hand-knit red caps.

"Most people don't make two because they don't want to make me feel bad," she said, fingering the soft yarn. "But I love these." Blake had grown to five pounds. Carter's small body was folded up high under her heart, next to his brother.

Darbi had started sewing blankets for both twins. She'd asked the ultrasound tech to measure Carter's head so she could make a tiny hat for him to be buried in. When they were done sorting the nursery, Darbi leaned against her stepmom and the tears started, a sudden rush like water breaking.

By the front door, she'd begun a second garden. A yellow teapot rested on a chair set in among the verbena and a loganberry bush. They'd planted daisies there for Hope. They would plant something new for Carter.

Two weeks later, I drove to the hospital for the birth. Darbi's door in the obstetrics wing was easy to find. She'd papered it over with ultrasound pictures of the twins, each image carefully captioned. In the last one, Carter appeared to gaze down at Blake. "Brothers forever," the caption read.

Inside, the room hummed with visitors as more family arrived. Dr. Walker strode in, wearing a purple polka-dot tie and his trademark cowboy boots. He'd come by to check on his patient before changing into his scrubs for the delivery. Darbi laughed when she saw the boots. She'd bought a miniature matching pair for Blake, in honor of the doctor who had saved him. The visitors linked hands and circled around Darbi. They prayed for Blake and Carter. Mike stroked her stomach, and for one last moment, they were all together before the hospital staff wheeled her away.

In the operating room, two Plexiglas warming beds stood side by side. Dr. Walker, in scrubs now, worked quickly to free Blake from Darbi's womb. At 9:58 A.M., an eager, insistent cry filled the room. Blake had arrived.

Mike and Darbi clutched hands, their faces turned in new-parent disbelief toward Blake, who squalled in his warmer. Dr. Walker kept working behind the drape that separated him from their joy until Carter slipped quietly into his hands, as fragile as a paper doll. A nurse wrapped him quickly and laid him, for a moment, in the bed beside his brother.

Grief comes in waves, like contractions.

A few days after the birth, Darbi and Mike gathered with friends and family to bury Carter next to their firstborn, Hope. Two small bouquets of baby white roses, one wrapped in pink, the other in blue, rested on the grave site. Darbi held Blake, who was less than a week old, against her breast. She kissed the dark blond hair on his sleepy head and started to cry. Mike, silent and drained, held her hand.

The family's pastor assembled the group under two old Douglas firs. He had seen their large extended family through many life transitions. "This is a mixed reality," he began. "But we celebrate death and life, for God made both of them." The pastor closed the brief service with a prayer, then many of those gathered wrote farewell messages on blue balloons. Singing softly, they released them to the sun.

Darbi watched the last one fade into a baby-blue sky, then turned back to Blake. Visitors closed around them—friends, family, the squad mates from Mike's firehouse—drawn by the magnetic pull of a new infant. They peeked under his blanket with its firefighter motif. They cooed and touched his hands. Mike and Darbi smiled and recounted their first baby stories.

A few miles away, daisies bloomed in Hope's garden.

I WALKED AWAY FROM the funeral that day feeling sad, but also strangely lighter, as though a weight had lifted off with those balloons. You could not choose sorrow, but you could choose joy. I remembered Darbi's words.

You have to choose to have hope, no matter what happens to you.

People tend to confuse hope with positive thinking or optimism, but it's fundamentally different from those things. Psychologists say hope is not so much an attitude as a kind of framework for moving forward in life. Hope is believing you have choices, and that there's a path forward, even if it's not the one you expected to be on.

One of the hardest things after any significant loss is giving yourself permission to laugh, love, and enjoy life again. I didn't want to be one of those people others pitied for being unable to move on, for refusing to rejoin the stream of life. At the same time, I felt guilty when I laughed or enjoyed myself, as though I were negating the enormity of Christopher's loss. And people assumed if I laughed, I must be "over it." I murmured excuses to get out of any kind of celebration—birthday parties, staff picnics, holiday gatherings, and especially baby showers. I expected going would be too painful.

But through Darbi's story, I realized that experiencing joy and celebrating that of others didn't have to minimize or replace my own loss and grief. One was not at the expense of the other. I could hold both without betraying Christopher's memory.

A few months after I finished Darbi's story, a group of women at work invited me to a baby shower for one of our colleagues. This time, I said yes. Before the appointed day, I went to shop for a baby gift. I wandered through the infant department, touching tiny onesies and rattling little toys. I picked up a plush giraffe and pet its silky mane. Finally, I settled on a set of soft receiving blankets.

"Boy or girl?" the woman behind the counter asked as she wrapped them in paper with a yellow teddy bear print.

"Girl," I said. She unfurled a pink ribbon.

I hugged the box to my chest as I walked out, feeling unexpectedly happy for this new life coming into the world. I hoped the blankets would fold her in as much love and joy as Christopher's life had brought to mine.

VII.

ON SCARS

(LAURA)

CHAPTER 19

The year Christopher died, a massive wildfire ravaged the area around the mountain town of Leavenworth in the Cascades, two hours east of Seattle. As a child, I'd learned to cross-country ski there during winters and hiked the trails above the valley when they were ablaze with yellow aspens in the fall. I'd loved taking Christopher there when he was little. We picnicked on the rocks by the Wenatchee River and watched inner tubers spin down with the current. "Fish," he'd sign, making his hands swim through the air and pointing to them. The first time he did it, I'd swept him into a big hug, thrilled he'd made his first metaphor.

The motel where we usually stayed had a large walk-in closet. He dragged his pillow and blankets inside and claimed it as his own. "Little house," he signed. He taught himself how to roll downhill at a nearby park, which put him into fits of dizzy giggles. One day he picked a dandelion at the bottom. "Look," I signed, making a V with my fingers and pointing to my eyes, then to the flower as I blew. Its tiny white windmills took flight like a puff of smoke. He hooted in astonishment.

The year of the fire, more than twenty-four hundred firefighters from twenty-four states descended to save the town and surrounding forests. More than 180,000 acres burned. A haze of smoke hung in the air as far as Seattle, turning the sky blood red at sunset. It took five months to put the fire out.

I drove there in the aftermath. A forest of ghostly tree trunks, feathery against the charred flanks of the mountains, marked the fire's course like a scar. The town itself had been spared the fire. I pulled into the parking lot of the small motel where Christopher and I had stayed. The dark beams and white plaster of its faux Bavarian facade remained intact, but it no longer looked like the castle of Christopher's imagination, merely the serviceable, slightly shabby way-stop motel it was. I got out to get some air, my knees wobbly. Cars sped past me on Highway 2. I wanted to scream at them. Make them stop. Time had spun to a halt for me with Christopher's death, but the rest of the world drove on by as though nothing had happened, everyone else passing through and moving on. I wanted a mark, the way the mountain wore its scar, to make them pay attention. Scars were what made pain visible. I wanted the Braille of a scar to press, a place to touch to remember. I wanted to tell someone my story, Christopher's story, but no one stopped to listen.

Years later, Billy's burn therapist would put my feelings from that day into words: *The thing about scars is they tell a story*. Stories *are* our scars. We can trace the arc of them. Let others see where we've hurt and where we've healed.

Those who have had their own aching and profound losses mark them in different ways. Years after I met him, my friend Mike lost his young niece in a horrible accident. Mike had always hated tattoos. After his niece's death, though, he began one that has grown into nearly a full sleeve. The images wind down his arm and leg, marking her life and death. People ask him about his ink, and he tells the story.

Researchers have found that deaf children who haven't been formally exposed to either speech or sign language still develop a language of gestures to share their experiences and get their ideas across. Linguist and author Steven Pinker called this a "language instinct." I'd argue there's also an instinct toward story—a fundamental desire to shape what's happened to us. Stories are our cultural DNA. They're how we communicate with each other, how we pass along our wisdom and experience.

My friends and colleagues sometimes seemed baffled by the kinds of stories I gravitated toward. They probably speculated about my preoccupation with trauma and death. The stories weren't depressing to me. They were testaments to the enormous transformative power of loss. The people who shared their lives with me showed me that. Their experiences had changed them, and in turn changed me. They taught me empathy. They taught me courage. They taught me humility. They saved me.

We need happy stories, too, and I did those along the way as well. I wrote about a ninety-six-year-old man who tried to skydive his way into *The Guinness Book of World Records*. I wrote funny animal stories about baby elephants and sassy crows. But it was the harder ones that stayed with me.

Mary Karr, author of *The Liars' Club*, was the keynote speaker at a conference I attended one year. After her talk, a middle-aged woman approached the microphone to ask a question. Before the woman could get her words out, she started to cry. She finally choked out that reading Karr's story was like reading her own. Karr came down from behind the speaker's podium and embraced her. We need these stories to recognize ourselves, to bear witness, and we need them no matter how long it takes to tell them.

My grandmother Laura taught me that.

THE YEAR MY GRANDMOTHER turned 105, it occurred to me she might be the oldest surviving female veteran of World War I. Almost all the women who had served in the Great War were gone by then. Ignored when they came home and forgotten by subsequent generations, most had never had a chance to tell their stories.

My grandmother had graduated from nursing school in 1917, the year the United States entered the war. Like many of her classmates, she'd enlisted. But the war was rarely mentioned after her return. Many of the nurses' experiences were more intense than those of their husbands, boyfriends, and brothers, so they didn't talk for fear of embarrassing the men. Social pressures against women doing "men's work" also enforced their silence. My grandmother had shared little over the years, even with my grandfather, who had served on a submarine chaser in the navy. She'd met him while in nursing school, a few years before they both enlisted, and married him six years after she came home from the war.

When I was young, her other accomplishments were more real to me—her lemon cake and skilled watercolors, her prized garden and the stories she told of growing up on a farm. Her military service had been such a small sliver of her life. It hardly seemed significant as I was growing up. I couldn't remember the contours of the war drawn in history classes, let alone picture my grandmother serving at five of its bloodiest fronts in France. They were just names printed on thin brass bars, clasped to the ribbon of her Victory Medal in a glass box on her wall: AISNE-MARNE, OISE-AISNE, YPRES-LYS, MEUSE-ARGONNE, DEFENSIVE SECTOR.

I'd seen a cache of letters once that she'd written to her parents from overseas. The letters were tucked in a cardboard box at the bottom of her china cabinet. Written in her spidery script on Red Cross stationery, the letters were brittle with age and folded into carefully slit-open envelopes. There were packets of them, neatly rubber-banded together, with ACCEPTED AS CENSORED stamped across the front, along with the eagle seal of the American Expeditionary Forces. I wasn't allowed to open them.

With each subsequent generation, the story faded further.

"It was too sad," my grandmother said to explain her silence. "So many hurt boys. Seeing the stumps and their bones . . ." She didn't finish. It wasn't until her nineties, at the urging of my aunt Mary Lou, that she finally began talking about her experiences in France, which in turn spurred her to write a brief memoir for the family.

The reporter in me knew that if my grandmother was indeed by then the oldest known living female vet of that war, it was an angle that might interest my paper. I pitched the idea to John Engstrom, the features editor at the time. It took a little convincing—generally reporters didn't write about themselves or their families—but when I told him I had the letters I'd once been forbidden to read, he jumped at the opportunity to hear the story in her own words. I immediately booked a flight to California to interview her at the retirement center where she'd lived for some thirty years.

THE MEADOWS—PERCHED AT the top of a steep hill overlooking the town of Los Gatos—was practically a second home to me. I'd been going there since childhood, before the sleepy Victorian town had morphed into a busy Silicon Valley suburb. My family stayed at a little adobe motel with a Mediterranean-tiled pool at the bottom of the hill. The drugstore across the street still had an aging, mirror-backed soda fountain. I hung out by the magazine racks or by the pool, daydreaming about my future. My memories of Los Gatos are like pencil marks on the wall of my growing up. First crushes, first boyfriend, college, first job, marriage, all duly considered as I swam laps in the pool between visits with my grandmother.

When I went up to see her, I'd sit by her chair in its window alcove, listening to the click of her knitting needles. She had big hands, gnarled with time, hands that had hammered and sawed and washed and cooked. Hands I thought could fix anything. She was always busy with them, whether making a mosaic table or wiring a lamp she'd built herself. Typically, she read only after the sun went down, a habit left over from her farm childhood. "Otherwise, it's a waste of good daylight for getting chores done," she'd say.

Her feminist leanings were not lost on me, her only granddaughter, even at an early age. She'd told me once how she'd run into some French officers on cavalry horses at the beach near Dunkirk one day. She'd asked to ride, and they let her, but kept hold of her reins, which wounded her pride. When one of them later showed off by riding up a steep sand dune and down the other side, she pulled her horse free and rode up and down the same dune.

"He was so angry," she said, and laughed. It was the only story from the war she ever told me.

When my grandmother first moved to the Meadows in the 1970s, she had her own small studio apartment. She ran pottery classes for the other residents and subbed at the front desk. She ate meals in its dining room. Now she lived in its skilled nursing unit, sharing a room with another resident. Every day, staff helped her get up and wheel outdoors to the patio. Over the years, she'd told me the secret to a long life was to spend some part of each day outdoors, and she intended to keep at it. I found her there on my last visit, dozing in her wheelchair, her face tipped to the sun and her knees covered with a red tartan blanket.

"Is that you?" She startled awake when I kissed her cheek. Her voice still held the half croon and faint trace of her Massachusetts upbringing, an accent peculiar to the town where she'd grown up. I checked again that she wanted to talk to me about the war. Her answer was firm. "If I don't, who will?" she asked.

For the next three days, we sat together on the patio beside a lemon tree as I looked for pathways through her memory that would take me back to the western front of France in 1918, the war zone that had separated her from her youth. She was still beautiful, her olive skin remarkably smooth for her age. She'd only recently abandoned the long hair she'd kept wound in a bun her whole life for a silvery bob. Though her eyesight and hearing were failing, there were still flashes of her keen mind and wicked sense of humor. I read to her from her memoir and she began to tell me the stories she remembered from the war. They started with a scene she could not shake:

"Do I look bad?" the soldier pleaded. Half his face was gone. She hurriedly dressed what remained. There were more men moaning on gurneys in the rain outside the operating tent. Her hands shook from the chilling damp seeping through the canvas walls. Blood smeared across her nurse's uniform, and her thin leather boots were coated with mud. She worked quickly, trying to block out the sound of limbs dropping into enamel pails as surgeons sawed through mangled flesh and bone.

"I can still hear it," she said. Her voice wavered. She pressed the back of her hand briefly to her eyes. I pictured her, hunched over her patients in the operating tent, doing the same thing to stanch tears that none of them could afford.

She couldn't stay in that memory for long, so our conversations ranged over wide places in our lives. In the evenings, I would search out the stories I was looking for in the letters she'd sent home from the war.

CHAPTER 20

Laura was an unconventional woman even before she went to war. Born in 1893, she grew up on a small farm in East Taunton, about forty miles south of Boston. Her father, George, grew vegetables that her mother made into pickles they sold in town. The youngest of three daughters, one of whom died young, she was given the middle name Georgina for the son her parents didn't have. Though she went to a one-room school where boys and girls had separate entrances, there was no such division of labor at home. She learned to work the land accordingly. "Give me girls every time," her father liked to say.

"My sister and I proved to him we could do our share working the farm," she said, which still made her chuckle. When the call went out for volunteers to fight the war that had been raging across Europe since 1914, it seemed natural to do her share as well.

Her training hospital, working with the Red Cross, coordinated to staff Base Hospital 44. "Most of my class signed up for it," she said. She was sworn in on February 15, 1918, and sent to Fort Oglethorpe in Georgia for training.

When she signed up, women couldn't vote and men were deeply suspicious of those with educations. Only five years earlier, the sinking of the *Titanic* and the cry of "women and children first" had inflamed arguments about female roles in society. To traditionalists, the *Titanic* proved women belonged to a special class, one requiring protection by—not equality with—men. My grandmother thought otherwise.

Like the rest of the country, she entered the war with high spirits and a certain innocence. On March 4, 1918, she wrote her parents from training camp:

Do you know I have never had such a good time in my life as I have had this last two weeks. One thing I have learned already—and had to if I was to live at all—that is to dance. Can you imagine fox-trotting and waltzing with majors and captains?

Soon enough, she fell in love with a first lieutenant. Laura was a tall woman, but he was taller—six feet with brown hair and eyes, like hers, and a pleasant smile. His name was Pete. "I was twenty-four years old and nothing like that had ever happened to me before," she said. Back home, her social life had mostly centered on the annual clambake at her church or the occasional ride in a horse-drawn sleigh. She was distantly related to the poet Robert Frost, and proud of it. Whenever I read his poem "Stopping by Woods on a Snowy Evening," I imagined my grandmother as a young woman, listening to her sleigh horse giving "his harness bells a shake."

Training camp was a different world. In their off-duty hours, she and Pete and some of the other nurses and officers would picnic on Lookout Mountain. They took pictures of themselves against the rocks, gazing at the Tennessee River winding through the country below. Sometimes Laura borrowed pants from an enlisted man so she and Pete could ride horseback together. He taught her to march and stood at attention for her first parade.

One day, Pete hired a taxi and took her for a ride. They were kissing in the back seat when the car hit a railroad track. The impact interrupted the kiss, but not before it broke his front tooth. "Really spoke well of all the milk I drank on the farm," she said, and giggled. "He told his fellow officers he ran into a telephone pole."

That, of course, did nothing to discourage them. He snuck in to see her when she was on night duty, much to the consternation of the officer in charge of the ward. "When the officer of the day couldn't find me, he had a hunch and flashed his torch into the supply closet window," she wrote in her memoir. "This unromantic individual reported me to the head nurse."

The next day, she was put on duty in the psychiatric ward. There she got one of her first glimpses of the realities she would soon face.

"The first day I went into the ward after lunch, I found everyone cringing into corners or under their beds. A young fellow was brandishing a straight razor. I didn't know what was happening but went right up to him and yelled: 'Give me that!' He smiled and handed me the open razor."

There were other signs that fantasies of life in the military were about to end. One afternoon, a friend asked her to go horseback riding. She accepted, but at the last minute changed her plans and asked a fellow nurse to take her place. Later, she wrote her parents:

> She was so pleased to think that she was going for a ride, and in five minutes she was thrown and died three hours later. I never realized what taps meant before, until they sounded for her at the station. None of us have very much pep since it happened.

"We had no idea what we were getting into," she said to me eighty years later. She was not so very different from me at that age, full of naïve and hopeful expectations, fully unaware of what lay ahead.

ON JUNE 17, 1918, THE base hospital moved by train from Georgia to New York to prepare for the trip to France. The timing meant the nurses got to march sixty blocks in New York City's Fourth of July parade, one of the first times American military women had ever marched alongside men. More than seventy thousand marchers swept up Fifth Avenue in a spectacle that began in the early morning—"8:43 o'clock," per the *New York Times*—and stretched into the late afternoon. According to the *Times*, "The parade was favored by fortune; the weather was perfect." Thousands of observers lined the route. Salvation Army workers tossed donuts to the crowd from a float depicting soldiers getting coffee and donuts from workers at the front. The marchers represented not just US military divisions, but also their allies and more. The *Times* listed them out: "After the Street Cleaning Department band came the Red Cross division—200 nurses in their dark blue uniforms, as many in their white, with red and blue capes, and the Allied Theatrical Nurses, also in white. They carried a motto calling on women to enroll to fill up the quota of 25,000 nurses needed by the army and navy."

Laura was thrilled to march, but the parade also offered a reality check for how the rest of the country viewed women in the army. As women, they could earn neither the rank nor pay of the men, with few exceptions. On July 6, 1918, she wrote home:

> *It really was a wonderful parade. . . . They didn't say much about the nurses in it. We thought we were the whole show.*

Pete's division had moved to New York as well, and he continued to woo Laura with dancing and shows. They went to dinner at the Hotel Brevoort in Greenwich Village and he took her to see Mistinguett, the French actress with the "million-dollar legs." "At least, they were insured for that amount," my grandmother said, and chuckled. The fun ended, though, when Pete was called up before she was. She went to Grand Central Terminal to see him off. He gave her a diamond service pin as a pledge of love. She promised to write him through the war.

"It was a very sad parting," she said, then fell quiet.

But she'd had little time to dwell on it. Her orders came soon after. On July 14, 1918, Laura sailed on the troop ship *Northland* for the eighteen-day trip to Liverpool and Le Havre.

On the ship, she wrote her parents:

> *For a while, we slept in the 3rd class cabin, but when the portholes were closed day and night, the air became rather rank, so every night they sent some privates over and they carried our blankets up on the promenade deck. We were laid out in rows on both sides, but the air and sea are certainly wonderful, and I slept sound every night.*

One night, it rained, and they had to move to the ship's library, which disappointed a lot of the nurses.

> *Maude Caldwell and I decided to cheer them up, so I got up on the piano with my blanket and pillow and proceeded to sleep while Maud crawled up in a chair or two that had been piled in the corner. Everyone who came in had to laugh and presently the whole place was in an uproar. Madame came up from her little bunk and squelched us. . . . Most of us would like to be acquainted with the men but some have had visits from Madame in their state rooms. It's a pity we still have that fear of her, but I'm sure the girls would obey her quicker than they would the General.*

They entertained themselves by putting on plays and dancing:

> *Now mother, imagine us having such good times and everyone at home worrying their heads off about us. You know, Uncle Sam is pretty clever, and I am sure I have never been safer in my life.*

That month, about three hundred thousand troops went over. Officers told them not to throw anything overboard to avoid revealing their course to submarines that might be lurking below. Tucked in Laura's small army trunk was a box camera and developing fluid—despite warnings they were not to take pictures.

By August 4, she'd left Paris and arrived at her first post with Evacuation No. 7, a field hospital. Her first day on duty nearly leveled her.

"If it hadn't been the amputation ward maybe the shock wouldn't have been so devastating but helping dress those quivering stumps and hearing the laughter and jokes in spite of their misfortune was too much for me and I cried all that first day," she wrote. "I thought they had made a mistake by putting us through that experience so soon, but maybe it was for the good and I could stand anything after that miserable week."

Evac No. 7 would not be her final destination. "We were all lined up one morning and twelve of us were cut off right between Marion and myself. We called ourselves the 'dirty dozen' from then on. Marion went to Pougues-les-Eaux, about 140 miles south of Paris, with Base Hospital 44 and lived in a hotel for the duration." My grandmother, her friend Margaret Cooper, and the rest of the "dirty dozen" were issued helmets, gas masks, mess kits, and canteens and dispatched to Evac No. 5 in a town along the River Marne, closer to the front. From there, they headed straight into the horror of the first "modern" war.

Laura's unit totaled about one thousand beds and received casualties directly from the trenches. Each operating tent had ten surgery tables in use around the clock. At full capacity, the hospital had about forty-eight nurses, each handling twenty patients.

Nothing in their training had prepared them for the kind of nursing they had to do. The use of poisonous gases—mustard gas, chlorine, phosgene, and other toxic aerosols—had increased toward the war's end. The soldiers arrived on stretchers, their skin horribly blistered and gangrenous, the smell of the gas still coming off their bodies. "I sometimes got a whiff of the miserable stuff," she said.

Medical staff worked frantically to save what was left of the men's bodies, but the damage was frequently too great. Double amputations were common. Many soldiers died on the operating table. Sometimes they arrived, scared yet hopeful, their young faces untouched. Nurses cut away their uniforms only to find the men had nearly been shot in two. They could do little more than hold their hands as they died.

I knew none of this when Christopher was born. Back then, I was afraid to tell my grandmother about his medical condition, let alone that her first great-grandchild might not survive. It was the one phone call I nearly couldn't bring myself to make. I'd wanted his birth to be a proud and joyful moment for her. After he was born, I was afraid the stress of the news might bring on a heart attack or worse.

When I finally did call, she listened calmly, then resumed knitting him a sweater. I could hear the needles clacking over the phone. Later, when she learned Christopher was deaf, she gamely picked up sign language in her nineties. Though her arthritic hands could barely make the shapes, they communicated her love nonetheless. I had often puzzled over her stoicism. Now I understood where it had come from.

DURING THE BITTER COLD fall of 1918, rain was as relentless as the shelling on the western front. Conditions for the nurses were primitive at best. They pitched their camps in fields filled with viscous, sucking mud.

"When the wounded began to come in, the stretchers were laid on the ground and the corpsmen stripped them of their muddy clothes and deloused them, usually before we received them in the operating tent," she wrote, adding, "I did find one cootie on me once." The nurses worked in perpetual chill and damp, layering men's socks and underwear under their uniforms for warmth. They slept on the ground or on cots in their tents with little more than blankets. The sleeping bags they'd packed at the base hospital didn't catch up to them until just before the armistice.

She described the conditions in her letters home:

Trying to sleep here is terrible . . . and the flies are awful. You have no concept of French flies. We have to wear gauze over our face to keep them from biting. . . . The mud is the worst thing we have to contend with. The blankets on the cots hang over into it and then they get all wet and so dirty you dread to put them on the patient. Then the pillows and cots get wet through the tent. Believe me, it's some mess.

She tried to make light of it for her parents' sake:

I asked one of the French boys why [other soldiers] called [the French ones] frogs. He said, "Why not? It is so muddy here and it rains all the time." You don't have to mind being dirty over here, it is quite the thing, and if you wash too much you are considered odd.

They worked eight hours on and eight hours off, around the clock, sometimes subsisting on little more than beans and hardtack. Time off was fleeting.

I had the afternoon off today for the first time. With so much time on my hands I didn't know what to do so I slept till supper time. Then tonight we went out to get water in our canteens and took a little walk. . . . The moon looked so pretty tonight shining on the ruins.

She wrote home about some of her patients, too.

Margaret and I became very fond of one of our patients and kept him several days, trying to get him to talk. He was only about eighteen years old and had a bullet hole right in the middle of his forehead. All he could say was "glass," but he wasn't paralyzed. When he wanted something, we would keep asking him until we hit the right thing and he would nod his head. One day, Margaret sang "Over There" to him, and he followed along saying all the words. That was a great day for us. When he was evacuated, we went to the train with him and sat by his litter until the train pulled out.

Shells and poison gas weren't the only things costing lives along the front lines. There was another, stealthier killer at work. Flu struck down soldiers and nurses alike. More than four hundred nurses died in the line of duty, most from Spanish influenza, a virulent strain that swept the world in 1918 and 1919, killing at least fifty million people worldwide.

My grandmother fell sick with the flu immediately after the Meuse-Argonne offensive, one of the war's decisive battles. She spent several days in a coma. "I came to one day and found myself in a regular hospital bed in a little tent all by myself," she wrote in her memoir. "I hadn't seen a bed before, as all our patients were put on army cots when they came in and that's what we slept on, too. The head nurse took care of me and I'm sure she saved my life."

The nurses were also fighting a battle on a different front. Nurses were barely recognized, either at home or in the war zone. After receiving a letter from her parents with news that her town was displaying a flag for the nurses, she wrote back:

> I'm glad someone appreciates the nurses. The patients are the only ones here that do. We just have to fight for our very existence here.

When the army passed out tickets to receive donated Christmas packages from America, they skipped the nurses:

> Don't worry about our Christmas, no one over here worries about us, so why should you? We weren't given any cards or tickets or anything else, so we are just out of luck. S.O.L. they say in the army. When I get back, you won't understand my language, not because it is French or German either.

Humor helped the nurses survive. The hospitals followed the line of battle, moving camp by train. During one transport, she wrote:

> We were fortunate to have a toilet on board, but the men stopped along the way at different sidings. One of our nice doctors was caught with his pants down when the train started up unexpectedly. He really got an ovation from the crowd as he scrambled aboard clutching his clothes. We made fun out of every little incident and were hilarious at times.

Letters helped, too—especially from her lieutenant friend.

Had a letter from Pete. He may be in the next town for all I know. He censors his own mail but is a very good soldier and wouldn't say a thing that wasn't right. Some people at home think that your mail coming this way is opened, but it isn't ever. . . . Margaret Cooper got a letter from one of the girls at the base today. It surely must be a wonderful place, but we are satisfied with this wild and woolly life until the snow flies at least. . . . Our tent is pitched on a kind of a hill and even though I have my cot propped up, my head is usually lower than my feet, and sometimes I wake up and find the bunk has sort of skidded during the night and my head is outside, with the flap of the tent forming a bib. Oh, it's a great life if you don't weaken.

The bravado was for her parents' sake. Although the nurses were several miles from the front, they were still at risk. They learned to tell the difference between the sound of a German Fokker plane and the drone of the Allied ones, jumping for cover even before alarms sounded.

They sang to keep their courage up. After pitching tents near Ypres, she wrote:

The boys found three pianos while they were searching the dugouts. They say some of the dugouts the Germans had were carpeted. Last night they brought one of the pianos back to camp and put it up in the Red Cross hut. Someone was clever enough to tune it and a lot of the boys can play, so we had quite a concert.

The tent hospitals relocated frequently, often on twenty-four hours' notice, to where casualties were heaviest. They packed a dozen nurses to an ambulance and spaced their vehicles miles apart to prevent detection from planes overhead.

The devastation along our route was unbelievable. Houses just a pile of rubble, dead cows in the fields, bloated bodies of horses along the muddy roads where rats were scurrying out of the way. No one

at home has the faintest idea how they are getting killed here. I'm
sure no one realizes the suffering of the boys. It's their spirit that
affects me. I can watch them amputate a leg and dress a wound
that is open from the hip down, but when a boy tells you he is sorry
he lost his leg because it puts him out and he can't go back, well I
have to walk away.

Daily, the medical teams fixed men up only to send them out to be
shot to pieces again. At the same time, in the same tents, they worked to
save enemy prisoners—the same men Allied soldiers were trying to kill.

"At the end of my ward there were several wounded German prisoners, young towheaded, blue-eyed boys," she wrote in her memoir.
"A guard stood over them with a .45. Having American and German
patients together brought home the fact of how stupid any war is."

There were other absurdities.

"In 1918, blacks and whites were kept separate even when sick in
the hospital. White orderlies were supposed to give the personal care
to the men, but when one refused to give an enema to a black man, I
was so angry I put up a screen and took care of the patient myself. He
was very grateful and that was the only time I was ever thanked for
giving an enema."

Eight decades later, sitting together in the peace and quiet of her
patio, I asked her what was most different than she'd expected when
she'd enlisted. "The mud," she said. "And the blood."

The woman who had signed her early letters home "From your
soldier girl" and gaily referred to being "in the army now" had hardened
into a pragmatic realist and passionate pacifist. She would become a
lifelong believer in equal rights.

IF THE WAR BEGAN a personal transformation that defined the rest of
her life, it also began a transformation of women back home. After
more than fifty years of pressure from suffragists, it was partly the
women who served in WWI who finally prompted the government to
take action on the right to vote. In June 1919, less than a year after the

war ended, the US Senate passed the Nineteenth Amendment. Women were legally able to mark ballots for the first time in 1920. For Black women, though, the struggle to exercise voting rights would continue many more decades.

By breaking the military's gender barrier, the thirty-three thousand women who served in WWI spurred other social changes. By WWII, more than ten times that number joined the military, and at that war's end, thousands of them took up work in fields previously dominated by men.

But my grandmother couldn't have known back then—just as the war was ending—how it would affect her life or her country. She was simply excited to be coming home safely.

"About Nov. 7th, we began to hear rumors that the armistice was being planned. We didn't believe it, for we still heard the guns and the wounded were still coming in. Finally, one day, the 11th of November, everything became quiet about 11 A.M. and you wondered what was different," she wrote. "There wasn't a sound, for there were no birds to sing, or no cows to moo. We still couldn't believe it possible, as we had so many patients. A group of French trumpeters came in the afternoon and played for us, so that was the only celebration we had."

By the armistice, her unit had treated fifteen thousand casualties.

On November 14, 1918, she wrote her parents a last letter from the front:

Just think, no more camouflaged lights at night and no more bar-rage to listen to all night long. Above all, no more wounded men. I can't realize yet that this will be our last camping ground. This place we are in must have evacuated in 1914. The worst thing I saw was the ruins of an old stable. It was partitioned with stalls of slate and the whole building was made of brick. Only part of the four walls were in sight and in what was left of each stall was the skeleton of a poor old horse. There were ten that I could count. It must have been a pretty quick retreat. The countryside

we came through at Ypres was the worst I have seen yet. A new
track had been laid beside the old one, but all the debris was
still there. Iron rails bent and broken as if they had been made
of wood. Cars upside down just where they had landed during
the explosion, shell holes full of green water. One place where the
train stopped the boys discovered a dead German. His feet were
all they saw sticking out of a pile of bricks and box car or what
was left of it. Then as you looked as far as your eyes could see,
were just a few bare sticks that had been trees. It is some wasted
country. No matter what the allies ask now it will never make up
for what the people have lost.

It would be six more months before she got orders to go home.
With the war over, she traveled through Europe, spending time in
Monaco, the French Alps, and Paris. I have a favorite picture of her
from that time. She strikes a jaunty pose with a walking stick in the
Place de l'Opéra, wearing her uniform, a long wool coat nipped
at the waist, a brimmed hat, and black lace-up boots. She and her
friend Margaret had just spent nearly a month's wages on tickets to
see *Aida*, her first opera, and overstayed their leave to do it. "It was
well worth the bawling out we received," she said. In the photo, she
looks at the camera head-on and unflinching. It's how she'd learned
to view the world.

THOUGH THE SHELLING HAD stopped, the war continued to wound in
unexpected ways. While on leave in Nice, she bumped into a friend of
the first lieutenant she'd fallen in love with during training camp, the
man whose letters she'd read and reread when she was off duty. The
friend told her that Pete would arrive in the same city the next day.

She could barely contain her excitement as she headed to the train
to meet him. She recognized him right away, but even from a distance,
she sensed something seemed off. He'd lost weight and looked wan and
tired. She ran up to him, expecting to fall into his arms with a kiss.
Instead, he just nodded to her.

"We all got in a taxi and he saw that we got off at our hotel, then he went on to where the officers were staying," she wrote. Crushed that his feelings appeared to have changed, she sent the little service pin back to him by messenger the next day.

"I never saw him again," she said, sounding wistful even eighty years later. "But I'm sure he never forgot me. Every time he looked in the mirror, he would have seen that tooth."

When I asked if she knew what had happened to him in the war, she said she'd learned later that his best friend had been blown up beside him two days before the armistice. What she'd taken as rejection was likely shell shock.

On May 31, my grandmother at last boarded the steamship USS *Cap Finisterre*, bound for America.

"Coming into New York Harbor was unforgettable," she said. Even heartache couldn't dampen her exhilaration. The troops had strung toilet paper all over the ship like streamers on a cruise. Bands played. Tugboats and fireboats churned out to meet them. In a frenzy of excitement, she threw her blue straw hat at the Statue of Liberty.

She didn't know the celebration would be short-lived, that she was returning to a country not ready to hear her stories or those of the other women who served. She rode the train home to East Taunton, dressed in full uniform, her head high. No one said a word to her.

THE WAR INFLUENCED MY grandmother's outlook and actions for the rest of her life. "I decided I was done working with men," she said. She turned instead to the happier task of obstetrical nursing. Her nursing skills gave her a degree of economic independence still rare among women. Eager for more adventure, she struck out for San Francisco to visit her uncle, who was working as an engineer on the construction of the Golden Gate Bridge. She found work at the children's hospital there. When it was time to go home, she tried to get a job on the Dollar Line as far as New York. "They said I would have to sign up for the trip around the world. Sometimes I wish I had taken that cruise."

But by that time—1925—she was engaged to a young shoe sales-man who had grown up in the town next to hers. They married that year. She was thirty-two, relatively old for that era. Eventually, they had two children—the second, my father, when she was forty. They lived first in Minneapolis, then migrated in 1939 to Seattle, where my grandfather, a traveling salesman, sold shoes to stores in his territory, including Nordstrom, which began as a single shoe store in Seattle in 1901. My grandfather was frequently on the road. My grandmother lived a life not unlike a modern single mother, not unlike my own had been, filling many roles and fending for herself, a job the war had taught her well.

The war left other marks on her life, too.

She went to the battlefields two years before women got the vote. When she returned, she voted in every election she could until she was 103. Her patriotism, while not showy, ran deep. She said the experience of not being noticed or acknowledged on that last train home from her deployment was the most "forlorn and depressing of her life." She said it gave her empathy years later for the Vietnam veterans who came home to a hostile America. She would have members of the military over for dinner on holidays and she always put out the flag.

But perhaps the most enduring mark of my grandmother's experience in WWI was her lifelong recoil at the mention of war. The few times she heard dinner-table talk of battlefield exploits, she quickly stopped it.

"I've seen it," she would say when war talk came up. "That's why I'm a pacifist. I was there."

MY GRANDMOTHER DIED ON November 18, 1998, eighty years and one week after the Great War ended and two months after her story ran in the *Seattle Post-Intelligencer*. She lived long enough to read hundreds of letters and messages that came into the paper after the story ran—letters of gratitude for her service, letters by others sharing their own families' experiences with the war. They came from nurses and veterans, from teachers and history buffs, from callers who sounded very old and very young. One said, "This story is like *Titanic* meets *Saving Private Ryan*."

A few months after my grandmother died, First Lady Hillary Clinton, who was unaware of her death, sent her a personal letter. In it, she wrote, "I salute your courage, your commitment, your generosity, and your undaunted spirit. You are an inspiration to all of us, but especially to women today who can look to your work as an example of the contributions that strong women have made and continue to make to our country."

My grandmother was a lifelong Republican but would no doubt have been pleased nonetheless.

In April 1999, the French government posthumously awarded her the French Legion of Honor medal for her service. I went to the Consulate General of France in San Francisco with my parents and my aunt and uncle to accept it on her behalf. I don't recall the words the consul spoke, but I do recall the feel of the medal he laid in our hands, cool and heavy with its red ribbon and green-and-white enameled French cross. It was the first time I'd held a medal of hers. I thought back to the little box of them that had hung on her wall during my childhood. At last, I truly understood what they represented.

Three months later, on what would have been her 106th birthday, our family gathered at her grave on the other side of the memorial park from Christopher's. She had lived nearly a century longer than he had, seen Halley's Comet come and go twice, but it consoled me to know they were resting there together. She had been one of Christopher's favorite people. She'd let him ride in her motorized wheelchair, zooming to the dining room with him in her lap, her big hand cupped over his on the controls. One day when we went to visit, he spied the chair in the hall where she kept it parked. As soon as we entered her apartment, Christopher went into a flurry of signing, pointing from my grandmother to the door. "Please, please," he signed. "Open. Bicycle chair."

My uncle Emil, who had been a flight engineer, took him out "to look at it," and soon there was a commotion in the hallway. I peeked out to discover Christopher "driving" the chair himself with Emil running alongside. They were laughing so hard that Christopher had steered into a wall.

At the cemetery, my grandmother's two surviving great-grandchildren placed small American flags by her marker. They played ball while the rest of us stood in a semicircle under a shade tree and shared our stories. My father spoke of her love for animals and the church, how she would have seen the day as a joyous one to have us all together.

My cousin Steve spoke about the sense of wonder he felt whenever he entered her old garage workshop and about the heirloom he valued most. "Some people get the silver and the china," he said. "I got her hammer." The wood was worn and dark from many years of handling. It was studded with paint and chips of terra-cotta, having bashed up clay, among its many uses.

I remembered the garage, too—cool and mysterious with its assortment of junk and art projects. But it was the china cabinet she kept with her to the end I remembered most. When I was an age most children wouldn't have been allowed to look inside, she'd let me play with its delicate contents—pressed glass goblets turned purple from the sun, a ceramic bride doll she'd made of my aunt in her wedding dress, her prized Hummel figurines.

Later, when I was in college, my grandmother sent me a Chinese plate with intricate fretwork that I'd remembered seeing in the cabinet. There was some story behind the plate that I never knew. It had been broken into many pieces, and she had glued all the fretwork back together. The yellowed glue made a pattern like lace. The plate was how she looked at life: The art of life was in the mending—broken dreams, broken promises, broken bodies. You repaired what you could. You went forward, and your plate could still be full.

TWO YEARS AFTER MY grandmother died, my father and I went to France to tour where she'd served. We retraced the path her mobile medical unit had taken, driving through pastoral fields, past stone churches and small villages. Except for the cemeteries dotting the landscape, there was little to indicate the massive, bloody violence that had taken place there. We went during early spring and occasionally we'd see faint traces of the old trenches in farmers' fields. They surfaced as chalk lines, tilled up from the deep limestone layer where the trenches once carved into the earth. In the same way, her service had left its traces on us.

Though she had rarely spoken of the war, it had spoken through her. She'd encouraged us—her children and grandchildren—to follow our hearts, use our hands, and speak our minds, three things that had guided her own life. For me, use your hands translated into make yourself useful, whatever form that took, whether planting a garden, knitting a sweater, or tutoring a child. Follow your heart and speak your mind led me to journalism, and journalism gave me a sense of purpose. It let me give a voice to others, not just myself. And it let me be a witness, the way she had been a witness.

She'd told me once not to let fear rule my life, that we become what we're afraid of becoming. I puzzled over that for a long time, until I realized that if I let fear define me, then what I feared would come to pass. If I was afraid that I'd never love again but did nothing to confront that fear, I would not have love in my life. If I was afraid I would not find meaning after Christopher's death and did nothing to seek it, then I would consign myself to a life without a calling.

The thing I'd feared most after Christopher's death was losing my memories of him. I'd wedged them down so far in my efforts not to feel pain that I worried they'd be gone forever, and him with them. My grandmother helped me see we never really forget. Though she had not spoken of the war for eighty years, she could still recall it in vivid detail. The memories embed somewhere until they're needed. Until it's time to tell the story.

And when the time came to tell Christopher's story, I found him again.

CHAPTER 20

My grandmother showed me one more thing. I had tried to track down her lieutenant, curious to hear what he might remember about my grandmother, but I couldn't find him. Years later, my aunt told me my grandmother had burned her one picture of him when she turned one hundred years old.

It takes as long as it takes to let go.

VIII.

YELLOW WHISPERING BELLS

(CHRISTOPHER)

CHAPTER 21

For more than twenty years, Christopher's ashes sat in a brown cardboard carton, tucked into a bureau drawer at my parents' house. My mom held them for safekeeping when I returned to California after Christopher's memorial service. It comforted me to know they were with her. Even after I moved back, though, I could not face the disposition of his remains, could not let go of the physical elements of him, the carbon and bone. I knew he was not there. He was nowhere, and everywhere. I could not stop searching for him.

I'd see him in small boys at the park and on empty swings. I'd see him on the seat next to me on the plane. Then I'd blink, and he'd be gone. I searched for him in the faces of older boys, then young men, who were the ages he would have been, looking for traces of him in the way they laughed, the way their eyes sparkled, a certain posture of defiance.

His things were still in boxes as well. I clung to them for fear of throwing away the one thing I'd later regret. The boxes moved with me, unopened, from place to place as I downsized my life. Eventually, even my rented storage unit had to go.

I dragged the boxes home to unpack. Soon my floor was strewn with crumpled paper, books, and toys, an excavation of our life together. The living room filled with the moldering smell of decaying cardboard, and my hands grew smudged and dry from inky newsprint, an old familiar feeling from mornings at the newspaper. Though it was afternoon, I'd shuttered my blinds. I sorted alone, in silence, piling things to give away and things to keep. I worked quickly, fearing if I didn't, I'd haul it all back to storage and let the record of our life sink again under another layer of time. Some boxes were easier to dispatch, the items drained of their charge of memory. A long white box I'd left for last lay in the middle of the room.

When I could avoid it no longer, I picked the box up and cradled it on my lap in the dim light. I ran my hands across its yellowing tape. "Christopher's baby box," I'd written along the top in black marker. I didn't recognize my own hand, my letters back then looping and hopeful, before decades of typing had turned my handwriting to a scrawl. I took a pair of scissors, flared the blades, and made a quick incision, the way I'd watched surgeons do. The box fell open. My breath caught. There was the knit hat with the reindeer on it he'd worn to make his first snow angel, his little red cowboy hat, the ivory fisherman sweater my grandmother had knit him, his soft square elephant that had gone back and forth with him to the hospital during his first year. I picked up a pair of socks with sailboats on them and held them to my nose, searching for his little-boy scent. I stood and curled them in my fist, squeezing to try to feel the shape of his foot. They were so light. I nearly staggered under their specific gravity. *What is the word for the weight of absence?*

The tears I'd been holding back all afternoon—or perhaps for decades—started, softly at first, and then with the force of a river pouring through a crack in a rock. I clutched each item to my chest to dampen the drumming of my heart, before placing it in the middle of the room with his other things.

My grandmother used to say, "Three moves are as good as a fire." She'd mention it whenever I complained about packing for yet another move. I'd always assumed she meant that moving helps get rid of the debris that accretes to our lives as we go along. Later, I understood that it was more than that. I'd run across an article once that described how a compound in sage smoke causes the germination of a scrub herb called yellow whispering bells.

Yellow whispering bells. That something so delicate could result from something as violent as a fire seemed somehow absurd. Like hope. Yet that was what my grandmother had been trying to tell me: Three moves are as good as a fire, not for destroying things, but for making things grow. The thought centered me and calmed my breathing. I settled back into a rhythm. Christopher's Mickey Mouse alarm clock and the plastic pilot wings from our many flights up and down the West Coast went into a box to donate, along with a pair of blue sandals he wore to the beach and his windup toys.

There were boxes of photos and crates of files, too, untouched since I'd put them in storage. One read: "Christopher, final."

Inside was a manila envelope I didn't recognize. I pulled it out.

The return address was "Pomerado Hospital, Poway, CA Health Information Management Services." The envelope was postmarked two and a half years after he died.

My hands shook as I opened it and pulled out a stapled report: "County of San Diego, Medical Examiner." My stomach twisted. I'd requested, but never read, the autopsy report, unable to face the facts of his death the way I'd faced the medical details of his life. I'd never spoken with the last doctor who saw him. I didn't want to know the specifics of the final labs, the final blood tests, as though by denying them, I could in some small way keep the hope of him alive.

WE'D HAD NO WARNING anything was wrong. The medical marathon of the previous years had at last started to recede. I'd begun purging my fears for his health—what would happen if his body rejected the donated kidney, if his diabetes worsened, if we could no longer control his seizures—replacing them with more mundane concerns. Was his reading progressing well enough? Was he getting enough chances to play with friends? I lived in a bubble of hope for the first time in a long time.

The morning of New Year's Eve began like any regular lazy Saturday. I lounged in my robe on the old blue couch I'd hauled from Seattle to LA, a security blanket after my divorce. The couch had been my first "grown-up" furniture, a remnant of the Martha Stewart life I'd tried to construct as a newlywed, the same one where I'd first realized Christopher and I had bonded despite his perilous start in life. The house was unusually quiet, and I was taking advantage of the peace to write belated Christmas cards. Jim was in the other room watching football. Christopher had gone with Frank the day before to visit his grandparents two hours to the south. He wasn't supposed to be there, but we'd had an unanticipated surgical reprieve. The previous year, Christopher had broken his leg tumbling out of his wheelchair while visiting his father. His leg hadn't healed straight. It was the least of our concerns at the time. He'd been doing so well since, and with his transplant behind us, we started to think about fixing it. His doctors had been planning elective surgery to reset the bone. Frank had flown down from Seattle a few days earlier to be there for the surgery and to visit his parents, who lived near San Diego. At the last moment, though, Christopher's doctors canceled the surgery. Christopher had been coming down with a cold and, absent an emergency, it wasn't wise to operate. The hospital sent us home.

The unexpected downtime was a gift. On the way home with me, Christopher asked for ice cream. We stopped at our favorite Baskin-Robbins in Pasadena and each got a cone to share. Vanilla for him, rocky road for me, a ritual I'd loved from my own childhood when my father would take the family for ice cream on special occasions. We sat on the grass and traded tastes, then headed up the street to the video store. He never tired of checking out the same Disney movies—*101 Dalmatians* and *The Lion King* were favorites. He would flourish his Video Row card when I'd hold him up to the counter to pay. The clerks, who all knew him, would laugh. We drove by a garage sale and stopped, something we often did together, me searching for finds for the antiques booth, him looking for treasure. That day, I loaded an old wicker writing desk into the back of my car. He insisted on hauling home a vintage Coca-Cola cooler.

"Red box, put toys, beautiful," he signed, swirling his hand in front of his face in approval.

With the surgery on hold, Frank had asked for some extra visitation time to take Christopher down to visit his folks. I figured it would be good for all of us. Christopher loved being with his dad and grand-parents, and the truth was I wanted the break. It would give me a chance to catch up on the bills and errands that never seemed to get done in the hubbub of caring for him.

Just before nine A.M., the phone rang. Frank's mother, Mary, was on the line. Her speech sounded garbled and pressured. I had to ask her to slow down. Christopher had fallen ill; his stomach hurt. He was on his way to Pomerado Hospital in Poway on the outskirts of San Diego, near where they lived. He was in an ambulance.

I tried to stay calm. Christopher had had more than a few ambulance rides in his life. It may have been new for his grandmother, but it was probably nothing. I hung up and immediately called Christopher's regular doctors to alert them so they could have him transferred to UCLA, where staff knew his complicated history. Jim came out of his office to see what was happening. I reached the renal doctor on call at UCLA and described what I knew about the situation, which wasn't much. She didn't seem too concerned—said she'd talked to Frank the day before and it sounded like a touch of the flu. After I hung up, I called the emergency room in Pomerado. They put me through to Frank.

"What's happening?" I asked.

"I don't know. They won't let me in," he said. He sounded bewildered and far away.

"Won't let you in where?" My voice started to shake. I'd assumed he would be able to assure me that the run to the hospital was only a precaution. That Christopher just had a bad stomachache and was already back to himself, probably entertaining the paramedics who'd brought him in.

"I'm in the ER," he said. "They're still working on him."

He couldn't tell me more. I hung up, truly alarmed for the first time. One of us was usually at Christopher's side, no matter what. Being kept outside the room signaled something different.

I paced the living room of our rented bungalow. The Christmas tree was still up. Christopher's presents lay beneath it—a vintage electric train we'd assembled together after scouring flea markets for its cars, the automatic pencil sharpener he'd asked for. A pack of pencils, some he'd already enthusiastically sharpened to stubs, lay beside it. I rolled a pencil in my fingers, like a prayer bead, and waited.

Dr. Robert Ettenger, his main pediatric nephrologist at UCLA, called a few minutes later. I again started talking about transferring him to UCLA. This time my own speech was pressured and garbled. There was a pause. He asked what I knew.

"Nothing more," I said. He gave me his home phone number and hung up quickly. Something in me started to panic. He'd never given me his home phone before. Later, I thought he must have already known something and didn't want to be the one to break the news. After minutes that seemed like hours, Frank called back.

I picked up the phone. I don't remember saying hello.

"Christopher died," he said. His words sounded so matter-of-fact, so disbelieving. So utterly inadequate to describe the shock wave that followed.

Between the not knowing and the knowing, a world vanishes. I screamed like someone falling off a cliff. I screamed like someone running from a train. I screamed like an animal being torn apart.

THE NEXT MINUTES AND hours have vanished from my memory, sucked into the gaping black hole of my life imploding. My journal tells me people began arriving. They brought food. They took over the mechanics of notifying people. My parents flew down from Seattle. Usually, when they'd arrive, Christopher would whoop and spring out to meet them. Now we sat in stunned silence and tried to think what to do next. I picked out clothes for Christopher. Frank arranged to accompany his body back to Seattle.

In the nightmarish days that followed, I became convinced he'd swallowed one of his hearing aid batteries—that somehow that was what had caused his death. I'd had a running battle to keep him from putting the batteries, the size of an M&M, in his mouth. He'd always had an odd attraction to metal objects. Years earlier, he'd swallowed a penny, which we'd discovered only later while he was getting X-rayed for an unrelated problem. I was sure that must have been what had happened. That it was my fault. *I'd killed him.* At night, my heart fibrillated wildly, rapid and random, like a rabbit darting this way and that in the shadow of a wolf.

Nothing seemed real. For days, I stood outside our little bungalow and waited for the school bus to come down the street. If his bus would come, it wouldn't be true. Christopher would kiss me and run toward the bus with his Batman lunch box, on his way to his "big school." I'd follow him up the steps of the bus and check his seat belt, remind him through the window to put his homework on the table for his teachers, Mrs. Parker ("Mrs. P") and Mrs. Lambert ("Mrs. L"). The bus driver would wave and the doors would exhale shut. Christopher was always looking when I signed "I love you" as the bus pulled away. Then he'd be off in a sweet rush to his own big world with big things to do.

The bus never came.

Doctors said there was no way they could have known, nothing anyone could have done to prevent the abdominal blockage that killed him. They seemed as shocked as we were. Their empty words of explanation offered no comfort.

The what-ifs would torture me for years. I second-guessed my decision to let him go that weekend. If his own doctors had known sooner, perhaps they could have saved him. I could not forgive myself for my final failure.

I wasn't there to say goodbye.

I LOOKED DOWN AT the medical examiner's report in my lap and at the remains of Christopher's life, now spread around my living room floor. The room had grown darker as the sun faded toward evening. I lit a lamp and forced myself to read the autopsy report:

> **Cause of Death**: *Strangulated small bowel.*
> **Due to**: *Congenital mesenteric band.*
> **Manner of Death**: *Natural.*

Congenital. All these years, I'd thought of the abdominal blockage as yet another consequence of his original birth defect—the obstructed urinary tract that had led to the grim procession of complications he'd experienced since his birth, each one triggered by the one before.

The report laid out a different story: Christopher was born with the medical condition that killed him. Another tiny developmental glitch, unrelated to the first, laid down long ago and previously undetected, had arisen and declared itself. Our seven years together had been a borrowed gift.

The report proceeded in meticulous detail, noting the exact locations of the scars from his various surgeries. His body, his medical record.

His lashes and eyebrows were noted as "unremarkable," as were his brown hair and brown eyes. *It's not true*, I wanted to shout at the medical examiner. How could he not know just how remarkable they were—how those eyebrows, dark and dancing, conveyed as much about his state of mind as any sign language. How I used to joke with my friends that such long, dark lashes would one day make girls swoon. How much I missed running my hand through his silky hair, feeling the fine shape of his head beneath.

The report continued, a clinical dissection:

Cardiovascular System: The empty heart weighs 130g. . . .

So small. So specific. The weight of a T-ball, of fifty cents in pennies. My empty heart, heavier beyond measure.

I felt dizzy. My hands were trembling so hard I could barely turn the pages to close the report. Stapled to the front was a xeroxed copy labeled "Emergency Department Note":

Chief Complaint: Cardiac Arrest.
On arrival, the patient is unresponsive . . . asystole on the heart monitor.

I read the line again, stunned. It meant his heart had been flatlined when medics loaded him into the ambulance. Flatlined when he rolled into the ER and the frantic team began the code. Flatlined the whole time I was on the phone with his doctors at UCLA, trying to find a way to get him transferred home. Above his signature, the attending physician noted:

*At 9:26 a.m. after 20 more minutes, the patient still remained in
asystole, and I felt that progressing would be futile, and the code
was called at that point in time.*

As I read the words, a strange thing happened. A sudden, unexpected
relief flooded through me. Christopher had been gone from his body
even before he'd arrived at the hospital. He would not have known if
I were there to hold his hand and stroke his face, to press him to my
heart to calm his fears and mine. He would not have been comforted
by my presence.

I could not have said goodbye.

And I realized something else, something it had taken me more
than two decades to understand. The fact that I wasn't there to say
goodbye to him wasn't what I needed to resolve. It was that I didn't
want to say goodbye. If I did, he would be gone forever, something I
feared I could not survive.

I folded the report and put it back in the file. Put the rest of the
items I'd sorted into bags.

I saved a few things—the letters his classmates had written me, his
favorite red sweater, and a Buzzy Bee pull toy he used to drag down the
street behind him, its antennas waving and yellow wings spinning so
furiously it made strangers stop and smile. The rest I took to Goodwill.
I imagined another child might like to have them.

That night, for the first time in many years, I dreamed of Christopher. I surfaced in that moment between sleep and waking to feel the
weight of his little body against my breast, his cheek pressed against my
vocal cords, the way he sometimes did when I sang to him. He would
nestle there, feeling the vibrations like hummingbird wings. He felt so
real, warm and heavy. Scientists say mothers carry the cells of their
babies in their bodies for years. Perhaps his cells were the seeds of my
dreams. It made me happy. I struggled to stay under. As the day dawned
and the dream dissipated, the feeling lingered. I felt him with me.

CHAPTER 22

There is something called complicated grief, or in clinical terms, persistent complex bereavement disorder. It's when you cannot accept a death. When you cannot resume your own living after a "normal" period of sorrow. I don't know whether a clinician would apply the term to me. I do know this. After Christopher's death, I lived in fear. I was afraid of forgetting who Christopher was, of letting go of him. Afraid I had failed him in his life and death, that I hadn't been there to say goodbye. I lived warily, avoiding entanglements of all kinds, especially relationships, especially children. I dissociated from my own life, living in an orbit that let me slide frictionless through my days, interacting only with my small circle of close friends, who were exceedingly patient with me.

Not long after I'd met him, my friend Mike, the cave diver, invited me along to scout a stretch on the South Fork of the Snoqualmie River called "Fall in the Wall"—a waterfall stair step of linked drops on a pass in the Cascades, an hour east of Seattle. By then, his new passion was white-water kayaking and he planned to run the stretch in the spring. It was winter then, though, so I bundled up and hopped in his car, excited to be outside. Halfway to the pass, I asked him, "What if the trail is snowed in?"

"What trail?" He laughed.

We plunged through hip-high snowdrifts toward the banks of the river. I ducked under the trees, shaking down whole boughs of snow. The air sparkled and glistened. We found the river by the music of a trickle of water playing over frozen falls. I realized I hadn't needed a trail to arrive in a new place.

Mike loved exploring remote spots, the less mapped the better, and took me along when he could. "Hikes with Mike," I called them. Sometimes the excursions ended in tears—mine—after particularly nerve-racking drives up steep canyons, or when we went too far into the woods. He walked me to the edge of my comfort zone over and over until I started to feel more confident in my own sense of direction.

One day, he put me in a kayak on a river. He paddled his own boat backward, facing me, as we shot down the Powerhouse stretch of the lower Snoqualmie River, a popular spot for beginners.

"Paddle, paddle," he shouted at me. But instead of digging into the water, my paddle flailed in the air. One of the edges of my boat caught, and I swerved into a train of small whitecaps. The waves galloped under the shell of my kayak. Ahead of me, a large rock loomed out of the water. I threw my hands up to protect myself. Mike paddled hard upstream toward me, but it was too late. I flipped upside down, trapped in the boat by the neoprene skirt that covered the cockpit to keep the water out. Suddenly, there was only churning green light and the low rumbling white noise of water strafing rocks along the riverbed as the current dragged me downstream. Time slowed. I swallowed what felt like the whole river. I couldn't remember how to eject underwater. My paddle was gone.

Then, just as suddenly, someone yanked my head up by the neck of my dry suit. I gulped a giant breath of air. Mike pulled me toward his boat, mine still upside down, until my cheek rested on his bow, our two kayaks knocking side by side.

"Now use your hips," he said. He was extremely calm. I could barely hear him over the rushing river and my pounding heart. I snapped my hips hard, the way he'd shown me on land, and my kayak righted. I clung to his boat the rest of the run until we eddied out near shore. Late afternoon light pooled on the river. The sky pinked up like the flank of a rainbow trout. I felt the pull of the river. I wanted to go again.

That spring, as the glaciers melted, Mike taught me how to read water and run a river, how to find the "green V," a tongue of smooth water that marked the way through the chaos of the flow. He taught me how to avoid the churn of "holes," created by water pouring over hidden rocks, and that the way to escape a hole was not to try to claw toward the surface, but to sink to the bottom of the river and let the slower water there carry you to safety.

On sunny days, I'd scoot off the bank of the river in my kayak, carve across the eddy line, and let the current catch me. It felt like banking into a turn, like flying, that moment when you stop resisting and let go. I learned to roll up to keep from drowning.

AFTER THAT, I LEARNED to dance, throwing myself first into the Latin rhythms of salsa and eventually sinking into the Argentine tango. In tango, I learned to lean on other people, to let them lean on me. The dance reconnected me to my body, then to a partner, and eventually to the closeness of a new community of friends.

I learned to sail, seeking wind in the San Juan Islands of my home state, in the Whitsundays near the Great Barrier Reef, and in the Ionian Sea off the coast of Greece. I navigated by line of sight, which suited my new life. I let the wind carry me close to joy.

One night, I lay on the bow deck of a sloop in the Whitsunday Islands and gazed at the Southern Cross above me. My friend Jim Erickson and I were at anchor, and the boat drifted in slow circles with the night breeze.

How many stars? I thought of Christopher's long-ago question. I could feel him jumping into my arms.

Astronomers say you cannot find a star in the sky by looking straight at it. You must instead search with your peripheral vision. The anatomy of the eye is more sensitive to starlight at the edges of the retina. We can be looking directly at something and not see it yet find it when we look away. I had found Christopher after all. He was still there, in my heart. He had never left. I did not have to say goodbye.

I HAD A COUNSELOR who used to ask me periodically, "What's the worst that can happen? If you can imagine it, you can imagine how you will survive." She likened grief to being swept down a river. "Every so often, you wash up on the bank, where you can get a breath. Knowing you've made it to the bank before means you can again."

The people I met through my reporting at the paper helped get me to the bank of the river. I had to take this journey through stories, had to report out my own life by interviewing people who were going through something hard of their own. Their stories let me put my experience into words, the words I couldn't find in the beginning.

Psychologists have a theory about trauma. People unconsciously reenact the trauma in different ways throughout their lives in order to master it. Sometimes the reenactments take the form of disturbing dreams. Sometimes they manifest as behavior patterns. People try to repeat relationships or situations that echo the trauma. They may be aware of what they're doing. Often they are not. The reenactment is how the brain processes repressed trauma. Many years after the fact, I realized that writing about these people for the *P-I* was my way of reenacting. I was, in essence, telling the same story over and over again, looking for a different ending.

I had an elderly neighbor once, named George, who lived across the street from us in Pasadena. We used to chat each morning when he'd set out on his daily walk, with a sandwich tied in a bandana on a stick he carried over his shoulder. He'd long since retired from Caltech and often pestered me for projects he could do to help me around the house. I once had to shoo him off my roof, where he was bent on nailing down some loose shingles, even though I'd told him I didn't want him up there for fear he'd fall. He was in his eighties.

One day he said to me, "Sometimes people come into your life as though out of the fog. They step out of the fog for a while, and then they disappear again." It was true of him. It was true of so many of the people who crossed my path in my reporting.

We are all somebody else's marker along the way. Recently, I spoke with my friend Kathy Ruccione, the nurse who had gone to Christopher's class all those years ago to help break the news of his death. I was fact-checking some details of that day. She mentioned that her son, Daniel, still remembers exactly where he was sitting and what the weather was the morning she told him Christopher, his best friend, had died. Christopher was a piece of his story.

Seth and Billy, John and Rose, Shali and Gerri, Darbi and my grandmother—each became a piece of my own story. They'd shown me how to be brave, and also that it was all right not to be. They'd shown me how to find balance, how to move forward, how to make peace with what we don't control, that sadness does not mean the end of joy.

There are many kinds of strength. What survives a fire is different from what survives a flood. When Christopher was little, he loved playing "rock, paper, scissors," exclaiming when his hand trumped mine. It was just a game to him. To me, it was a reminder of all the different ways materials are strong. Paper can bear surprising load weight, but its shear strength is no match for scissors. The compression strength of granite can overcome the tensile strength of steel. My reporting showed me that people, too, bring different kinds of strength to their situations. Seth brought his acceptance of his future; Shali, his discipline; Gerri, her gratitude. They'd helped me find my own.

And I'd discovered a bit of Christopher in each of them, his enthusiasm for life in Seth, his stubbornness in Rose, his sense of humor in Shali, his acceptance of himself in Billy and John. In telling the stories of these people, I discovered they were also mine. They lifted me out of the particulars of my specific grief. Loss, the need to reinvent and redirect, to honor and survive, is a universal story. Their stories are all our stories.

They'd reminded me, too, that we all die in the end, no matter how good we get at coping with what's thrown our way. The prize is not cheating death, or avoiding loss, because none of us get to do that. Detaching from life is no guarantee of safety. The antidote to fear is living the moments we have the best way we know how. Christopher had taught me that.

One day, we were out walking in our old part of Pasadena, a neighborhood called "Bungalow Heaven" for its oak-lined streets and Craftsman homes. We pulled a red wagon behind us, for him to ride in if he got tired, and made a game of naming things as we walked.

"Cat," he signed, making whiskers when he spotted one on a neighbor's deeply gabled front porch.

"Bicycle," I signed back, rotating my fists like pedals and pointing to where one lay on the lawn of the next house over.

"Cat bicycle, go playground," he signed.

"Cat swing, cat slide, cat chase dog," I signed back, making him laugh.

He pointed to our shadows, lengthening along the bumpy sidewalk.

"Word?" he asked in sign, pushing the thumb and index of his left hand against the side of his right index and looking up at me. I ratcheted through possibilities in my brain, coming up empty. He giggled at having stumped me, then made the signs for "sun" and "picture."

Sun picture. That was how he looked at the world. Where others saw darkness, he saw light.

THE YEARS SINCE CHRISTOPHER died have been marked with many anniversaries. There are the obvious ones—dates of birth and death. The less obvious ones have been harder. There was the day at the Department of Motor Vehicles when I realized he could have been one of the fuzzy-faced boys coming out with their learner's permits. There was the year many of my friends' children left for college and the year Barbara's daughter, the one born a week after Christopher, had a baby of her own.

Your children grow older with you, even in imagination. I watched the kids I knew maturing, the girls growing curvy and graceful, the boys, strong and deep-voiced. They rented first apartments. Picked first loves. Endured first heartbreaks. Needed their parents less and less.

I realized I, too, had a mother's task left to do—letting go of the boy Christopher was and the young man I wished he had become.

On February 10, his birthday, I will take Christopher's ashes from my parents' house. I will drive over Stevens Pass to a spot near Icicle Creek where we liked to go when he was little, where we'd sit on the bank of the river in bright sunlight and watch the white curls of the rapids, furling and unfurling against the rocks.

There's a bridge nearby where the water slips slowly under. I used to carry him there, against my chest. We would lean over together to watch the wind throw its net of ripples on the water.

I will go back there to that bridge and stand over the middle of the river. I will hold Christopher's story in my heart and give his ashes to the wind.

EPILOGUE

One morning in early January 2009, I got a call to get to work as soon as possible. By the time I arrived, people were milling around the city desk, like bystanders clustered around the scene of an accident. An executive from the Hearst corporation took the mic and stepped into the middle of the ring, a police scanner murmuring behind him. We listened, arms folded and faces ashen, to his prepared speech. Our paper was going on the auction block. We had sixty days.

News folks are realists. We knew we had just been pronounced dead. Still, we reacted with the stunned disbelief of people who get a sudden call about a loved one. People hugged and huddled in small groups. We shuffled off in silence to start notifying relatives. We drank bourbon out of paper cups.

For many of us, the staff was like a large, not always functional extended family. We knew each other's backstories and idiosyncrasies, knew who had phoned for a paycheck advance from Las Vegas, who was trying to have a baby, and who was having an affair. Life inside the city room was as full of daily drama as the life we documented outside it. We held each other up through cancers, deaths, divorces. We bickered bitterly, the way siblings do, over perceived favoritism—who got more time or inches for a story. But we stood together in a fight.

I'd grown up at the paper, felt privileged to have had a front-row seat to life unfolding. A quarter century later, I'd lived through my personal share of good news and bad, deaths and divorces, debilitating illnesses, my own and others'. My colleagues saw me through it all.

Over the next two months, we went about our daily duties while trying to ignore the countdown. The newsroom took on the air of a picked-over estate sale. We parted out equipment: battered paper boxes, filing cabinets, and dented pica poles. A giant shredder squatted in the middle of the newsroom, turning decades of notes into confetti. We took souvenir shots of ourselves under the famous spinning globe that had lit the night sky since the 1930s.

One day, the managing editor, David McCumber, glanced up mid–news meeting from the bullpen table, took off his glasses, and rubbed his eyes.

"What happened to the jungle?" he asked.

The other editors looked confused. It took me a few moments to realize he was referring to Upton Sinclair's famous muckraking book. A shadowboxed copy had hung above my desk in his line of vision for years.

Sixty-six days after learning our fate, I wrote the obit for the paper. It began:

> The Seattle Post-Intelligencer, *the region's pioneer newspaper and the city's oldest continually operating business, a newspaper that both shaped and was shaped by the community it covered, prints its last edition Tuesday—nearly a century and a half after its forebear first rolled off a hand-cranked Ramage press promising to be "the best and cheapest promulgator of all sorts of useful information."*

The paper had managed to get out even after its presses burned to the ground in the Great Seattle Fire of 1889, had endured through eleven moves and at least seventeen owners. It survived the newspaper wars of the nineteenth century, which one publisher once described as a time when newspapers "lived hard and died easy."

We used to affectionately call the *P-I* "the Daily Miracle." Now we were out of them.

Newsprint had been a central part of my life since childhood, when I'd helped my brother with his paper route. My mother, and her mother before her, diligently clipped the paper each morning for coupons and articles to send to friends and relatives. My father would settle in a chair after work and hold the paper up to read, a ritual we knew better than to disturb.

Journalism was a calling. Stories in the newspaper were what connected us to each other and to our community. Stories had seen me through my own worst times. Now the paper that had saved my life was winding down its own. Even as the newspaper folded, though, its stories lived on. They live on in the lives they changed. Like mine.

What sustains us, and what endures, are our stories.

I REMAIN GRATEFUL TO the people in this book, who shared their lives with me during extremely difficult circumstances. Their stories, of course, continued after our paths crossed. I recently caught up with as many as I could.

Since I wrote about him, General John Shalikashvili has passed away. His son, Brant, told me it had been a tremendously difficult journey for his father to recover from that first stroke, but that he gained enough ground to continue some of his speaking engagements and serve on several corporate boards. "My dad always fascinated me, because there was a steely resolve beneath that surface, yet as my dad I never felt like that resolve was a weapon, but a determination to do whatever it took to achieve what he believed in," Brant wrote in an email. "I always say he worked on the things he cared about until the week he died. He remained committed especially to Fisher House and the National Bureau of Asian Research, among others. With the help of his caregivers, he was able to continue to get out and about and visit with friends until he went into the hospital for the last time."

A second stroke claimed his father's life in 2011 at age seventy-five. Shali was buried with full military honors in Arlington National Cemetery. President Obama, quoted in the *New York Times*, said: "Shali's life was an 'only in America' story. By any measure, he made our country a safer and better place."

To Brant, though, he was a dad first. "He was a funny, kind and loving man that was always there when his son needed him. I miss him every single day."

JOHN SWANSON STILL RUNS a charter boat business, but he's added a few others along the way. He sold Christmas trees for fifteen years and bought a dump truck for another side business he still runs. He and Jamie added a third son to their family as well. They spend a lot of their time outdoors, camping and snowmobiling.

"Keeping up with three businesses and three boys has kept us busy and as of just recently has finally panned out that we can get away and enjoy a bit of travel," he wrote me. "It has been a long road and struggle to get to that point but makes it all that much more worth it when sitting on the beach with a margarita in hand."

He's got more time to read books now, too, something his schedule hadn't allowed until a few years ago. "The only time I actually get a chance to read is during the summer and I have since read a couple dozen books. Almost every one of which has been a true story and ironically, most of which have been about overcoming adversity in one way or another. Funny enough, that hasn't been intentional exactly, but I guess really, that's what makes a good story."

In a curious twist, John survived another harrowing incident: He was buried by an avalanche while snowmobiling. The video of his rescue went viral.

DARBI AND MIKE ALSO expanded their family.

"Our story has continued with the ups, downs and sideways of life," she wrote me. "Blake is in high school and is passionate about writing and producing music. I don't ever take for granted the miracle that he is." They went on to have one more biological son, Tyler, and adopted two girls from the foster system. The girls are two months apart in age. Almost twins. Darbi works for their school as a behavioral support person.

"I hope I can tell you the story of how they came to us," she wrote. "It is beautiful and heartbreaking."

I went down to Portland a few weeks later to meet her kids.

"It's been a minute," said Blake, shaking my hand. The baby I'd seen born had grown into a young man with a deep voice and sandy hair. As a kid, he would sometimes look in the mirror and imagine he was looking at his brother, Carter. One of his younger sisters brought down a WELCOME sign she'd made for me, and then the whole family settled around the fireplace to catch me up.

Darbi, as warm as I remembered her, recounted how they'd had a scare with her pregnancy with Tyler but were overjoyed when his birth went uneventfully. He's now nearly as tall as his brother.

"After that, though, we decided we were done with being pregnant," said Mike, who still works for the fire department. So they decided to adopt a foster child. They were excited to welcome their first placement, a baby girl, only to have her taken away a few months later when a distant family member stepped in. Darbi was crushed, but they pressed on with a second placement, another little girl.

"Then one day the caseworker called and said she had some news she needed to deliver in person," Darbi said. She prepared for what she was sure was going to be more bad news. When the woman from the agency arrived, it was to tell Darbi that their first foster baby was available again for adoption. She and Mike were thrilled. Their lives now are full and busy.

On my way out, two pinwheels caught my eye as they twirled in a small garden along their front path—one for Hope and one for Carter.

BILLY PREFACED HIS EMAIL to me with these words: "I'm getting married!" He spent much of his twenties traveling, or as he put it, "wandering, more or less." He worked as a kayak guide in the summers and at ski resorts in the winters, "living the dirtbag lifestyle." He also traveled in New Zealand and Australia for a year each, working as a fruit picker.

"Turning thirty was a pivotal year for me. I really began ironing out what I want to do with my life and have spent the last year working towards those goals." He has a job at a drug and alcohol inpatient center and volunteers with the Juneau fire department as a firefighter and EMT. "My ultimate goal is to work in some capacity as a teen advocate, helping young people find purpose and their voice at such a trying time in their lives." He and his fiancée are expecting their first child.

ROSE TRACKED ME DOWN herself a few years ago in search of a copy of the story to give to her friends.

"I'm doing great," she wrote. Two years after Aries's arrival, she and Alex had a little girl they named Alchemy, born on Halloween. "Aries is into computers and Alchemy is a ball of energy and so artistic."

She and Alex divorced, but he lives close by and she has a new love in her life now. She used part of her settlement from the accident to buy some land and a house north of Seattle. "I have been renting rooms out, so we have a full house, but I don't mind. Lots of people to talk to."

She remembered that I had told her once I had a son who had died. "I just wanted to say that I'm glad if writing the story about that year of my life helped you cope with anything you were going through," she wrote. "It really helped me to deal with some things as well. While you were doing it I was going through a lot of emotional issues as I'm sure you can imagine. But having you guys come around and talk to me kinda got me out of dark places and made me get out of bed and do things. When I read the full story even to this day it makes me tear up."

SETH DIED OF COMPLICATIONS from a heart attack three years after his story ran in the *P-I*. He was one month shy of his fourteenth birthday.

I'd braced for this day, but when it came, it still hit hard. Word spread quickly around the newsroom. Journalists in general are a stoic bunch. Bad news is an occupational hazard. But he was more than type on a page to my colleagues. Many who stopped by my desk that day to say they were sorry to see him go had tears in their eyes.

I sat quietly at my desk for a few minutes, absorbing the news, then went outside to sit on the *P-I*'s patio overlooking Elliott Bay. The day was bright and breezy. Sailboats crisscrossed the water. I leaned back and watched the globe spin slowly against the sky. Seth's world had gotten so big.

In the year after the *P-I* published his story, offers poured in from people who wanted to give Seth experiences. He flew in a stunt plane, even handling the controls, and was made an honorary sheriff's deputy, a lifelong goal of his. He got to visit ancient ruins in Mexico with his parents and travel to New York. He got a personal tour of the newsroom, shaking hands politely with the people who had helped make his story happen. He learned how to blow glass at my brother's studio nearby.

I was happy for that, and grateful I'd had a chance to know him. He had widened my world, too. I sat until I'd composed myself before going back in to call Patti. She told me that in the weeks before his death, Seth had been too weak to go on a planned camping trip. Instead, they'd spent time in the flower garden they'd made together. He planted a small rosebush, which they were watching bloom. I pictured them there with their hands in the dirt together, and thought of the Little Prince caring for his thorny rose, a small emissary to teach us how to love what we will necessarily lose.

Patti said something else as well. "So many people have added to the person he is—all the people he got to enjoy," she said. "They all have their little fingerprints on him, and he has his on them." I loved that image. It comforted me to think the same was true of Christopher.

I went to Seth's funeral to say goodbye. The entire town turned out to celebrate the life of the little boy they had loved. Afterward, they filled the high school gym with tables of food—every kind of casserole and barbecue imaginable. Mounds of desserts. He would have loved it. I could imagine him perched in the middle of the party, orchestrating games for the little ones, his plate filled with ambrosia. *I hit the jackpot.*

On the way back home that day, I thought about my time on the river with him. The anticipation of not knowing the outcome, the promise of the unseen, placing yourself in the realm of the possible and casting. This is what makes a life seem long in childhood. A few weeks after we'd gone fishing, he'd caught an eighteen-pound steelhead, his personal best. Then he'd released it.

ONE CRISP FALL DAY, twelve years after his death, I drove up to visit Seth's parents, who still live in the same house in Darrington. I turned up the little winding road through the woods to their house, and a small sign to the left caught my eye. SETH'S CREEK, it read. I smiled, thinking of how his spirit had infused this place. Patti came out of the house as I arrived and gave me a big hug. Kyle joined us a while later, muddy from working outside. We sat around their kitchen table and laughed and cried and traded stories. They'd just gotten back from Montana, where they'd taken Seth's cousin Tristan, who had just turned twenty-one, for his first hunting trip.

Every year, they gather their extended family for an annual camping trip on Seth's birthday. They play all the games he loved and hold a fishing derby in his honor. They still host a weekly Bible study as well. "Seth is with us all the time," Patti said. Kyle got up and retrieved a quilt he'd had made for Patti from Seth's favorite T-shirts. A friend had sewn the story of Seth's life into it. In the middle was a stitched outline of a drawing he'd made of the house he'd told his mom he was building for her in heaven. On the insides of their wrists, Patti and Kyle each have a small tattoo in Seth's handwriting that reads "Buddy," their pet name for him.

A couple of years after Seth died, they lost his little dog, Bullet. He got out one day and didn't come back. They think coyotes got him. "I didn't expect it to hit me so hard," Kyle said. "But that felt like this connection to him." It took a long time, but they have a new dog now, a sweet black lab that chose them. Its name, coincidentally, when they adopted it, was also Bullet. They figured Seth was looking out for them.

Patti still follows some of the progeria families, but the reunions no longer happen. The kids, though, are living longer—more often into their early twenties, she said, thanks to advances in treatments.

Seth's ashes are scattered in the woods where we had walked that day.

GERRI SURVIVED HER BREAST cancer. She and Bob are active with Physicians for Social Responsibility. For years now, they've been traveling to Gaza to help residents there. She still runs the moms group out of her living room every other Tuesday. I recently rejoined it and recognized some of the moms from years ago. Most of the faces, though, are new ones. This past October, I went again with the moms to the beach. I drove over the Coast Range, red maples dappling the light, and then hit the marshy flats on the beach side of the mountains in the late afternoon, the golden hour. A murmuration of starlings swirled up in front of me, making brushstrokes against the sky as exuberant as any of Christopher's kindergarten paintings. I passed a buttercup-yellow house set in a clearing, the color startling against the shadowy green backdrop of the forest. It was as though the house had concentrated all the available sunlight and released it at once, throwing it into the air like a handful of bright gold coins. "Sunshine house," I signed to myself, and smiled.

By the time I arrived at the beach house, it was dusk, and Gerri already had a pot of mushroom risotto simmering. During these weekends, she filled us with comfort food as though we were hungry children, which in a sense we were. We ate to the music of waves pounding outside the house.

After dinner, she passed out notebooks and asked us to write down two things: what we were grateful to our children for and how we were surviving. I wrote how Christopher's gift to me was a way of looking at the world through his eyes. I wrote how when I walked, I noticed little bits of beauty everywhere—the tinsel on an abandoned Christmas tree, a crack in a wall someone had filled with a tiny mosaic, the kinds of things he'd have noticed.

I wrote how Christopher had loved the day-to-day machinations of the household. He loved pushing buttons on the blender and putting birdseed in the feeders. He loved to water plants and vacuum. When I changed a light bulb, he'd point and whoop in wonder. He saw a world full of ordinary miracles.

Now, I do.

ACKNOWLEDGMENTS

To borrow a phrase from Patti Cook, so many people have had their little fingerprints all over this book. I want to first thank Jennifer Herrera of David Black Agency, who believed in this project from the start. You have my deepest gratitude, Jenny, for helping me find my voice and then finding the exact, right home for this book.

And for giving the book a home, Jamison Stoltz of Abrams Press, whose insights and deeply thoughtful edits made the book what it is today. Your infectious love of books and sense of humor even as the world kept crashing around us made this journey ever so much easier. I'm so glad my book proposal made you cry on the subway home that day.

Huge thanks also to Shanna McNair and Scott Wolven of the Writer's Hotel for guiding this book into the light and for the amazing writing community they have built through the TWH workshops. I'm so proud to be a part of it. I'm indebted to my intensive workshop leaders, Saïd Sayrafiezadeh, Elyssa East, and Meghan Daum for helping me refine my ideas and my craft. To my fellow workshop participants, thank you for holding me up and keeping me going.

Thank you as well to Donna Talarico-Beerman, founder of *Hippocampus*, for gathering memoir writers together for Hippocamp each year—truly, a place where magic happens. Lancaster will always feel like this book's birthplace.

Claudia Rowe, Mike Lewis. and M.L. Lyke, my fearless first readers and writing comrades—thank you for your friendship and your honesty over the years. To my new writing friends, Jennie Shortridge and Jennifer Haupt, I learn something new from you each time we meet. Anna Quinn, thank you for believing in this book. Who would have thought that all our high school daydreaming on the dock would have led us here?

I would not be the writer I am today without my *P-I* editors: Rita Hibbard, Scott Sunde, Laura Coffey, Bill Miller, Duston Harvey, John Levesque, and the late John Engstrom. I use something I learned from each of you in my work every day. Special thanks to *P-I* executive editor David McCumber for inspiring me with his own words and sharing his love of story. And to the rest of my *P-I* and KUOW families, thank you for all the laughter and the inspiration. You've kept me going all these years.

To the many people who made Christopher's life both possible and rich, and who have held me through it all, I am beyond grateful for your love and friendship. And finally, but most especially, to my family, whose love sustains me.

It took many hands to make this book happen, including all the ones behind the scenes at David Black and at Abrams Press. I'm grateful for every one of them.